# THE
# IRISH DIASPORA
# IN AMERICA

# THE
# IRISH DIASPORA
# IN AMERICA

*Lawrence J. McCaffrey*

*Indiana University Press*

**BLOOMINGTON**

**LONDON**

*Published in Canada by Fitzhenry & Whiteside Limited, Don Mills, Ontario*
MANUFACTURED IN THE UNITED STATES OF AMERICA

**Library of Congress Cataloging in Publication Data**

McCaffrey, Lawrence John, 1925–
  The Irish diaspora in America.
  Bibliography
  Includes index.
  1. Irish Americans—History.  I. Title.
E184.I6M115  973'.04'9162  75–23894
ISBN 0–253–33166–8  1 2 3 4 5 80 79 78 77 76

TO

*My father: John McCaffrey*
*in gratitude*

AND

*My children: Kevin, Sheila, and Patricia McCaffrey*
*in hope*

# Contents

ACKNOWLEDGMENTS     ix

1   Introduction: Irish Pioneers of the American
Ghetto     3

2   Ireland: English Conquest and Protestant
Ascendancy, 1169–1801     11

3   Ireland: The Rise of Irish Nationalism, 1801–1850     30

4   Refugees from Disaster: The Irish Immigrants,
1822–1870     59

5   The New Immigrants, 1870–1922     70

6   Communities in Conflict: American Nativists and
Irish Catholics     85

7   Irish-America and the Course of Irish Nationalism     107

8   Irish-American Politics     138

9   From Ghetto to Suburbs: From Someplace to No
Place?     152

RECOMMENDED READING     179

NOTES     188

INDEX     209

# Acknowledgments

I want to thank David Doyle, my former colleague at Loyola University of Chicago and now a member of the history faculty at University College, Dublin, for permitting me to read large portions of his Ph.D. dissertation—"American Catholics, Native Rights and National Empires; Irish-American Reaction to Expansion, 1890–1905"—and for allowing me to use portions of his work as evidence to support my assertions concerning Irish-American political opinion and social mobility. I also express my gratitude to Maryann Valiulis, my friend and a graduate student in Irish history at Loyola University of Chicago. She has read my manuscript and offered valuable suggestions for improvement.

My most important debts are to my family, first of all to my father, the late John Thomas McCaffrey, who came from the Cuilcagh Mountain region of County Cavan. He aroused and encouraged my interest in Irish studies, and his instructions in the Irish historical experience, emphasis on intellectual matters, magnanimity, courage, and liberal spirit made me appreciate how much I owe to my Irish and American Irish heritages and to immigrants like him who struggled against many adversities in urban America to create a new life and better opportunities for their children. My wife Joan Elizabeth McNamara McCaffrey, whose ancestors came from Counties Clare and Cavan, has always been my best friend and the sharpest yet most sympathetic critic of my writing, sharing my interest in things Irish, sacrificing her own time to read and comment on my manuscripts, lifting my morale in bleak periods. She and my happy-go-lucky and good children Kevin, Sheila, and Pat, have inspired me with the hope that the best in Irish-America has not and will not completely fade away.

In this book I have used revised portions of essays that I have previously published: "Pioneers of the American Ghetto," *Illinois Quarterly,* September 1971; "Catholicism and Irish Identity," *Holy Cross Quarterly,* Spring 1974; "Daniel O'Connell and the Irish-American Nationalist and Political Profiles," *O'Connell Bi-Centenary Volume,* editor, Donal McCartney (Dublin, 1975); and "The Conservative Image of Irish-America," *Ethnicity,* Autumn 1975.

*Evanston, Illinois*
*August 1975*

# THE
# IRISH DIASPORA
# IN AMERICA

# I

# Introduction:

# Irish Pioneers of the American Ghetto

Since the civil rights movement in the 1950s initiated the black quest for identity, dignity, and power and stimulated a resurgence of white ethnicity, historians have been forced to review traditional interpretations of the American experience. As a result, many have decided that their academic discipline has tended to present an establishment version of American history. For too long a period, American historiography has concentrated almost exclusively on the activities and values of the dominant, Anglo-American Protestant class to the neglect of ethnic and racial subcultures, adhering to a form of sophisticated nativism.

Unfortunately, in redressing the injustices of the past, many ethnic-studies scholars have substituted exaggeration for distortion, isolating their subjects from the multidimensional flow of American history. But in general, revisionism to contradict the melting pot thesis has improved the content of American studies. Now non–Anglo-American Protestants can appreciate American history as participants rather than as aliens. But despite the recent emphasis on the contribution of minority groups to the total American experience, Irish-America has received little attention from the scholarly community. At a time when publishers are producing a plethora of ethnic-studies series, few volumes are dedicated to the American Irish. And few minority-group culture programs in colleges and universities pay tribute to them.

Perhaps the Irish are virtually ignored in this ethnic-studies boom period because most of them have become so successful in the United States that they no longer pose a social problem or a political crisis. As part of suburban rather than urban America, they seem physically, linguistically, economically, and culturally indistinguishable from Anglo-Americans.[1] There seems to be little ethnic consciousness left among the many Americans who emphasize their Irishness, particularly around March 17, but who at the same time take tremendous pride in the degree of their assimilation into the national mainstream. Such fading cultural identity discourages Irish-American interest in the history and literature of their Old and New World ancestors, and few young scholars with Irish-Catholic backgrounds seem eager to investigate their own ethnic group.

I suspect, however, that the notable absence of discussions of Irish-America in ethnic-studies publications and classrooms has little to do with fading Irish identity and assimilation into the American mainstream. In fact, from my own experience in the classrooms of an urban, Catholic university where a large majority of the students are Catholic ethnics, I have concluded that the present generation of college-age Irish-Americans are more interested in studying their ethnic origins than Poles or Italians are theirs. Today's American Irish, sure of their place in the general society, can afford to cultivate their Irishness; lacking such social confidence, Poles and Italians seem more interested in establishing credentials as good and successful Americans than in preserving ethnic identities. In my opinion, the neglect of Irish-American ethnic studies is a conscious act by a portion of the academic community, an attempt at revenge against an old adversary.

American scholars have always felt uncomfortable in dealing with the Irish, because the Irish have controlled the American Catholic church since the early nineteenth century, and "Anti-Catholicism has always been the anti-Semitism of the American intellectual."[2] A large majority of scholars, particularly in the fields of history and the social sciences, operating from an eighteenth-century Enlightenment set of prejudices, have traditionally viewed Catholicism as an anti-intellectual, authoritarian monster threatening the liberal American system. Their criticisms of Catholicism have often been personalized in attacks on its Irish leadership. Although American intellectuals often express fondness for the Italians, a people who seem to wear their Catholicism more lightly than the Irish and who sing romantic songs and eat exotic foods, and although they express pity for the "poor Poles" whom they find ignorant and stupid, they hate the "puritan," "aggressive" Irish who run the Catholic church like a spiritual empire.

Tensions between establishment intellectuals and the Irish, however, have involved the question of power as much as the issue of anti-intellectual Catholicism. Intellectuals have for a long time competed with the Irish for position within the Democratic Party. They have tried to urge the party toward an uncompromising, ideological liberalism, while the Irish have insisted on a pragmatic concern with bread-and-butter issues and winning elections. In most instances the conflict between the pragmatic Irish and intellectual liberals has resulted in a victory for the former. When the ideologists have gained control, as they did when George McGovern became Democratic presidential candidate in 1972, the result has been a disaster at the polls and a massive, conservative electoral swing.

Irish power—both Catholic and political—has haunted and infuriated academic liberals. They often patronize objects of their concern with a humanitarianism that is a mixture of empathy and contempt. But when the Irish were victims of racism and discrimination, academic liberals were not sympathetic to their plight. And the Irish were one oppressed minority who refused to be patronized. They were not hospitable to establishment champions, and they defended their own interests, always distrusting the sincerity and integrity of Anglo-American liberalism. In retaliation, the academic community has ignored the Irish, refusing to accept them as a significant portion of American society or as an ethnic culture worth scholarly attention.[3] Perhaps some scholars have even patronized the ethnic-studies boom in an attempt to capture Irish ethnics and remove them from the pragmatic influence of Irish politicians.

Ignoring the Irish when presenting the mosaic of American cultural diversity is a major distortion of the reality of American history. It is impossible to examine American prejudice and pluralism or the development of American cities without confronting the Irish presence. Historical analysis demands the presentation of problems in an evolutionary context, and for this reason the Irish are perhaps the most important of all American ethnics; their experience offers the most useful case study. This volume will present the Irish as the pioneers of the American urban ghetto, previewing the experience of almost every other ethnic, religious, and racial minority that followed them into the cities of the United States.[4] The Irish were the first unwanted aliens in the new republic, the first targets of hate and violence. American nativism, a cultural child of English parents, defined itself in terms of the centuries-old conflict between Anglo-Saxon Protestants and their Catholic enemies. In the United States, the Irish filled the same role as in the United Kingdom: they were hated, papist subversives, the slinky agents of popery. Their obnoxious social behavior—the fruit of an impoverished culture and alienation—only reinforced prejudices that were essentially religious but that also contained the rudiments of racist ideology.

The Irish role as pioneers of the American urban ghetto had positive as well as negative results. They were more than just passive victims of nativism. In their efforts to overcome hate and discrimination and to achieve respectability in the United States, the Irish cultivated ethnic pride, fostered self-sufficiency, and exploited political talents to achieve power. Irish responses to the challenges of Anglo-American prejudice established precedents for identity-seeking and survival politics that have influenced the conduct of other minority groups.

Irish-America is also an interesting case study of the relationship between European and American ethnic experiences. Before the recent interest in minority-group studies, examinations of non-Anglo-American Protestant whites in the United States tended to accent accommodation, acculturation, and assimilation, de-emphasizing the European components of their personalities. Contemporary ethnic studies place more emphasis on the European backgrounds of Americans, but it is still not enough. For example, most studies of the American Irish pay too little attention to both the cultural and psychological luggage that these people transported with them across the Atlantic and the continuing links between Ireland and America.

It is true, of course, that Irish immigrants were probably the least sophisticated Europeans entering the United States in the first half of the nineteenth century. But they did have a culture and a history—a painful record as victims of conquest, colonialism, serfdom, tyranny, prejudice, poverty, and famine. Most Irish people entering the United States between 1818 and 1870 came as refugees from disaster, people running away from misery and death rather than rushing toward freedom and opportunity.

While these nineteenth-century, Irish immigrants landed hungry and culturally and technologically impoverished on the American shore, seeking survival in the New World as an alternative to extinction in the old, their unfortunate experience in Ireland did positively influence their adjustments to life in the United States. Perhaps the most important thesis of this book is the assertion that the Irish of the American Diaspora remain part of the totality of Irish history. Irish emigration from Ireland and immigration into the United States linked Irish, British, and American history. For example, the same close associations between Irish and Catholic identities that inspired Anglo-Saxon Protestant prejudice in Britain and Ireland as well as Anglo-American Protestant prejudice in the United States also gave the frightened immigrants a means of bridging Old and New Worlds and easing the problems of adjustment to a strange environment. Catholicism also provided a focus for unity in the Irish ghettos, creating an Irish-American community out of a people who arrived in America with diverse loyalties to parish, townland, and county. Through Catholicism, the Irish developed a solidarity which was expressed in Irish-American nationalism and political power.

But the famous Irish-American political style is rooted in Irish history as well as in American Catholicism. The Irish political personality was shaped by confrontation with British imperialism and colonialism. In their efforts to free themselves from anti-Catholic Penal Laws and to achieve national independence, the Irish learned to compete within the context of the Anglo-Saxon Protestant political system. They became particularly adroit in the techniques of mass agitation, political organization, confrontation, and liberal, democratic politics. They expressed their nationalist ambitions in the rhetoric of British liberalism, and the words and values of liberal democracy became essential elements of Irish political and nationalist theory. Such politicization meant that, although the Irish arrived in this country culturally and technologically unpolished, they were politically sophisticated and prepared to challenge Anglo-Americans for power within the structure of their own system.

While the Irish historical experience taught Irish-Americans how to function in Anglo-America, in time the educational process was geographically reversed. In the second half of the nineteenth century, the American Irish took the reins of Irish nationalism. Their hatred for a British system that had degraded them in Ireland and had forced them into exile and their search for respectability in America through the establishment of an independent European homeland made the Irish-Americans more passionately committed to a free Ireland than those who remained at home. Irish-American money and commitment to liberal, democratic republicanism sustained Irish nationalism, contributing significantly to the final success of the liberation movement. And in their efforts on behalf of Irish independence, the American Irish set precedents for the use of ethnic power to manipulate American foreign policy.

Frequently this book argues that liberal intellectuals, in criticizing the conservativeness of American Catholicism and its Irish leadership, have libeled both an institution and a nationality. Despite the charges of opponents both within and outside the Catholic church, the influence of the Irish on American Catholicism has been, for the most part, liberal rather than conservative. The European and American traditions of the Irish, their familiarity with two contrasting cultures—Anglo-Saxon Protestant and Roman Catholic—and their domination over American Catholicism and urban politics placed them in a position to solidify Catholic ethnics into a larger religious community. And because of their essentially liberal political commitment, the Irish were the only Catholic group that could have led an American Catholic church with a diverse European immigrant constituency into an accommodation with the dominant, Anglo-American Protestant culture. Irish domination of Catholic American affairs has liberalized the American Catholic church and prevented the construction and maintenance of permanent walls of hostility and suspicion between Catholics and most other Americans. Irish control of Catholic America has also made possible that unique quality of American life—consensus existing side by side with cultural diversity—preventing a suffocating dullness and conformity, sustaining an essential unity.

Even the social and economic mobility of the Irish, their

speedy assimilation into the middle-class mainstream, qualifies rather than eliminates them as objects of ethnic study. Are the same people who pioneered the American urban ghetto now establishing precedents for the future "progress" of other ethnics, both black and white? Does the present degree of assimilation of Irish-America indicate that the myth of the melting pot will become a suburban reality? If so, is the change from unwelcome alien to respectable, middle-class suburbanite a progressive or retrogressive move?

In evaluating the late twentieth-century Irish community whose values approximate those of Anglo-American Protestants, the historian and social scientist can begin to ask some fundamental questions about the future of ethnic America. Have the Irish in their successful search for respectability been adequately compensated for abandoning their ethnic cultural identity? Has their trip from Irish Catholic, urban neighborhoods to suburban melting pots been a journey to achievement and contentment or an excursion from someplace to no place? Is the history of Irish-America an ethnic success story or a warning to other groups that they should be wary of surrendering ethnicity for the sake of assimilation? These questions are complex, the answers cannot be simple, and they will be a long time in coming.

# 2

# *Ireland: English Conquest and Protestant Ascendancy, 1169-1801*

Ireland's long and violent association with English imperialism began in 1169 when a number of King Henry II's knights arrived in the country. These Norman freebooters came on invitation of Dermot MacMurrough, deposed king of Leinster, to help him regain the throne he had lost in a civil war in 1166. Mac-Murrough persuaded one of his new allies, Richard fitz Gilbert de Clare, known as Strongbow, to join forces by promising him the hand of his daughter in marriage and succession to the kingship of Leinster.[1] After Strongbow and his associates landed in Ireland, however, they quickly made it clear that they were there to stay and that their ambitions exceeded ruling Leinster. The Normans began a military sweep through the country, winning victories with superior weapons, armor, and horses and securing conquered territory with castle fortresses. The Irish, divided by clan and regional loyalties and factionalism, could not muster a united front.

Worried that Norman victories in Ireland might mean that his vassals were about to establish an independent, rival state in the neighboring island, Henry II in 1171 crossed over to Ireland and received the homage of his Norman barons and a few Irish clan chiefs as lord of Ireland, a title Adrian II had first conferred by papal grant. The pope, an Englishman, blessed and ratified the Norman conquest of Ireland, not as a gesture of ethnic loyalty but as a means of forcing individualistic Irish Christians and their anarchistic church to accept the authority of Roman Catholicism.

In the struggle between Normans and Celts, Irish disunity was a more decisive factor than English military superiority. England represented a new and dynamic Europe, Ireland the old and static. While other parts of Western civilization were in the process of evolving through feudalism toward centralized nation-states, Ireland had remained a clan society where major chiefs reigned as monarchs over seven petty kingdoms. When the Normans arrived, Rory O'Connor was Ard Rhi (high king) at Tara, but since tribal and territorial interests took precedence over any concept of nation, his title was more nominal than real.

Although Gaelic Ireland lacked the institutional framework and loyalties essential for political nationhood, she certainly had cultural unity.[2] A common language rich in literary tradition, laws reflecting the customs and values of the entire island population, and the unique character of Celtic Christianity welded the Irish people together. Much of the personality of Irish cultural nationality was displayed in Celtic Christianity, which was indeed quite different in practices, attitudes, and institutions from the church in England and on the Continent. And in Ireland the Roman presence remained vague and remote.

Following the collapse of the Roman Empire in the West, Irish monks played a major role in re-Christianizing and recivilizing Europe. The dynamic intensity of Celtic Christianity was manifested in a renaissance of art and learning as well as in zealous missionary activity. But with the development of the papal monarchy and Roman religious imperialism, Celtic Christianity slowly retreated from the Continent to Britain and finally back to its original Irish base. Another blow to the Irish

church was Danish raids, which concentrated on monastic centers of wealth and culture, forcing Celtic Christianity into a
long period of decay and corruption and draining much of the
vitality from Irish culture. When the Normans began their
conquest of Ireland, both Celtic Christianity and Irish culture
had slipped from the golden peaks of the past, but a rich tradition of literature and art still survived in the country. In the late
twelfth century, the Irish were probably more culturally sophisticated than many other Europeans, certainly more so than
their English "guests."

Exploiting the chaos and jealousies within the Irish tribal
system, the English invaders enjoyed a century and a half of
territorial conquest in Ireland, replacing old Gaelic political
and economic institutions with Continental and English feudal
and manorial practices. But early in the fourteenth century, the
Irish launched a counteroffensive, forcing the English to assume a defensive posture. This reversal was due to a number of
factors, among them that the Irish had adopted Norman military tactics and weapons and had entered into an alliance with
the Scots against the common English enemy. From 1315 to 1318,
Scottish liberator Edward Bruce and his Irish allies almost
drove the English into the sea. But the anarchy at the core of
the Irish clan system reasserted itself at the moment of victory,
preventing the sustained unity and cooperation necessary to
completely purge the English presence. Clan chiefs fought to
retain local power rather than restore Irish sovereignty. Once
secure in their own little "countries," they would be as likely
to battle with one another as to fight the foreigner.

Assimilation probably did more to retard the English conquest than did improved Irish military skills or the Scottish
alliance. While Irish clan chiefs were adopting Norman feudal
and manorial institutions, Norman barons in turn were embracing the values, customs, and language of Gaelic Ireland. Geography and marriage encouraged the assimilation of the English
invaders. Isolated in predominantly Irish areas, Normans married native women and after several generations, with the ex-

ception of their names, not much was left of their English origins. Far from the Leinster core of English rule in Ireland, Normans in Munster, Connacht, and the southern fringes of Ulster cultivated an Irish life-style, resembling clan chiefs in their manners and resentment of outside controls.

From the early fourteenth until the early sixteenth century, the unassimilated English in Ireland were more interested in maintaining areas they already controlled than in expansion, confining their energies within the province of Leinster to a garrison region called the Pale. This defensive mentality was expressed in the Statutes of Kilkenny. Passed by an Anglo-Irish parliament in 1366, these laws were an early example of apartheid in Western civilization, an attempt to protect minority values and institutions from the threat of a dynamic, majority, native culture. According to the statutes, the English in Ireland could not associate with the native Irish, marry their women, wear their costumes, speak their language, adopt their children, or utilize the services of their priests.

In 1509, when Henry VIII ascended the English throne, he was actually lord of three Irelands rather than one: the Pale or Anglo-Irish Ireland, Gaelic Ireland, and the ambiguous in-between. Covering the present counties of Dublin, Louth, Meath, Westmeath, Kildare, and Kilkenny, the Pale resembled a miniature England in language, cultural loyalties, and institutions.

Although the relationships between Irish minor chiefs in their little "countries," and the major chiefs who dominated vast areas, and between tenants and landowners in Gaelic Ireland beyond the Pale were often similar to those between vassals and lords in feudalism and lords and serfs in a manorial system, the native Irish still lived within the borders of a separate cultural nation. Their laws reflected Irish values, and their judges (Brehons) arbitrated legal disputes between contending parties, punishing with fines rather than with physical retribution. The influence of the church, the weight of public opinion, and the scorching satire of poets (bards) helped enforce judicial decisions. And since in the Irish tradition the family was a corporate whole, the complete tribe bore the responsibility for the crimes, debts, and sentences of its members.

Differing attitudes toward primogeniture formed a major distinction between the natives and the Anglo-Irish, a distinction with both property and political implications. Unlike the English and Anglo-Irish, who passed on property and the political authority associated with it to the eldest male heir, the Irish elected their chiefs from among the leading male members of each clan, and the successor (taniste) was chosen before the death of the chief (taoiseach). All sons received a portion of their fathers' lands (gavelkind). Theoretically, the election of chiefs was supposed to guarantee the succession of talent; more often it encouraged civil wars among candidates for the taniste, intensifying the anarchy of the clan system. Becoming a clan chief involved the ability to survive civil war and assassination attempts—requiring as much luck as skill—but at least it meant the victory of strength and cunning if not moral virtue.

Religious life in Gaelic Ireland also differed from that of the Pale. Natives wore their Catholicism more lightly than did those in the English colony, and they continued to have little respect for or contact with Rome. Bishops and abbots came from the families of clan chiefs, married or kept concubines, and passed on dioceses or monasteries to their sons, sometimes described as nephews. Clan chiefs usually married in civil ceremonies, divorced easily and frequently, and often were involved in polygamous relationships. The Irish were not hypocritical about their casual sexual encounters; bastardy did not even exist as a concept in Irish law. Irish men freely acknowledged their paternity on the claim of a mother, and sons of both wife and mistress shared equally in their father's inheritance and in the right to be considered as candidates for his office as clan chief. Among the clergy, only the mendicant friars—Franciscans, Dominicans, and Carmelites—represented orthodox

Western Christian values and practices. They tried to live and teach the austerity of the Christian ideal to the wild and exuberant Irish.

While the Pale represented the core of the English colony, Ulster in the North was the essence of Gaelic Ireland, an area barely touched by the invading culture. On the fringes of the Pale and in Anglo-Irish Connacht in the West and Munster in the South, culture, institutions, language, dress, and religious practices represented a fusion of Anglo and native-Irish cultures. The feudal nobility in these areas were more Irish than Anglo, but they tried to maintain close relationships with their Anglo-Irish peers in the Leinster Pale as well as with their neighbors, the native clan chiefs.

In an effort to enhance the national and international prestige of the Tudor monarchy, both Thomas Cardinal Wolsey and his successor as the king's minister, Thomas Cromwell, advised Henry VIII to jettison the defensive strategy of the Pale and convert his claims in that country from shadow to substance. Taking their advice, the king during the 1530s crushed the power of the Fitzgerald Earl of Kildare, the leader of the Anglo-Irish aristocracy in the Pale, and in 1540 he persuaded the leading clan chiefs outside the Pale to surrender their lands to him, receiving them again with English titles to use as his vassals—the O'Neill became Earl of Tyrone, the O'Donnell Earl of Tyrconnell, the O'Brien Earl of Thomond. In 1541, an Irish parliament dominated by Anglo-Irish barons but with a sprinkling of clan chiefs recognized Henry as king rather than lord of Ireland.

Henry's new title and the feudal policy of surrender and regrant certainly violated the Gaelic institutional structure, but they were more symbols of English domination than actual indications of any significant change in the Irish power structure. Concerned with English and Continental affairs, tight-fisted Henry refused to spend the necessary money to employ a bureaucracy adequate to control Ireland. Beyond the Pale, Ireland remained Gaelic in culture, tribal and chaotic in political organization. Henry's real impact on the course of Irish history was the introduction of the Reformation rather than the superficial paraphernalia of English feudalism. The Reformation was a decisive event in the long struggle between the Irish and English because it erected a definitive religious-cultural barrier between the two peoples, one that intensified hate and impeded assimilation and reconciliation. This barrier would be maintained by Anglo-Saxon Protestants and Irish Catholics on both sides of the Atlantic Ocean.

Anxious to have a male heir and frustrated in his efforts to obtain an annulment of his marriage with Catherine of Aragon, aunt of the Holy Roman Emperor Charles V, Henry in 1534 broke with Rome, declaring English religious independence and his own leadership over the church in territories under his political jurisdiction. Both the English and Irish parliaments passed Acts of Supremacy confirming the king's religious claims. Irish bishops, Anglo-Irish feudal lords, and Gaelic clan chiefs all accepted the new state religion.

Tudor quarrels with the pope had little relevance for the Irish, who were Catholics rather than papists; their loyalty to Rome was much less than that of their English enemies. And Irish lords and chiefs, like representatives of the aristocracy all over Europe, accepted the principle "cuius regio, eius religio" —the religion of the prince should determine the faith of the people—because union of church and state was a valid method of securing public order and tranquility. In addition, the change of religious leaders from pope to king did not interfere with the devotional life of the people. Although Henry confiscated the wealth and property of Irish monastic establishments, keeping much of the spoils for the royal treasury and distributing the rest to loyal Anglo-Irish barons and clan chiefs, his rejection of papal supremacy did not affect theology or liturgy. The Irish continued to attend mass and receive the sacraments; they remained essentially Catholic.

Things changed during the reigns of Henry's children, Edward VI (1547–1553) and Elizabeth I (1558–1603). The churches of England and Ireland became officially Protestant, mostly Calvinist in doctrine, and English authorities insisted that the Irish renounce Catholicism to prove their loyalty to the Crown. This ultimatum offended the Irish, who considered English efforts to change their religion as a form of cultural imperialism and an attack on their Irishness. Unlike the English, the Irish had no motive for abandoning Catholicism. In England, Scotland, and in certain places on the Continent, various forms of Protestantism became both political and cultural expressions of national self-consciousness; in Ireland Catholicism continued to symbolize the values, customs, emotions, and tastes of the people.

Fearing complete subordination to English cultural imperialism, the Anglo-Irish both inside and beyond the Pale joined the native Irish in resistance to the new religion. They negotiated with Catholic powers on the Continent, particularly Spain and later France, in an effort to obtain support in their opposition to Anglo-Saxon Protestant power. This religious dimension of the fight against English imperialism changed the character of Irish Catholicism, beginning the process of Romanization which was not completed until the 1860s, making the Catholic component the main feature of Irish identity. Jesuits and Franciscans flooded into Ireland as missionaries of papal-centered, counter-Reformation Catholicism. And the leaders of Catholic Ireland began to scorn Oxford and Cambridge educations for their sons, sending them instead to Continental, Catholic universities. Candidates for the priesthood studied in places like Spain, France, Belgium, and Italy. Although the English had used Protestantism as a crusading instrument to conquer and subdue Ireland, the results were far different from those they had anticipated. Anglo-Saxon Protestant imperialism worked politically but created stubborn cultural pockets of resistance in the Irish mind.

While most Irish and English historians have emphasized the significance to the British Isles of the conflict between English Protestants and Irish Catholics, the struggle also had European dimensions. During the sixteenth and seventeenth centuries, England was engaged in a series of wars against Spain and France to achieve and maintain status as a major power. Since its enemies were Catholic nations, the English government cultivated Protestant nativism as an ideological weapon. England's numerous wars against Continental Catholics and the religious propaganda aspects of those conflicts prompted arguments for total subjugation of Ireland. English leaders feared that the Spanish or the French would exploit Irish Catholic animosity toward Protestant England by providing troops to aid Irish liberation movements. And an Ireland occupied by either the Spanish or the French would place England geographically in a papist pincer, diminishing the effect of her sea power. So from the mid-sixteenth well into the twentieth century, militant, Protestant, anti-Catholic, English nativism coupled with British imperialism and national security needs provided the foundations for England's Irish policy.

During the reign of Elizabeth I, English armies conquered Munster and Connacht and pushed stubborn Ulster to the point of surrender. In her effort to permanently suppress the Irish potential for rebellion, the queen employed a plantation policy first tried by her Catholic sister Mary in Leix and Offaly. She seized about four hundred acres of Munster rebel territory and colonized it with Protestant loyalists from England. After Ulster Chiefs O'Neill and O'Donnell submitted to James I in 1603 and then left Ireland in fear of their lives in 1607, the first Stuart king took advantage of "the flight of the Earls" by branding them traitors, confiscating their vast estates, and "planting" the area with Protestants from Britain, many of them Presbyterians from the Scottish lowlands. Unlike the earlier southern plantations, where the major change was from Catholic to Protestant landlords, the Ulster scheme involved density, settling a variety of classes and occupations in the area to create the only sizable Protestant community in Ireland, sowing the seeds of the current religious-cultural crisis in the Six Counties.

In the seventeenth century, the Divine Right of Kings political theories and the governing style of James and his heirs antagonized the oligarchs who controlled the English Parliament, setting the stage for tension and civil war. Irish Catholics attempted to exploit divisions and conflict in England to recover "stolen property" and to restore the "national" religion. During the civil war between Charles I and parliamentary radicals in the 1640s, Old English in Ireland and Irish Catholics expressed loyalty to the Crown but rejected English domination and established an independent Irish parliament at Kilkenny. After he defeated the Stuart armies in Scotland and England, Cromwell crossed over to Ireland, crushed the Confederation of Kilkenny, confiscated rebel property, transferring it to English Protestant loyalists, and proceeded to drive Catholic leaders and their followers west of the Shannon River into Connacht.

Despite the plantations of Mary and Elizabeth in Leinster and Munster and the massive resettlement under James, before the rebellion of the 1640s Catholics still owned two-thirds of Irish property. After Cromwell's confiscations and resettlements, however, a small Protestant minority controlled three-fourths of Irish soil. Eleven years of resistance against British authority and the vengeance of Cromwell had diminished the Irish population by a third and reduced the Catholic masses to the level of serfs. The English transported many of them to the West Indies as slaves.

After the Restoration in 1660, Irish Catholics supported the Stuarts because they believed that Charles II (1660–1685) and his brother James II (1685–1688) were sympathetic to Catholic religious convictions and might even return some of the property confiscated by their predecessors. Aware of the loyalty of Catholic Ireland, James II, following his deposition by Parliament, decided to fight for his throne in Ireland rather than England. As before, an Irish war fitted into a wider European background. Led by the new English King William III, a European alliance was trying to contain the territorial ambitions of

France's Louis XIV, the Sun King. Because of his hostility to Louis, the pope favored the European alliance and thus was forced to sympathize with the Protestant cause in Ireland.

On the banks of the Boyne on 12 July 1690, William's Dutch, German, English, and Irish-Protestant army defeated James's French and Irish-Catholic soldiers. When Protestant victory became inevitable, James fled the battlefield and then Ireland, leaving his Irish supporters with a few French allies to struggle on alone against superior forces. Under the brilliant leadership of Patrick Sarsfield, Irish Catholics made a brave fight out of an impossible situation, gradually falling back on Limerick where they held out against a massive Protestant siege.

Because he had to cope with other problems, such as maintaining the alliance against Louis XIV, William offered the Anglo-Irish and native Irish-Catholic leaders honorable terms of submission. According to the 1691 Treaty of Limerick, they were permitted to leave their country and to serve under Continental, Catholic monarchs on the promise that the Catholics left behind would not suffer either religious persecution or property confiscation. So the leaders of the Catholic aristocracy sailed off to France, leaving their dependents protected by a piece of paper that relied on the integrity of the English government and its Anglo-Irish Protestant planter colony.

William was a politician, not a Protestant fanatic. His native country, the Dutch Republic, had experimented with a policy of religious tolerance as a pragmatic alternative to civil war between Catholics and Calvinists. The English king now was prepared to apply this same flexible approach to the religious tensions dividing England and Ireland. To him, stability and unity were more important political objectives than Protestant Ascendancy or Catholic humiliation. But British and Irish Protestants demanded a total victory over their "seditious" Catholic enemies and insisted on vengeance. In the 1690s and during the early decades of the eighteenth century, the British and Irish Parliaments, purged of Catholic representation, enacted laws abolishing the civil rights of papists and outlawing Catholic worship. Carefully considering the intensity of British and Irish Protestant anti-Catholicism, William and his successors decided that it would be impolitic to resist the popular passion and reluctantly assented to anti-Catholic legislation.

The resulting Penal Laws in Ireland were more thorough and severe than those in Britain, covering all aspects of the political, social, economic, and religious lives of Catholics. They exiled Catholic bishops, forbade the entry of priests into the country, outlawed religious orders, and restricted the movements of resident secular clergy. If rigidly enforced, the exile of bishops and the restrictions against priests entering Ireland would have eventually eliminated the Catholic clergy. In addition to attacking the fundamental institutions of the church and curtailing Catholic worship, the Irish Penal Laws also relegated Catholics to subcitizen status. They could not vote, sit in Parliament, hold commissions in the armed forces, serve as government employees, establish schools, practice law, possess weapons, or purchase property. If the son of a Catholic landowner became a Protestant he could seize his father's land, reducing his parent to the status of life tenant.

Penal legislation completed the division of Ireland into two distinct communities. A Protestant minority, including Church of Irelanders and nonconformists, owned ninety-five percent of the country's property and enjoyed a complete monopoly over political power.[3] The Catholic majority, which constituted seventy-five percent of the population, held only five percent of the property and paid tithes to support the Protestant religious establishment. The English conquest and Protestant Ascendancy had reduced most Catholics to the condition of illiterate, impoverished serfs working for alien masters. Members of the small Catholic aristocracy and gentry that had managed to survive the Penal Laws were quiet and humble, hoping to avoid trouble by insisting on their loyalty to the Crown. Restrictions on the increase of Catholic property encouraged the growth of a substantial Catholic middle class, particularly among those in the provisions trade. Members of the Catholic aristocracy, gentry, and middle class were forced to send their children abroad for advanced schooling, and significant numbers of the Catholic upper class continued to seek military careers serving Bourbon and Hapsburg kings.

Some Protestants who wrote, supported, and enforced the Penal Laws did so to root out the "evils" of popery, hoping that persecution would force the conversion of a large section of the Catholic population to the "true faith" of Christ. But terror rather than proselytism was the essential purpose of anti-Catholic legislation. Protestants in Ireland were an outnumbered English garrison constantly fearing a slave revolt that might cost them their property and perhaps even their lives. The Penal Laws expressed planter paranoia and were designed to guarantee a permanent dominance of the minority Protestant Ascendancy by demoralizing and dehumanizing the native Catholic majority. The psychology was impeccable: debased and frightened slaves, more concerned with survival than human rights, do not make good revolutionary material.

Because Protestant politicians and police officials did not invest much money or energy in enforcing the religious category of the Penal Laws, Catholicism continued to flourish. In fact, by the end of the eighteenth century, the Catholic church in Ireland was a much healthier and more dynamic institution than it had been in 1691. Repression inspired reform, and persecution improved the quality of the hierarchy and clergy, reinforcing ties between Irish and Continental Catholicism and increasing the influence of the Vatican in Irish-Catholic affairs. Some members of the Catholic aristocracy and gentry did defect to Protestantism, often to protect their property and to retain social status and political influence. But with few exceptions the peasant masses remained loyal to the old religion.[4]

Despite the continued commitment of the overwhelming majority of the Irish people to a Catholic church revitalized under the lash of persecution, the Penal Laws accomplished their main purpose. Physical and psychological terror did de-

moralize Irish Catholics, and their fear and insecurity strengthened Protestant Ascendancy.

There were of course some exceptions to Catholic timidity in
the face of terror. Not all Catholics quietly submitted to tyranny and serfdom. In the eighteenth and early nineteenth centuries, Catholic associations and committees, representing the
aristocracy, gentry, and middle class, frequently petitioned the
Crown and the Irish Parliament for the repeal of laws depriving
them of civil, religious, and property rights. And many Catholic
peasants joined secret societies to protest high rents, tithes paid
to the Protestant church, and excessive dues demanded by their
own priests or to protect themselves from Protestant tenant
farmers attempting to drive them off their farms.[5]

Agrarian secret societies adopted a variety of names: Whiteboys, Captain Moonlight, Molly Maguires, Defenders, and Ribbonmen, and they used violent methods of intimidation: burning hayricks, destroying buildings, maiming cattle, and
sometimes assaulting landlord agents, tithe collectors, and
other peasants who dared occupy farms of evicted members of
their own class. Through much of the eighteenth and into the
early years of the nineteenth century, a guerrilla war raged in
parts of rural Ireland between secret societies and the forces of
law and order. Agrarian terrorism did help force a reduction
in the financial pressures exerted by the Protestant church and
by landlords on the native peasant population.

Some commentators on Irish history have interpreted the
agrarian secret societies as the embryo of revolutionary nationalism. While such a thesis makes fascinating reading, it takes
tremendous liberties with historical reality. Secret societies
were concerned with local economic grievances and, in the case
of the Ulster border counties, with sectarian interests. They did
not wage war on the manorial system in an effort to destroy
landlordism, and they never articulated any concept of an Irish
nation.

Anglo-Irish Protestants rather than native Irish Catholics

first delineated an Irish political nation. In the course of the eighteenth century, with the Catholic majority demoralized by physical and psychological terror, Protestant planters began to relax and lose their identity as members of an English garrison colony. In time they themselves became Irish patriots, resenting British restrictions on Irish commerce and British political sovereignty.[6] Anglo-Irish Protestant patriotism grew concurrently with and shared the same principles as Anglo-American patriotism in the North American colonies. Both planter populations protested the burdens of British political and economic imperialism, insisting on the role of new adults no longer dependent on the protection of mother England. Anglo-Irish Protestant and Anglo-American patriots both expressed their principles and ambitions in the rhetoric of English Whiggery; they exalted John Locke as the philosopher of their ideals. And both movements were logical extensions of the myth that Parliament fought the Stuarts to enhance individual liberty, the root of the Social Contract, when Parliament's real objective was the defense of a landed oligarchy.

Anglo-Irish and Anglo-Americans affirmed allegiances to British culture and institutions while at the same time arguing that British tyranny denied them their natural rights as human beings and their constitutional privileges as British subjects. They argued that these rights and privileges could best be protected in local legislatures freely discussing and deciding local issues.

During the late 1770s and early 1780s, the courses of Irish and American history were further linked when the Americans resorted to a war of liberation to emancipate themselves from the British Empire. During this war, Anglo-Irish patriots exploited British weaknesses in Ireland to eliminate many of the restrictions of British imperialism that shackled Irish commerce and limited the authority of the Irish Parliament. With most of the Irish army serving in North America and the combined French and Spanish navies in control of Atlantic sea-lanes, Ireland was left without adequate protection against possible invasion. When neither the Irish nor the British governments could muster an Irish home army, Anglo-Irish patriots organized a force called the Volunteers and then used it to threaten the British government, demanding a free Irish Parliament and the end of British mercantilist limitations on Irish trade. Responding to the pressures of Anglo-Irish Protestant opinion and Volunteer intimidation, the British Parliament in 1779–1780 removed restrictions on Irish commerce and finally in 1782 surrendered its claim to legislate for Ireland.

From 1782 until the end of 1800 there was an Irish nation, but it was exclusively Protestant. Although Henry Grattan, the most prominent and talented leader of the patriot cause, argued for a nonsectarian Ireland and warned his fellow Protestants that they could never really be free as long as the Catholic majority remained slaves, most Anglo-Irish Protestants were convinced that total repeal of the Penal Laws would lead to Catholic power at the expense of Protestant property and political influence. They refused to admit Catholics to first-class citizenship in the Irish nation, insisting on the permanence of Protestant Ascendancy.

In the 1790s, the threatened invasion by the armies of the French Revolution compelled the British government to court the support of English and Scottish Catholics by repealing many of the Penal Laws in Britain and urging similar concessions from the Irish Parliament. Such pressures did persuade Irish Protestants to lift some of the burdens of prejudice from the Catholic community. The Parliament permitted Catholics to operate schools, practice law, hold commissions in the army below the rank of colonel, lease property on a long-term basis, and vote in parliamentary elections if the property they occupied earned a rating of forty shillings for tax purposes (the "40s franchise"). And Parliament even endowed a Roman Catholic seminary at Maynooth, County Kildare, mainly to prevent young seminarians from soaking up the revolutionary ideology pervading seminaries on the Continent. Despite these concessions, however, Catholics remained pariahs, excluded from Parliament and political office. Even the 40s franchise was an essentially useless concession because without a secret ballot Protestant landlords controlled the votes of their Catholic tenants. If a tenant dared to openly vote his convictions against those of his landlord, he risked eviction.

Not only Catholics were dissatisfied with the constitution of the Irish-Protestant nation; many Anglo-Irishmen expressed discontent with the extent of their victory over British imperialism. Complaining that the Irish Parliament like its British counterpart represented the interests of the aristocracy and the landed gentry, middle-class radicals agitated for popular sovereignty, and the French Revolution inspired and encouraged their hopes for change. In the 1790s, under the leadership of Theobold Wolfe Tone, Protestant radicals in Belfast and Dublin organized the Society of United Irishmen to express their liberal, democratic ideology. Instructed by their Jacobin cousins in France and exasperated by government repression in Ireland, the United Irishmen ranged beyond parliamentary reform, finally insisting on establishing a democratic republic through a French-supported revolution. In order to achieve a united front as a prelude to revolution, Tone appealed to the Catholic population for support, strongly endorsing Catholic Emancipation and pledging a nonsectarian Irish republic.

Anticipating an insurrection, the Irish government arrested a number of United Irishmen and moved militia troops, mostly Catholics, into Ulster to seize arms and intimidate potential rebels. When revolution did come in 1798 it was a badly coordinated fiasco and, predictions of Irish nationalists to the contrary, Protestant, middle-class radicals and Catholic peasants did not unite to liberate Ireland from tyranny. Catholic peasants in Wexford fought a bloody religious and class war against Protestant landlords, and Orange militiamen brutally punished them for the effort. Revolution in Ulster was as sectarian in tone as it was in Wexford. More influenced by the bigotry of the Orange lodges than the idealism of United Irishmen, Protestant rebels in Antrim and Down were less than enthusiastic about cooperating with Catholics in a struggle to create an ecumenical Irish republic. When a small French force finally landed in Mayo in August 1798, after the uprisings in Wexford, Antrim, and Down, confused Catholic peasants greeted Gen. Humbert on the shores of Killala Bay and promised to help him defend the pope and the Blessed Virgin. Although the French fought well, they were outnumbered and short on provisions. Without adequate local support they were forced to surrender to Gen. Packenham.

While the rebellion of 1798 created martyred heroes to spice the legends and ballads of Irish nationalism, the immediate result was the reduction rather than the expansion of Irish liberty. British politicians and frightened Irish Tories viewed the events of '98 as an effective argument against Irish sovereignty. For some time, British leaders, particularly Prime Minister William Pitt, were apprehensive about the Irish situation, fearing that Protestant, middle-class radicalism and Catholic discontent were open invitations to French intervention. Again the prospect of an Ireland in enemy hands threatened British security. Since Pitt and his cabinet colleagues doubted that the Irish Parliament could preserve law and order in that troubled land, they decided that the final solution to the Irish Question was a legislated union between the two islands.

Pitt instructed Lord Lieutenant Lord Charles Cornwallis, and Chief Secretary Lord Robert Stewart Castlereagh to persuade the Irish that a union with Britain would serve the interests of both countries. Cornwallis and Castlereagh told Irish Protestants that the British connection would guarantee stability in Ireland and assured Catholics that it would result in their emancipation. Pitt and his Irish agents in Ireland were sincere in their promise to relieve Catholics from the remaining restrictions of the Penal Laws, realizing that the Union could never work unless the Irish-Catholic majority entered the United Kingdom as first-class citizens.[7]

Irish Protestant opinion divided on the Union. Invoking Locke and his Irish disciple William Molyneux as authorities, some Anglo-Irish patriots insisted that the British connection would endanger Irish political and economic interests. Irish-Protestant patriot Henry Grattan emerged from retirement to protect the British legislative concessions of 1782. Orange Protestants also opposed the Union, but for more selfish, sectarian reasons. They warned that a Westminster parliament might destroy Protestant Ascendancy in Ireland by submitting to the pressures of Catholic agitation. Anti-Catholicism also motivated Protestants who favored the British connection. They were convinced that Protestant, middle-class radicalism allied with Catholic agitation and the ideology of the French Revolution was a more dangerous threat to Protestant Ascendancy than the risks involved in the Union. Protestant advocates of the Union argued that British power would defend their interests in Ireland, claiming that British anti-Catholicism would frustrate Pitt's effort to merge the issues of Catholic Emancipation and the Union.

In 1799, the British Parliament approved the principle of Union with Ireland, but a majority of the Irish House of Commons remained either opposed or uncommitted on the subject. A year later, after vigorous debate in Ireland, considerable pressure from the British government, and a generous application of funds and Crown patronage, the Irish Parliament by a narrow majority finally agreed to its own extinction. On 1 January 1801 Ireland officially became part of the United Kingdom of Great Britain and Ireland.

# 3

# *Ireland: The Rise of Irish Nationalism, 1801-1850*

The Act of Union changed the multidimensional Irish Question from a problem of external British security into a perennial internal crisis, the most persistent and emotional issue in British politics. Irish problems and protests and British responses to them transformed economic and political institutions and altered the shape of the empire. They also destroyed governments and political careers. As an experiment, the United Kingdom intensified rather than diminished ethnic and cultural tensions between Anglo-Saxon Protestants and Irish Catholics. Current events in Northern Ireland indicate that Britain still has not escaped the implications of the Irish connection.

From the very beginning of the Union, the United Kingdom Parliament fulfilled the pessimistic prophecy of anti-Union, Anglo-Irish patriots; it governed the two islands in the interests of industrial Britain and at the expense of agrarian Ireland. One hundred Irish M.P.s in a 658-member House of Commons (this number was increased to 105 after the 1832 Reform Bill) and twenty-eight Irish peers and four bishops in a House of Lords numbering about 360 members had little influence over the course of government policy. And Irish-Protestant opinion lost its significance as time went by. Throughout the nineteenth century, the Protestant patriot tradition kept fading, and most Irish Tory and Whig M.P.s, as representatives of the British colony in Ireland, were dependent on the Union for the security of a minority ascendancy. And in order to maintain the British connection, they acquiesced in the sacrifice of Irish to British interests.

While the Union failed to achieve harmony for a number of reasons, the religious issue was the most important factor. When British politicians refused to concede Catholic Emancipation as a package deal with the Union, they sealed the doom of the United Kingdom. Since the Irish-Catholic majority entered the new constitutional arrangement as far less than first-class citizens, it became impossible for them to develop British loyalties like Scottish or Welsh Protestants. When Prime Minister Pitt attempted to honor his pledge of civil rights to the leaders of Catholic Ireland, George III flew into a rage, declaring that he would never violate his coronation oath or Protestant conscience by consenting to equal citizenship for papists. George IV shared his father's hostility to Catholic Emancipation and his determination to preserve the remnants of the Penal Laws. On several occasions a practical and enlightened majority in the House of Commons indicated a willingness to scuttle the bigotry of the seventeenth century, but the House of Lords and British anti-Catholic public opinion joined the Crown in insisting that Catholics must remain outside the structure of British politics.

Poverty and religion were inseparable aspects of the Irish Question. For the most part, Irish Catholics were landless serfs, the victims of an inefficient manorial system that had vanished from the rest of Western Europe. And anti-Catholic prejudices limited the ability of British politicians to confront the essence of Irish poverty by reforming the cruel agrarian system. Many British saw the Irish as savages innately inferior to Anglo-Saxons and interpreted Catholicism as a manifestation of the superstitious, irrational, and lazy Celtic disposition.

Despite its most prominent role, anti-Catholicism was not the only obstacle to social and economic reforms in Ireland. Right-wing Tories, the Whig center, and the radical left all insisted on the free exercise of property rights as unassailable economic dogma. They argued that any significant change in the Irish land system, any modification of landlord rights in favor of tenant-farmer security would establish precedents endangering the rights of property throughout the United Kingdom.

Irish nationalism emerged from the failure of the Union to confirm Catholic civil rights and alleviate Irish poverty. In the first half of the nineteenth century, three men—Robert Emmet (1778–1803), Daniel O'Connell (1775–1847), and Thomas Osborne Davis (1814–1845)—respectively represented the myth, reality, and ideology of the Irish struggle for freedom.

Emmet, a younger brother of Thomas Addis Emmet, one of the cofounders of the Society of United Irishmen who later had a brilliant career in New York state politics, was a Trinity College Protestant. With Tone dead and his brother and other United Irishmen in exile, young Emmet attempted to keep the spirit of republican democracy alive in post-Union Ireland. But in 1803, a revolution that he planned degenerated into a Dublin street brawl and Emmet was arrested, convicted of treason, and sentenced to death.

As a revolutionary leader Emmet was a disaster, a conspirator who failed to obtain French support for an Irish insurrection, and a man who could not keep his mouth shut. Informers easily penetrated his organization; even his defense attorney was a government agent. After his conviction for treason but before receiving the death sentence, however, Emmet made a speech from the dock that transformed a pathetic failure of a revolution into a glorious legend. In his statement to Judge Lord Norbury, the jury, and the people of Ireland, he defended his revolutionary nationalism, condemned British oppression, and called on future generations of Irishmen to take up his burden. Emmet concluded his speech by asking the Irish people to postpone any memorials to his memory until his cause was successful: "When my country takes her place among the nations of the earth, then, and not until then, let my epitaph be written."

With his death on the gallows, Robert Emmet joined Wolfe Tone, who had committed suicide when his captors had refused him the honorable death of a firing squad, at the top of what would become a long list of martyred Irish nationalists. More talented men would serve Ireland, and many of them would accomplish a great deal for their fellow countrymen, but none would match Emmet as a popular hero. His youth, idealism, zeal, and oratory captured the imagination of the Irish masses. Emmet's portrait was enshrined in many Irish homes; parents memorized his speech from the dock and recited it to their children. Many fathers and mothers, particularly in Irish-American communities, named their sons Robert Emmet or just Emmet. Thomas Moore, the first popular bard of romantic Irish nationalism, contributed to the Emmet myth. In a poem entitled "Oh, Breathe Not His Name" he reminded readers of his hero's final request:

> Oh, breathe not his name! let it sleep
>   in the shade,
> Where cold and unhonored his relics are
>   laid;
> Sad, silent, and dark be the tears that
>   he shed,
> As the night-dew that falls on the grass
>   o'er his head.

Moore also celebrated Emmet's romance with Sarah Curran and at the same time exalted his motives and cause in "She Is Far From the Land Where Her Young Hero Sleeps":

She is far from the land where her young hero sleeps,
    And lovers around her, sighing;
But coldly she turns from their gaze, and weeps,
    For her heart in his grave is lying.

He had lived for his love, for his country he died,
    They were all that to life had entwined him;
Nor soon shall the tears of his country be dried,
    Nor long will his love stay behind him.

If Emmet contributed to the inspirational myths and legends of Irish nationalism, Daniel O'Connell created its reality. Considered by many to be the greatest figure in the Irish freedom effort, he made Irish Catholics rise from their knees and demand the dignity of free men.[1] Intellectually, O'Connell was a philosophical radical, a disciple of Godwin, Paine, and Bentham, and his nationalism was an extension of a liberal concern for human rights. As a young man, influenced by the religious views of the Enlightenment and the philosophers he admired, O'Connell had been a skeptic. Later the Catholic civil rights cause he represented and the influence of his wife Mary converted him into a pious Catholic. Still he remained a liberal democrat, committed to freedom of conscience and separation of church and state, completely opposed to the reactionary political values of the Vatican. O'Connell never intellectually harmonized his political convictions and his loyalty to the Catholic church, but he was too powerful for the Vatican to condemn as it had French Catholic leftists Montalembert, Lacordaire, and Lamenais.

Considering violence negative, destructive, and antagonistic to Irish freedom, O'Connell rejected revolutionary tactics, arguing that the peasant masses could not compete on the battlefield against the discipline and weapons of British soldiers. To him, revolution in Ireland meant the destruction of property, the loss of lives, and the expansion of tyranny. Pointing to the

abortive rebellion of 1798 to prove his thesis, O'Connell blamed
the Society of United Irishmen for the demise of the Irish
Parliament and the creation of the Union, and in 1803 he
strongly argued that Robert Emmet deserved to be punished for
the violence he unleashed. Insisting that organized public opinion could work as the most effective instrument of Irish freedom and reform, O'Connell decided to mobilize the Irish
masses for political action, using Catholic civil rights as the
issue to galvanize energy and enthusiasm.

Coming from a Catholic, aristocratic background, O'Connell
had taken advantage of the modification of the Penal Laws to
study law in London and Dublin and became the most successful young barrister in Ireland. In 1815 he took charge of the
Catholic Committee, which at the time was dominated by the
Catholic aristocracy, gentry, and middle class and annually
petitioned Parliament for a repeal of the remaining Penal Laws.
Henry Grattan, still an Irish-Protestant patriot and advocate of
Catholic equality in the House of Commons, presented Catholic Committee petitions to the British Parliament.

While agitating for Catholic Emancipation, O'Connell constantly emphasized that the ultimate goal of his energies was
repeal of the Union and restoration of the Irish Parliament in
College Green. In his campaign against the British connection,
he considered himself a disciple of Locke, Molyneux, and Jona-
than Swift and a spokesman for the eighteenth-century patriotic
tradition. Anything but a narrow sectarian, O'Connell rejected
a Catholic Ireland as an alternative to Protestant Ascendancy,
but the realities of the Irish situation forced him to couple
Catholic Emancipation with Irish nationalism. He realized that
most Protestants were committed to the Union and that the
future of Irish self-government depended on the activities of the
oppressed Catholic majority. And he knew that Catholic
Emancipation was the only issue that could overcome the tor-
por that pervaded the majority community. To Irish Catholics,
their religion was the symbol of their cultural identity, the only

proud possession salvaged from a humiliating historical experience. But there were some influential Catholics who were opposed to combining Catholic and nationalist issues, and this controversy over strategy was a major factor in the destruction of the Catholic Committee.

In 1815, Grattan worked out a compromise on the Catholic Emancipation issue with some important British leaders. In exchange for Catholic civil rights in the United Kingdom, the Vatican would assure Parliament that it would not appoint unfriendly bishops to sees in Britain and Ireland. Most governments in Catholic countries already enjoyed the privilege of vetoing episcopal appointments, so the selection of bishops by a committee of loyalist Catholic laymen or a veto of papal choices by a British king was not really an innovation. This compromise had an excellent chance of being adopted in Britain, and powerful forces at the Vatican were willing to forfeit some of their control over the hierarchy in the United Kingdom to establish friendly relations with the world's leading government. Many members of the Irish and British Catholic aristocracies, gentries, and middle classes also were delighted with an arrangement which promised them opportunities for professional, political, and social success, seats in Parliament, distinction at the Bar.

O'Connell quickly dashed these hopes, however, by refusing to endorse Grattan's compromise arrangement, and he carried the Catholic hierarchy with him. In arguing against the plan, he insisted that it would give the British government control over the Catholic church in the United Kingdom and that such a prospect violated his liberal convictions concerning the separation of church and state. What he did not say—and most obviously meant—was that British controls over Catholicism would destroy the identity link between that religion and the Irish. And O'Connell thought it more important to cultivate Irish self-consciousness as a foundation for nationalism than to promote the political, social, and professional interests of members of the British and Irish Catholic upper and middle classes or to facilitate harmonious relations between London and Rome.

O'Connell's rejection of the compromise divided and then destroyed the Catholic Committee, and the Catholic Emancipation movement languished in Ireland and in Parliament for nearly ten years. The spark was reignited in 1823 when O'Connell collaborated with Richard Lalor Sheil and Sir Thomas Wyse, two leaders of the procompromise faction of the committee, to create a new organization called the Catholic Association. In its early days the association failed to overcome the lethargy in Catholic circles, but in 1825, O'Connell devised a tactic which invigorated the Catholic Association, making it the most powerful instrument of public opinion in the United Kingdom.

Catholic Association dues of one pound per year were high enough in impoverished Ireland to restrict membership to the more prosperous classes. In an attempt to broaden his base, O'Connell decided to add an associate membership category requiring dues of only one shilling a year, which could be paid in a lump sum or more slowly at the rate of a penny a month or a farthing a week. He asked priests to promote associate memberships among their flocks and appointed rent collectors to harvest the shillings, pennies, and farthings. In their Sunday sermons, Catholic clergymen described emancipation as both a holy and patriotic cause, and Catholic peasant and urban working-class people flocked into the association. The burgeoning membership of the emancipation movement served to illustrate the extent of Catholic bitterness as well as O'Connell's hold on the Irish masses. And the new membership category also gave the association the financial means to conduct a vigorous campaign for civil rights.

Joining the association had a powerful psychological impact on the Catholic poor. A shilling a year was not a great deal of money, but to the average Irish peasant it represented a major sacrifice. A shilling donated to the Catholic Association often meant giving up alcohol and tobacco, two popular escapes from the misery of poverty and boredom. But through such a sacrifice the people found identity, hope, and dignity. Participation in the struggle for Catholic Emancipation began to liberate the Irish people from their slave mentality; they began to think like men and women who belonged to a nation with a future.

In the general election of 1826, the Catholic Association tested its strength against the Protestant Ascendancy. O'Connell and his associates endorsed and worked for Protestant candidates who opposed the Penal Laws. Waterford was the critical constituency; there, the association challenged the mighty Beresford family, which had long held a monopoly on the House of Commons seat. Clerical influence clashed with landlord power as tenant farmers marched to the polls accompanied by their priests. And to the consternation of British and Irish Tories, the 40s franchise peasant voters dealt landlordism and Protestant Ascendancy a near-fatal blow. Their Waterford victory influenced similar decisions in a number of other counties.

Two years later, the Catholic Association decided on a bolder challenge to Protestant Ascendancy, and again Irish peasants rallied to the cause. In a County Clare by-election, voters chose O'Connell himself over the incumbent, C. E. Vesy Fitzgerald, a member of the Duke of Wellington's Tory cabinet, forcing the British government into a difficult decision. Wellington and his chief lieutenant Sir Robert Peel, the home secretary and leader of Tory forces in the House of Commons, could either accept the reality of Catholic strength or they could ignore election results in Ireland and refuse to begin dismantling the Protestant Ascendancy. The latter choice involved a serious risk of civil war because it might persuade Irish Catholics to abandon constitutional avenues and rely on physical force as an instrument of change. Since the Irish-Catholic masses were expecting some kind of victory, a government effort to put them down through force could have been costly in terms of life and property. And any British military intervention would have been an admission of moral and political failure by conceding that the Union had not worked and reaffirming that the Irish-Catholic majority were conquered people, not an integral part of the United Kingdom.

O'Connell kept reminding Wellington and Peel that they had only two choices: reform or revolution. And the British leaders ultimately decided to violate their Tory principles and their Protestant consciences for the sake of a healthy United Kingdom and continued law and order. At Wellington's and Peel's urging, Parliament in 1829 passed a Catholic Relief Bill, and George IV reluctantly signed it. Unfortunately for the "health" of the United Kingdom, the government's concessions to Catholic demands contained as much vindictiveness as generosity. Since the 40s franchise freeholders could no longer be counted on to follow their landlords' orders at the polls, the Catholic Relief Bill stripped them of their franchise.[2] In addition, the government forced O'Connell to recontest and rewin his Clare seat before permitting him into the House of Commons; it also outlawed the Catholic Association and insisted that Catholic M.P.s take an insulting oath of allegiance.

The immediate benefits of the 1829 relief bill were less than revolutionary: upper and middle-class Catholics gained increased political, social, and professional opportunities, but the peasant masses continued to exist as manorial serfs or as members of a wretched, urban proletariat. However, although the legislation of 1829 fell far short of the jubilant expectations of the Irish-Catholic masses, this step toward total emancipation was an important event with implications not only for Ireland but for all of Western civilization as well as the English-speaking world.

The Catholic Association was the embryo of modern Irish nationalism and served as the model for other constitutional reform movements all over the United Kingdom. As part of the agitation for Catholic civil rights, O'Connell had instructed the Irish masses in the art of democratic politics, turning them into political sophisticates. Through working toward emancipation, Irish Catholics both learned to manipulate the British constitutional system and acquired the confidence to do it. And the Irish who emigrated to North America entered a similar Anglo-Saxon environment already equipped with political weapons to compete for power against Protestant cultural foes.

In addition to encouraging further reform efforts in Ireland, O'Connell's success against the Protestant Ascendancy inspired all liberal democrats fighting for change in the bleak mood of Metternich's Europe. The Catholic Emancipation struggle in Ireland paved the way for Jewish and black liberation movements throughout the Western world. On the negative side, the Catholic victory over Anglo-Saxon and Anglo-Irish Protestant prejudices strengthened the intensity of anti-Catholic passions throughout the United Kingdom. Fearful of eventual, complete victory for the Catholic democracy, Irish Protestants bound themselves even closer to Britain as the ultimate protector of their lives, property, and political power.

During the early 1830s, O'Connell sat in the British House of Commons in a dual capacity—as leader of an Irish nationalist movement dedicated to repeal of the Union and as a prominent Benthamite Radical advocating prison and legal reforms, black and Jewish emancipation, and complete political democracy. Because of these multiple roles, he injected Irish nationalism with a strong commitment to the basic principles of liberal democracy, a contribution that had a profound influence on both British and American history.

Although he served with energy and skill in the House of Commons, O'Connell had little confidence in the British Parliament as a vehicle for Irish freedom and/or reform. He wrote in 1840:

It is vain to expect any relief from England. All parties there concur in hatred to Ireland and Catholicity; and it is also founded in human nature that they should, for they have injured us too much ever to forgive us.[3]

Despite this profound insight into the psychology of hate and prejudice, O'Connell was prepared to go to any lengths—even cooperation with British politicians—to achieve some improvement in the Irish condition. In the 1834 Lichfield House Compact, the Irish leader verbally agreed to an alliance with British Whigs. In exchange for a promise of good government and remedial legislation for Ireland, he pledged to give the Union an opportunity to work and to stop agitating against the British connection.

The Lichfield House Compact had some immediate, beneficial results for Ireland. In 1831, even before the alliance, the Whigs had given the Irish a national primary-level school system. To reduce religious controversy and hostility, the national schools concentrated on a nondenominational approach to secular subjects but permitted the various churches to provide supplemental religious instructions for their own members. At first Protestant leaders protested such "Godless education," and Catholic spokesmen welcomed it as an opportunity to raise the cultural level of their own people. Later, however, Irish nationalists, encouraged by their Catholic bishops, condemned the national schools while Protestants in turn defended them. The nationalists attacked the schools as agents of British cultural imperialism, and Catholic bishops derided them as instruments of Protestant proselytism. Protestants, on the other hand, claimed that nondenominational, government education was better than a system under the control of the papist hierarchy. By the middle of the nineteenth century, however, the national schools had already become denominational with Catholic priests running school boards in areas with Catholic majorities while Protestant parsons performed this same function in Protestant districts. And although the national schools did teach English history, literature, and language and undermined the use of Irish, schoolmasters often adopted a nationalist point of view, and advancing literacy provided an audience for nationalist propaganda.

To fulfill their promise of remedial legislation in the 1834 Lichfield House Compact, the Whigs sent Thomas Drummond to serve as undersecretary at Dublin Castle. Drummond reduced the strength of Protestant Ascendancy by appointing Catholics to a number of Irish government offices, but despite this, O'Connell decided that the Whigs had failed to live up to their part of the bargain.

In protesting the shallowness of the Whigs' Irish policy, O'Connell pointed to the new Irish Poor Law as illustrative of the inability of British politicians to understand the uniqueness of the Irish situation and to the recently-passed Irish Municipal Reform Bill as evidence that the British were not prepared to trust Irish Catholics with political power. He considered the reform bill to be a pale imitation of a more liberal measure passed for Britain, but he reserved most of his anger for the Irish Poor Law. He described the workhouse system it proposed as totally inappropriate in a country where a third of the population qualified as paupers and where taxes to support that number in workhouses would reduce another third to the level of mendicants.

Although his opposition to Irish municipal reform and poor relief was vehement, O'Connell remained loyal to his pact with the Whigs, keeping Lord Melbourne's cynical and lethargic administration in office. But he started to send out signals that Ireland was dissatisfied with inaction and angry with false promises. O'Connell was preparing the ground for a large-scale attempt to repeal the Union.

When O'Connell's old enemy Sir Robert Peel became prime minister in 1841, the Irish leader decided it was time to abandon efforts to work within the parliamentary system for Irish reform and to return to the tactics of mass agitation. He organized the

Loyal National Repeal Association, modeled after the old Catholic Association. By 1843, O'Connell had managed to weave the strands of widespread reaction against the Irish Poor Law, resentment against continued British misgovernment, and the enthusiasm and organization of Father Theobold Mathew's large temperance group into a massive repeal movement that exceeded in members and wealth the Catholic Emancipation effort of the 1820s. A major factor in the success of the repeal association was the contribution of the Young Ireland movement, a group of bright young men who helped create the ideology of Irish cultural nationalism.

Thomas Davis, like Robert Emmet a Protestant and product of Trinity College, seemed to epitomize the intelligence, idealism, and romanticism of Young Ireland. In autumn 1842 he and two friends, John Blake Dillon and Charles Gavan Duffy, began to publish a newspaper called the *Nation* as an expression of Irish cultural nationalism. Dillon was a middle-class Catholic from Mayo who had attended Trinity College with Davis, while Duffy, an Ulster Catholic from Monaghan, had acquired considerable experience as a journalist in Belfast. All three attended the King's Inn in Dublin and during breaks from their legal studies discussed the need for an Irish nationalist ideology. These conversations culminated in the decision to publish the *Nation* as the voice of Irish cultural identity.

O'Connell's nationalism had been a logical extension of Whig patriotism and Radical values. He believed that an Irish parliament would protect individual rights, elevate the dignity of the Irish people, and promote the economic prosperity of their country. While he admired British political theory and institutions, O'Connell doubted the possibility of complete Irish assimilation into the United Kingdom because Britons and their parliamentary representatives did not understand or respect Ireland or her people.[4] O'Connell's nationalism was more pragmatic than ideological, essentially pro-Irish rather than anti-British. In contrast, Young Irelanders were enemies of all things British, insisting that their country must be a separate cultural as well as political entity. They represented an Irish version of the general European Romantic movement, which was at least partially inspired by a reaction against the ugliness and urbanization of the Industrial Revolution. To Young Irelanders, Britain was the essence of urban industrialism, and British domination of Ireland was a cultural imperialism attacking a more spiritual, agrarian way of life. They wanted to de-Anglicize Ireland, to purge the Irish mind and soul of alien materialism. Young Irelanders believed that the dogmas of political economy so dear to O'Connell embodied the coarseness and materialism of British urban, industrial culture.

In the columns, editorials, essays, and ballad poetry of the *Nation,* Duffy, Dillon, Davis, and their associates encouraged the Irish people to be aware of their history, language, and traditions. In addition to their own contributions, the editors encouraged readers to submit articles and creative literary efforts on Irish subjects. Unlike so many romantic, cultural nationalists in other parts of Europe, most Young Irelanders rejected racism, refusing to pit Celt against Anglo-Irishman. They emphasized a nationalist creed embracing the total Irish historical experience, insisting that the descendents of Celts, Danes, Normans, Elizabethans, and Cromwellians could all claim Irish nationality. This cosmopolitan attitude was clearly expressed in Thomas Davis's poem, "Anglo-Saxon and Celt":

> What matters that at different shrines
>     We pray unto one God?
> What matters that at different times
>     Our fathers won this sod?
>
> In fortune and in name we're bound
>     By stronger links than steel;
> And neither can be safe nor sound
>     But in the other's weal.

Unfortunately, the reality of the Irish historical experience contradicted the Young Ireland version of the past and hope for an ecumenical future.[5] To Anglo-Irish Protestants it mattered a great deal at what shrines Irishmen worshipped God and when their fathers won Irish sod. They rejected O'Connell's and Young Ireland's invitations to participate in Irish nationalism, insisting that the Union sheltered them from the property lusts and political ambitions of a dangerous Catholic democracy led by the clerical agents of an ambitious Vatican.

Although Young Irelanders failed to touch the minds and hearts of Protestant Ireland, their message reached Catholics. The eight thousand subscribers to the *Nation* were only a small portion of the numbers exposed to Young Ireland's brand of cultural nationalism. Repeal reading rooms featured the *Nation,* and local "scholars" trained in national schools read its message to their illiterate friends and relatives in peasant cottages scattered throughout the country.

Despite his organizational genius, Young Ireland's gospel of cultural nationalism, and the enthusiasm of the Irish masses, O'Connell could not honor his pledge to the people that 1843 would be "the Repeal Year." Trapped by the glory of past successes, he misjudged the situation and the intentions of his opponents. When O'Connell again used organized Irish mass opinion to confront Peel with the alternatives of reform or revolution, the British leader refused to retreat. This time he made it clear that he would risk civil war to preserve the Union because it was essential to the security of the United Kingdom and the empire. Tory, Whig, and Radical M.P.s announced that they would support the prime minister's resistance to repeal.

When O'Connell finally realized that British politicians viewed Catholic Emancipation and repeal of the Union as completely separate issues deserving different kinds of responses, he began to slow down the repeal agitation, pleading with his followers to obey the law and to avoid violence. In October 1843, O'Connell decided to abide by a government proclamation banning a large repeal meeting scheduled for Clontarf, a Dublin suburb. Many a nationalist hothead would have welcomed a showdown with the British authorities, but the Irish leader would not permit his people to be killed by trained soldiers. His decision to conform to the law ended repeal as a significant expression of Irish nationalism. Shortly after the Clontarf meeting crisis, the British government arrested O'Connell along with some of his lieutenants, including Duffy, and prosecuted them on charges of sedition.

A Dublin jury convicted the men, and the judge levied fines and sentenced them to a year in prison. But after O'Connell and his associates had spent only a few months in Richmond Jail, the British Law Lords in a three-to-two decision (three Whigs and two Tories) decided that the leaders were victims of an improper indictment and a packed jury and ordered them freed. Irish nationalist opinion interpreted O'Connell's release as a great victory over British tyranny and injustice. The people lit celebration bonfires and a large crowd cheered O'Connell's carriage as it moved from the prison to his home in Merrion Square, Dublin. Unfortunately, O'Connell, approaching 70 years of age, was too old and dazed by his prison experience to generate enthusiasm for another large-scale protest. Speechifying rather than action became the routine of the Loyal National Repeal Association.

Still, the failure of repeal in 1843 was not a total defeat for O'Connell. His success in rousing the Irish masses forced Peel to reconsider Britain's Irish policy and the implications of Protestant Ascendancy. In 1845 and 1846, after he was certain that law and order had been restored in Ireland and that insurrection was no longer a threat, the prime minister introduced a comprehensive program of reform in an effort to destroy nationalism. This strategy involved fragmenting the Irish nationalist movement into its component parts—priest, peasant, lawyer, merchant, and shopkeeper—and attempting to give each class an identity of its own that would supersede loyalty to any abstract Irish nation. For example, Peel provided the Catholic hierarchy and clergy with a Charitable Bequests Act facilitating the inheritance of property by the church and a permanent endowment with an increased income for the Catholic seminary at Maynooth. The prime minister intended both of these concessions as initial steps on the road to an eventual dual religious establishment in Ireland.

While Peel directed his main efforts toward removing the Catholic clergy from the vortex of Irish agitation by nurturing a dependence on English generosity, he also wanted the Catholic middle class to develop attitudes similar to those of their Protestant counterparts in Ireland and Britain. To achieve this goal, he provided them with opportunities for higher education in the newly constructed and staffed Queen's Colleges located in Galway and Cork.[6] The prime minister recognized peasant discontent by appointing a commission chaired by Lord Devon, an Englishman who owned an Irish estate and was sympathetic to the lot of Irish farmers, to investigate relations between landlords and tenants as a prelude to legislation that would increase the latter's economic security.

O'Connell blocked Peel's attempt to separate nationalism from its Catholic roots by frightening Irish nationalists with a warning that an alliance between Britain and the Vatican would endanger the freedom cause by removing Catholic bishops and priests, the agents of the movement, from the center of agitation. The prime minister's overtures to Irish Catholicism also antagonized British anti-Catholics. They were particularly incensed by Peel's proposal to endow Maynooth, "the classroom of papist treason." And his scheme to woo the Irish middle class through the Queen's Colleges was opposed by Catholic bishops who praised Peel for the Maynooth grant but condemned him for emphasizing a nondenominational education for Catholics. They refused permission for Catholics to attend the secular Queen's Colleges or to hold faculty or administrative positions in the new institutions. Land reform as envisioned in the appointment of the Devon Commission encountered the intractable resistance of British upper and middle classes' commitments to unrestricted property rights. Despite Peel's slight success in weakening the fabric of Irish nationalism by concessions to Irish grievances, his reform legislation did change the condition of the Catholic church in Ireland, and it established precedents for the consideration of future British politicians.

Following O'Connell's release from prison and his decision to cool passions in the ranks of Irish nationalism, relations between the old leader and his Young Ireland allies rapidly deteriorated. Temperament, personality, and ideological differences contributed to tensions within the repeal association. Romantic, uncompromising Young Irelanders complained about O'Connell's pragmatic tactics and his willingness to cooperate with British Whigs to achieve reform. They argued that collaboration with Whiggery demoralized Irish nationalism. As an aging hero, O'Connell no doubt was subject to the petty jealousies old leaders usually display toward bright, ambitious young men coveting their place. And people around him, particularly his son John, who envied the talents of Davis, Duffy, and Dillon, distorted the message of the *Nation*, feeding the old man's fears and suspicions.

O'Connell was convinced that Young Ireland's efforts to deemphasize sectarian differences between Protestants and Catholics was motivated more by religious indifference than by Christian tolerance. And he feared that the constant praise for former Irish rebels like the United Irishmen that appeared in the columns of the *Nation* encouraged the Irish people to abandon constitutional nationalism for physical force. In 1846, O'Connell decided it was time for a showdown with Young Ireland. He insisted that they formally agree that association members must never advocate revolution for Ireland or leave the organization. Unable to comply with this ultimatum, Young Irelanders walked out of Conciliation Hall, the association's headquarters, and organized the Irish Confederation primarily to promote Irish cultural nationalism and harmony between Catholics and Protestants. The new organization did attract middle-class nationalists in cities and towns, but the peasant masses, led by their priests, remained true to O'Connell and Old Ireland.

Early in its history as a separatist repeal movement, the confederation also was split by tactical and ideological quarrels inspired by the fiery zeal of a new member, John Mitchel. After Thomas Davis died of scarlet fever in 1845 and while John Blake Dillon was recuperating from a bout with tuberculosis, Charles Gavan Duffy had to bear most of the responsibility for editing the *Nation* and managing confederation affairs. He did have the help of William Smith O'Brien, an M.P. and Protestant landlord from Clare who resigned from the Whig party in 1843 and enlisted in the repeal association, and in 1845 Duffy also recruited Mitchel, an Ulster Protestant with a brilliant and passionate style of journalism, to take Davis's place at the *Nation.*

Mitchel, who hated Britain and British culture, came under the intellectual influence of James Fintan Lalor, another contributor to the *Nation,* who insisted that the agrarian question demanded priority over political dissolution of the Union. Lalor argued that "the land of Ireland for the people of Ireland" should be the first consideration of the Irish Confederation and urged a rent strike as means of destroying the landlord-tenant system. Mitchel accepted Lalor's economic premise and built on its foundation, recommending the nonpayment of taxes as well as rents as a tactic to paralyze British rule and destroy landlordism in Ireland.

Since O'Brien and Duffy remained confident that Irish nationalism should attract Protestant support, they rejected Mitchel's suggestion because it encouraged class and sectarian conflict. They also pointed out that the nonpayment of rates would increase the suffering of Irish peasants by reducing funds available for famine relief. Duffy and O'Brien recommended the formation of an Irish parliamentary party which, as the voice of Irish opinion in the House of Commons, would serve as a political alternative to Mitchel's economic radicalism. They foresaw a time when the Irish party would be strong enough to demand repeal of the Union and be prepared to deliver the consequences if British M.P.s refused Irish independence. According to this plan, nationalist M.P.s would withdraw from Westminster, return to Dublin, and establish an Irish parliament that would be supported by Irish public opinion and local government agencies. A majority of the Irish Confederation preferred the Duffy-O'Brien strategy to the plan Mitchel proposed, so the latter left the organization and the *Nation* to start his own newspaper, *The United Irishman,* which advocated a revolution against British tyranny and instructed its readers on the techniques of guerrilla-style street fighting.

Shortly after the split in the Irish Confederation early in 1848, revolution broke out in Paris and spread to Germany, the Hapsburg Empire, and Italy. Inspired by the general feeling of the European left that the days of the old regime were numbered, Young Ireland abandoned constitutional for revolutionary nationalism. Mitchel rejoined the confederation, and O'Brien led a delegation to Paris to seek the aid of the leaders of the Second French Republic for an Irish liberation movement. Courteous but cautious—they did not want to antagonize British politicians and endanger England's recognition of their coup d'etat —French Republicans warmly hosted the Young Irelanders but sent them home without any pledges of aid.

Finally, the British government in 1848 pressured Young Irelanders into a premature rebellion through coercion laws and the arrest of many confederation leaders, including O'Brien, Mitchel, and Thomas Francis Meagher. After juries freed Meagher and O'Brien, the government rushed special legislation through Parliament which allowed it to convict Mitchel of treason and send him off on a prison ship to Van Dieman's Land, now Tasmania. Continued government pressure and arrests—Duffy went to jail to await trial—convinced confederation leaders that they could no longer postpone a strike for Irish freedom.

Young Irelanders were excellent journalists and intelligent nationalists but hopeless revolutionaries. Their middle-class respect for property rights, in combination with their unrealistic efforts to court Protestant gentry support, prevented them from devising the kind of cold-blooded, destructive, guerrilla-war tactics that might have produced a few victories. And they never seemed to understand that Irish peasants suffering from hunger and disease were hopeless revolutionary material. Carelessly planned, without public support or adequate equipment, O'Brien's insurrection ended in a comic-opera skirmish with the Royal Irish Constabulary in a Kilkenny cabbage patch. Shortly after an inglorious defeat, O'Brien and many of his associates were tried and convicted of treason and sent to Australia as political prisoners. Other Young Irelanders managed to elude capture and left the country for exile in France or North America.

As 1848 came to a close, Young Irelanders seemed to be pitiful failures. But as the nineteenth century progressed, the mythology and needs of Irish nationalism transformed the farce of 1848 into a heroic enterprise, moving Young Irelanders into the pantheon of Irish martyrs for freedom. The editorials, essays, and ballad poetry of the *Nation* became the scriptures of Irish cultural nationalism. Exiles took the gospel of Young Ireland with them on their journeys across the Irish Sea and the Atlantic Ocean, cultivating it in the fertile soil of ghetto discontent.[7]

\* \* \*

Up to this point the emphasis in this analysis of the Irish Question has been on the religious, political, and cultural dimensions of the conflict between Irish Catholics and Anglo-Saxon and Anglo-Irish Protestants. But most Irish Catholics were more concerned with food and land than they were with

Catholic Emancipation or repeal of the Union. And after the victory of Catholic Emancipation, the land question developed as the most important element in the clash between Irish nationalism and British and Irish Unionism.

In the middle of the eighteenth century, Irish peasants were the most miserable representatives of their class in Western Europe. Their standard of living was probably lower than that of black slaves in North America. Peasants fortunate enough to have rented farms usually occupied less than fifteen acres—five was the average—and many residents of rural Ireland were agricultural laborers or bog squatters attempting to feed large families with the produce of an acre or less. Irish peasants lived in mud huts, usually windowless, with dirt floors and a hole in the thatched roof to serve as a chimney. Cabin interiors were dirty and smoky from turf fires, constant rains turned dirt floors into mud holes, and thatched roofs, although attractive from a distance, hosted a variety of vermin. Since animals were precious—their sale paid the rent—large families shared their wretched hovels with pigs and chickens. These unsanitary living conditions resulted in heavy infant mortality and high death rates from tuberculosis and diseases associated with diet deficiencies.

Most of the scanty information about the habits and personalities of eighteenth-century Irish peasants came from the pens of English and Continental visitors. Travelers in Ireland were appalled by the poverty in rural areas and criticized the cruelty of the manorial system. They described Irish peasants as happy-go-lucky, shiftless, emotional, courteous, generous, and generally good-natured but easily provoked into violent rages. In summary, the outsider saw the Irish-Catholic peasant as childlike, needing guidance and discipline.

There is, of course, some truth in stereotypes. Servitude, poverty, and a constant struggle for survival degrade human nature, encouraging personality weaknesses rather than strengths. In Ireland, the domination of alien landlords and the serfdom of the native population did produce lazy and inefficient farmers, and poverty and insecurity encouraged the excessive consumption of alcohol, which fueled violence. Since humility is a mask that slaves frequently don for survival purposes, Irish peasants were courteous, often to the point of obsequiousness.

Visitors, however, saw only the superficial traits of the Irish peasant character; they could not distinguish between the mask and the reality. Anger seethed in the peasant soul, often boiling over into clashes between families and party fights between Catholics and Protestants in the border counties of Ulster. In frustration, many Irish peasants expressed their anger against the system by joining agrarian secret societies. Whiteboys, Defenders, and Ribbonmen represented the brutalization of the Irish peasant, his need to express his despair in violence because he could not articulate needs through the Irish political, social, economic, and legal systems, which looked after the interests of the Protestant Ascendancy.

During the eighteenth century, most of the Irish peasantry outside the province of Leinster still spoke Irish, and wandering bards taught them Gaelic legends and folklore. Aisling poems, a popular form of literary expression, promised a return of the Gaelic order through a restoration of the Stuart dynasty. But despite the claims of modern Irish nationalists, there were few Gaelic cultural influences left in the peasant environment. Songs and stories of a former aristocratic, Gaelic society or hopes of returning Stuart kings had little relevance for Irish serfs. Some Gaelic values no doubt survived English invasion, conquest, resettlement, and persecution, but native Irish culture had been transformed into what was essentially a rural, peasant, Catholic culture similar to life-styles in most parts of Italy, Poland, Portugal, or Spain. Catholicism, not Gaelic culture, was the essential ingredient in the Irish life-style. Catholicism was a source of comfort in a painful existence, a touch of beauty in an ugly environment, an outlet for pent-up emotions.

It served to dampen violence and provided a hope of salvation, a bond of unity, and a source of identity.

Although it seems impossible, the Irish rural standard of living actually fell from 1750 to 1845. A massive population increase was most responsible for the decline. All of Europe experienced this population explosion, but the percentage of growth was highest in Ireland. From 1725 to 1841, the Irish population expanded from about three million to more than eight million, putting tremendous pressure on a static, inefficient land system. Competition for farms increased rents, leading to the subdivision of holdings that were already too small for efficient cultivation and decent family incomes.

Population experts have explained the eighteenth-century population boom in terms of the Industrial Revolution, arguing that improved technology provided more and cheaper food, pipes to carry away sewage and bring fresh water for drinking and washing, inexpensive clothing, and the beginnings of preventive medicine. This thesis certainly applied to industrial Britain, but as one social historian, Kenneth H. Connell, in *The Population of Ireland* (1950) pointed out, industrialism had little significance for Ireland. There the most dramatic population increase took place without a varied diet, cheap clothing, sewage disposal, or preventive medicine. In Ireland the population explosion was a product of increased fertility. In Ireland boys married at sixteen, girls at fourteen, and they had large families, considering children a blessing from God. Infant mortality was high, but many children managed to survive dirt, fever, and malnutrition.

Cultivation of the potato as an almost exclusive food source also contributed to Irish population growth. Potatoes grew easily in bad soil, needing little attention, and an acre of them could feed a large family. During the last few decades of the eighteenth and the first four of the nineteenth century, Ireland exported grain and meat to Britain, but the peasant masses ate potatoes, selling their grain crops, pigs, chickens, and eggs to pay their rents. The average peasant consumed between ten and twelve pounds of potatoes every day, usually boiled and seasoned with a little salt. He seldom enjoyed the taste of meat, cheese, eggs, fish or bread, and milk was also a luxury.

The exclusive use of one food on the Irish peasant table, however, frequently subjected the rural population to the dangers of famine. Potato crop failures because of bad weather or disease resulted in many deaths from malnutrition and its allies, scurvy and fever. Frequent famines in the 1820s convinced many Irish Catholics to emigrate to North America.

Although famines were frequent and devastating, they were usually of short duration. In 1845, however, a potato fungus spread from North America to Europe, hitting Ireland the hardest because of the importance of the potato to the Irish diet. In 1845, the fungus destroyed almost the entire potato crop, and the disaster was complete the next year. The following winter was exceptionally severe, making it difficult for people to forage beneath the snow for nettles, weeds, and cabbage leaves. In 1847 the fungus did not appear, but farmers either lacked money to purchase seed or they had eaten what seed potatoes they did have. The next year optimism encouraged heavy planting, but the blight returned. Eighteen forty-nine was the last year for a diseased potato crop, but the effects of hunger, scurvy, fever, cholera, and low morale survived into 1851.

When the Great Famine began in 1845, the estimated Irish population was approaching nine million, with at least a third of that number below the poverty level. During the famine years, at least a million and a half people perished from starvation and related diseases. They died so quickly and in such large numbers that it was difficult to bury the dead. Rats, cats, and dogs fed on human carcasses. Famine also stimulated the process of emigration. Considerably more than a million people left Ireland between 1845 and 1851 to seek refuge in Britain and North America, mainly the United States.

Since emigrants often started without adequate provisions,

sailed in ships lacking adequate space, food, or sanitation facilities, and sometimes carried famine fever with them, a large number of transatlantic passengers died enroute to the New World. Voyages were nightmares for terrified refugees; they were sick from rolling seas, the stench below deck, hunger and fever; they were assaulted and cheated by brutal ship captains and crews. Those who did reach their destinations were often cheated of scarce funds by runners, grog and boarding-house keepers, and by sellers of real and counterfeit railroad, canal, or riverboat tickets. A number of immigrants landed without clothing, stepping literally naked into a new world. Most often these people were part of landlord-sponsored emigration projects. Seriously concerned for the welfare of their tenants, some landowners hired ships and sent their people off well-provisioned to what they hoped might be a better life. But there were others without a sense of decency, responsibility, or humanity who transported their tenants without adequate food or clothing, not to help them but to reduce their own contributions to poor relief.

Without a doubt, the Great Famine was the most dramatic and decisive event in modern Irish history. The experience of mass hunger, disease, death, and emigration had a negative influence on the Irish personality, encouraging despair, insecurity, paranoia, and hatred for all things British. Irish nationalism responded to the disaster with a number of crucial questions: since Britain was the richest and most powerful nation in the world and since Ireland was part of the United Kingdom, why had the British government permitted the export of Irish meat and grain at a time when the peasant masses were perishing from hunger? Why did the government fail to provide a sufficient food supply for the Irish people? These questions were mainly rhetorical; nationalists thought they knew the answer: genocide.

Were the nationalists right? Did British politicians attempt to solve the troublesome Irish Question by allowing a large portion of the Irish population to starve? This does not seem to be the case. Even without the exportation of agricultural products from Ireland, there still would have been a serious food shortage in the country after the failure of several potato crops. And many English politicians, civil servants, religious groups, and ordinary citizens did contribute money or otherwise help with famine relief efforts.[8] Peel's administration distributed imported Indian maize to the Irish people, and the Whigs spent millions of pounds for food distribution, public works projects, and soup kitchens. British physicians and civil servants, along with their Irish counterparts, and both Irish-Catholic and Protestant clergymen contracted fatal diseases while administering food, medicine, and spiritual comfort to famine victims.

Despite their exaggerated rhetoric, however, there is some validity to the arguments of Irish nationalists that Britain was guilty of grave atrocities in her response to famine in Ireland. In a way, many of the famine dead and exiled were victims of a kind of ideological torture and murder, because British politicians administered relief within the narrow confines of *laissez faire* dogma. Because the ideology of political economy was more important than people—particularly poor Irish peasants —Tory and Whig governments did not make an all-out effort to save lives in Ireland. They insisted that the Irish people must not lose their initiative by becoming dependent on government welfare, and they tried to prevent relief programs from interfering with normal trade and commerce.[9]

If English, Welsh, or Scotsmen had been dying of hunger and fever, British governments might have shown more concern. Religious and cultural prejudices as well as *laissez faire* dogma influenced British attitudes toward misfortune in Ireland. George Trevelyan, head of the Treasury and the man most responsible for Whig famine relief projects, considered the potato blight and its consequences a Divine punishment of a wicked and perverse people. And Nassau Senior, a prominent economist who advised Whig political leaders, viewed the Great Famine as a solution to the Irish population problem, regretting only its limited efficiency.

Some British newspapers and periodicals of the time also reflected British racial and religious prejudices. They argued that the Irish rebellion in 1848 had demonstrated that Irish ingrates did not deserve British help or sympathy. The influential Tory *Quarterly Review* in the late 1840s claimed that the famine attacked an inferior race, people who were victims of their own vices:

> all of civilization, arts, comfort, wealth that Ireland enjoys she owes exclusively to England . . . all of her absurdities, errors, misery she owes to herself . . . this unfortunate result is mainly attributable to that confusion of ideas, that instability of purpose, and above all, that reluctance to steady work which are indubitable features of the national character.

In Ireland famine memories left permanent psychological scars; in the ghettos of America Irish emigrants were even more bitter. They accused Britain of tyranny and murder and blamed her for their poverty and exile. The Irish of the Diaspora, nurturing famine hatreds and educated on the cultural nationalism of Young Ireland, became even more passionately pro-Irish and anti-English than those who remained at home. They would become a decisive factor in the Irish fight for freedom, and their experiences with Anglo-Saxon and Anglo-Irish Protestants in the United Kingdom would color their responses to the Anglo-American Protestant culture in the United States.

# 4

## Refugees from Disaster:
## The Irish Immigrants, 1822-1870

⚛

Contrary to pub talk on both sides of the Atlantic, Irish-Americans were not the decisive factor in the thirteen colonies' War of Independence. By 1790, in fact, there were only about 44,000 Irish-born residents in the United States, most of them Protestants and many of them Presbyterians from Ulster. Since the early eighteenth century, American and Canadian ships had stopped in Irish ports after delivering flax seed and lumber cargoes to the British Isles to pick up immigrants as ballast. An average ten-guinea transatlantic fare guaranteed that most of the Irish entering America were people of at least moderate means. The majority were artisans or tenant farmers, many of the latter doubling as handloom weavers. They came to the New World to find opportunities in a land further removed from the oppression of British mercantilism. And since most of them were nonconformists, rather than Church of Irelanders, they also fled Ireland to protest religious discrimination that relegated them to second-class citizenship within the Protestant social order.

Ulster nonconformists brought energy to their new country along with economic and intellectual skills and a commitment to democratic principles that speeded the maturation of America. Catholics, who constituted a smaller part of this early American emigration, were also farmers and artisans who had the ability to make an immediate contribution to a dynamic, emerging nation.

Most pre-1815 Irish Catholics who left Ireland, however, were poor people who went to Britain. Some of them helped to harvest crops in England and Scotland, while others supplied unskilled labor for industrial and transportation needs by digging canals, laying railroad track, driving and caring for horses, and loading ships, trains, and wagons. When they earned enough to pay rents to their Irish landlords, harvest workers tended to return home; gandy dancers (railroad workers), navvies (canal diggers), teamsters (wagon drivers), and stevedores (cargo handlers) frequently remained in Britain. Even before the Great Famine of the middle and late 1840s, Irish ghettos had emerged in Liverpool, Manchester, Birmingham, Glasgow, London, and other large cities in England and Scotland.

After 1815, the pace of Irish immigration to America rapidly increased. Among the factors prompting emigration were an economic recession in the United Kingdom that followed the Napoleonic Wars and a shift in Irish agriculture from tillage to grazing, resulting in consolidation of estates and evictions of small tenant farmers. Other emigrants feared the violence of secret terrorist societies like the Ribbonmen or wanted to avoid the increasing agitation for Catholic Emancipation and for the abolition of tithes to the established Protestant church. From 1815 to 1845, more than a million Irish immigrants entered the United States. In the early stages of this new wave of immigration, most of the newcomers were still Protestants, but then periodic famines and lower ship fares converted Irish immigration from a Protestant to a Catholic movement. Many of the new Catholic immigrants sailed first to Canada, some reaching their final destinations in the United States via Newfoundland, while others walked south from New Brunswick into Maine and eventually into the rest of New England.

Although the Great Famine (1845–1849) did not initiate this mass exodus from Ireland, it did a great deal to institutionalize emigration as a permanent feature of Irish life. During the grim years of potato crop failures, hunger, and disease, nearly two million desperate Irish refugees sought shelter in Britain, Canada, and the United States.

Malnutrition and its numerous physical and psychological by-products finally persuaded the Irish to abandon their traditional attitudes toward marriage and reproduction. Starting in the 1850s, famine memories encouraged fewer and later marriages, a decrease in the birth rate, and a reluctance to divide small farms. The average age of marriage in Ireland began a steady climb from the lowest to the highest in Europe. Economic strictures were given moral interpretations through a rigid sexual code taught by Catholic priests but partly shaped by British Evangelical Protestant puritanism. In spite of all this, the Irish population continued to exceed the available resources of its static, rural economy. Only one son could inherit the farm, and few daughters, even with beauty enhanced by dowries, could find men in a financial position to marry. Young people without land to work or prospects of marriage either entered the seminary or convent or followed the trails of emigration to urban centers in Britain and America.

Throughout the nineteenth and early twentieth centuries, Irish emigration to Britain remained steady. Fares for the short passages to Liverpool, Glasgow, and Cardiff were within the means of even the poorest tenant farmers and agricultural laborers. And going to Britain involved less of a commitment to permanent exile than did the long, transatlantic voyages to Quebec, Boston, New York, or New Orleans. Many refugees in Britain were comforted by the knowledge that their homeland was just across the Irish Sea, within easy reach. Still, America represented extensive opportunities and a cleaner break with an oppressive past. Many Irish immigrants in America, attempting to calm parental anxieties and to present an image of success, wrote letters home exaggerating the possibilities for the good life in the United States. These messages, along with enclosed money to purchase ship tickets for brothers and sisters, stimulated the process of emigration.

In the ten-year period from the beginning of the Great Famine in 1845 to the end of 1854, nearly a million and a half Irish immigrants arrived in the United States. Although the total emigration rate from Ireland slowed down in the postfamine period, from 1855 through 1870 more than a million Irish people, usually young men and women between 15 and 35 years of age, came to the United States. Since they constituted the first large group of people who were not Anglo-Saxon Protestants to arrive in the United States, Irish Catholics had the painful and dubious distinction of pioneering the American urban ghetto, previewing experiences that would later be shared by Italians, Jews, Poles, and other Slavs from eastern Europe, blacks migrating to the North from the rural South, Chicanos, and Puerto Ricans.

Although physically absent from their parishes and townlands in Ireland, emigrants continued to influence the course of life back home. Irish-American refugees from Irish poverty, particularly the women, were generous in sending hard-earned dollars to their relatives back in the old country. In the 13-year period between 1848 and 1861, although the Irish were on the bottom rung of the American socioeconomic ladder, they still managed to send almost sixty million dollars to Ireland. This sum was recorded in bank drafts and money orders of the time but does not include the many dollars enclosed in letters. While a quarter of this money—scrounged from the meager earnings of servant girls and unskilled manual laborers—financed the emigration of family members, most of the dollars that journeyed from America to Ireland went to improve the standard of living for relatives left behind. This money improved the Irish life-style and helped finance both constitutional and revolutionary nationalist efforts to free Ireland from British rule. Thus the letter from America containing news from loved ones, a gift of money, and perhaps a boat ticket was an important event in the cottages of rural Ireland.

The concentration of the Irish in urban residences and in industrial occupations in the United States seemed to contradict their agrarian heritage. According to the brilliant anthropogeographer, E. Estyn Evans, "The whole nature of Gaelic society was opposed to urban living"; cities were associated with foreign invaders and an alien culture.[1] But in the United States, the Irish as a group scorned the vast and fertile open lands of the West and the opportunity to buy farms at bargain prices, preferring to live in cities. In 1870, seventy-two percent of the American Irish were concentrated in seven urban, industrial states—Massachusetts, Connecticut, New York, New Jersey, Pennsylvania, Ohio, and Illinois—usually residing in communities whose population exceeded 2,500. Considering their agrarian roots, why did Irish immigrants decide to dwell in urban rather than rural America?

In *Boston's Immigrants* (1941), Oscar Handlin argued that Irish famine refugees really had no choice but to settle in cities along the East Coast because they lacked the funds to move west. While this explanation is true, money problems do not adequately explain the urbanization of the American Irish. Wealthier, prefamine immigrants also chose to live in cities, and when the Irish finally did begin to move west, most of them preferred places like Chicago, St. Louis, St. Paul, and San Francisco to farms.

Lack of skills was far more important than a shortage of funds in determining the Irish-Americans' decision to become city dwellers. Because manorialism and serfdom had not encouraged agrarian skills or knowledge, Irish peasants were among the most inefficient farmers in Europe and were not equipped for life in rural America. Irish agriculture traditionally was more a cultural life-style than an economic system, and Irish peasants still used only simple tools—the spade, the scythe, and the hoe.

Unable to cope with the techniques of large-scale American farming, the Irish in America, like those in Britain, had to start at the bottom of the urban, unskilled labor force. Women took jobs as servants or shirt makers in textile factories; men worked as stable boys; bartenders, bouncers, and pot boys in saloons; street sweepers; dockers; and canal diggers. Before the Civil War, Irish Catholics provided the muscle for canal construction in the United States. In 1818, three thousand Irishmen were digging the Erie Canal; eight years later there were five thousand Irish navvies working on four major canal projects. After the war, the Irish built the railroads east of the Rockies. Life on the canals and railroads was tough and unhealthy, encouraging the Irishman to drink his salary and troubles away.

Work on railroads and canals did move the Irish west, and military enlistments also scattered them around the country. Back in the United Kingdom, many Irish lads joined the British army or navy to escape the poverty and boredom of rural Ireland, to seek adventure and see the world, and to have a few shillings jingling in their pockets. In America, a large number of Irishmen also decided that military careers combined excitement with a kind of economic security. During the Mexican, Civil, and Spanish-American Wars, the United States government depended on the many Irish-Americans who served as regulars in the armed forces or who were quick to volunteer to defend their adopted country. In the United States the Irish had motives for fighting that were lacking back home. They had served Britain for gold and excitement; they fought for the United States out of love and patriotism.

Irish labor contributed much to the progress of the Industrial Revolution in America. Irish women often found jobs more easily than did their husbands or sons. As the first servant class in the urban North, Irish women paved the way for other minority-group women who followed them into the ghettos. But high male unemployment and the availability of only seasonal work or traveling labor jobs on the railroads and canals for men, coupled with high female employment, frequently had disastrous effects on family life and relations between the sexes.

Irish economic and social problems in the early and mid-nineteenth century were similar to present-day difficulties in urban, minority-group neighborhoods. Although some comparisons between early Irish and contemporary black ghettos are valid, the Irish did have more unskilled labor opportunities than do twentieth-century blacks. Technology and automation have drastically reduced today's job prospects for unskilled workers.

In addition to their lack of agricultural skills, the Irish were not psychologically suited for existence in rural America. Like other Catholic ethnics, they were community-minded, gregarious by nature, fond of visiting and talking. In Ireland small farms were so close together that they really constituted peasant villages. During the day there was considerable conversation across hedges and stone walls. In the evening neighbors visited, talked, sang, and danced in each other's cottages. In rural America, on the other hand, farms were often miles apart and families had to be self-sufficient, seeing neighbors only on Saturday shopping excursions into town or at Sunday church services. Some of the Irish who did settle in rural America sent letters home commenting on the depth of their loneliness. American cities were rough, tough, corrupt, dirty, violent, and unhealthy places to live, but the extroverted Irish found such urban areas congenial because they could live close to ethnic friends and neighbors.

Some Catholic bishops in Ireland and the United States worried that American urban life would destroy the religious and moral values of the transplanted peasants. They encouraged immigrants to bypass cities for a more wholesome, country environment and even sponsored experiments in agrarian settlement. For example, in the 1890s, John Ireland, archbishop of St. Paul, purchased a large tract of fertile Minnesota land and brought Belgian and Irish peasants over to farm it. The Belgians prospered, but the Irish quickly abandoned their fields to work in factories or on the railroad. The failure of Archbishop

Ireland's experiment to save the Irish from urban vice and brutality revealed the lack of agricultural skills among Irish farmers and their preference for community living among their own religious and ethnic group.

To many Americans, particularly members of minority groups who have worked or are working their way up from the poverty of ancestors, the word "ghetto" is loaded with bad connotations. They think of ghettos as unpleasant, unhealthy, violent, and as contradictory to the American ideal of one harmonious nation. They also believe that ghettos have had a strictly negative impact on the progress of the nation, frustrating social mobility and assimilation by freezing people into social, cultural, and occupational patterns by preserving cultures filled with poverty.

Ghetto life certainly does tend to exaggerate and perpetuate ethnic and racial vices and stereotypes. It did nurture Irish failure much more than it encouraged Irish ambition by cultivating the paranoia, defeatism, and feelings of inferiority planted by the past. But the negative aspects were partially balanced by some positive features. American urban life was cold, competitive, and hostile. Anglo-Saxon Protestants, who controlled the economic system, despised the Irish as barbarians, and members of the Anglo-Saxon Protestant working class hated and feared them as competitors on the labor market. In this unfriendly environment, Irish ghettos served as psychological havens, preserving traditions and values and perpetuating a sense of community among people who could have disintegrated in an oppressive situation.

The ghettos also functioned as halfway houses between two cultures. Although the Irish preferred to dwell among fellow Irishmen, they really lacked a practical alternative in the early and mid-nineteenth century. No one else wanted to live with or near them. Their lack of education, poor living habits, and rough social conduct offended native Americans. But despite the lack of skills and cultural deficiencies of the Irish-Catholic immigrants of the 1820s, 1830s, and early 1840s, these new citizens did work hard, began to find a place in the economy, and began to experience some degree of social mobility. By 1845, many Irishmen were moving into the ranks of skilled labor, and some even crossed the border separating the middle class from the proletariat. In their ghetto communities the Irish built churches and schools, and most of them lived quiet, decent, respectable lives.

Just when the American Irish began to overcome the handicaps of their own inadequacies and American prejudices, the famine drove new masses of Irish refugees to the American shore. Although famine immigrants were more economically and culturally sophisticated than the peasants who remained in Ireland, they nevertheless were poor, ignorant, and unskilled. The American economy could not easily absorb them, and they pulled down the entire Irish-American community from the modest heights of respectability that it had worked so hard and so long to achieve.[2]

Famine refugees increased the number of urban Irish ghettos in the United States and expanded the size of those that already existed. When the Irish started to move into sections of New York, Boston, Philadelphia, or New Orleans, other residents fled. The Irish did not know how to live in cities. The migration from agrarian to urban environment resulted in mental and psychological dislocation, accenting Irish vices and destroying Irish virtues.

Housing conditions in postfamine Irish ghettos were atrocious. People lived in old mansions and warehouses converted into crowded tenements or in wooden-crate or tar paper shacks. They also occupied stuffy attics and damp basements, taking turns using the few available beds. Fresh water and toilet facilities were scarce; sewage flowed through the streets and alleys, and fleas, lice, mice, and rats shared accommodations with their human hosts. Cholera and tuberculosis decimated ghetto populations, and mental disorders were common. A plethora of filthy grog houses offered the Irish temporary escape from the horrors of poverty and disease. In the ghetto, Irish girls sold their bodies to provide food and clothing for their families, and Irish boys prowled as muggers and petty thieves.

Irish poverty, crime, and disease placed a tremendous strain on the resources of urban governments and the patience of native Americans, who labeled Irish immigration a social plague that had descended on the United States. During the 1850s, 1860s, and 1870s, the Irish were America's law and order problem. In *Boston's Immigrants,* Handlin presents figures showing that from 1856 to 1863 at least half of the inmates of the Boston House of Correction were Irish. And in 1864, about three-fourths of the people arrested and detained in Boston were Irish. The situation that Handlin describes in this one urban center was typical rather than an exception. In other New England towns, in cities all along the East Coast, and in New Orleans the Irish constituted a majority of the people occupying penal and health institutions at the taxpayers' expense.

In tense Irish ghettos there was always the danger that poverty, drink, despair, and depression would explode into individual or mob violence. In 1863, the Irish poor, who had already contributed more than their fair share to the combatants and casualties in the Civil War, protested a new draft law, which permitted men to purchase substitutes to satisfy their military obligations. While Anglo-Saxon, Protestant, middle-class males could afford to buy replacements, lower-class Irish could not.

Complaints against the new conscription legislation were also manifestations of anti-black prejudices among the Irish. While Irish-Americans were champions of the Union, they were not friends of black emancipation. Their hostility to blacks contradicted the liberal and democratic spirit that O'Connell had given to Irish nationalism and seemed an inappropriate attitude for people who were also victims of bigotry. But since they knew that Anglo-Saxon Protestants considered them something of a human subgroup, perhaps the Irish expressed some sort of ego-defense through feeling and acting superior to another persecuted group. There were also economic reasons for anti-black sentiments among the Irish. Both free blacks and the Irish suffered from cultural and technological deficiencies and competed for unskilled jobs. There was some justification for Irish anxiety over such competition, for on occasion, American employers imported black labor as scabs to break strikes by Irish workingmen.

The anti-slavery movement also discouraged Irish support of black freedom. Quite often leading abolitionists, particularly the clergymen, were at the same time passionate enemies of Irish Catholics. While these men expressed concern over the cruelties of black slavery in the rural South, they seemed indifferent to the social injustices suffered by the Irish in the urban North.

Protests against the 1863 draft law escalated into riots in a number of cities. In New York, violence lasted for five days in July with mobs of angry, inebriated Irish people fighting the police, killing eleven blacks and an Indian mistaken for a black, burning a black orphanage, and destroying three million dollars worth of property. Finally, city officials had to call in the army to restore order. During the long disturbance, police and the military killed twelve hundred rioters and wounded many more while members of the mob killed three policemen and injured others. Interestingly, almost all of the policemen and a large number of the soldiers on riot duty were as Irish as their opponents.

In 1871, an Irish-Protestant Orange parade touched off another violent outbreak in New York City. When Irish Catholics threatened to prevent the Protestants from celebrating King William's 1690 victory over James II and his Irish army at the Boyne on 12 July, organizers of the parade sought and obtained police and military protection. During the procession, a sniper started shooting and soldiers protecting the parade route panicked, firing into the hostile crowd lining the street. When the shooting stopped, thirty-three people were dead and ninety-one were wounded, many of them civilians.[3]

# 5

## *The New Immigrants, 1870-1922*

Although emigration never again reached its famine peak, throughout the last half of the nineteenth century the Irish kept leaving their country, most of them on their way to America. From 1870 to 1900, more than one and a half million Irish immigrants entered the United States, an annual average of more than 50,000. The number of Irish emigrants at any one time during this period depended in part on the quality of harvests. The early and mid-1860s and the first few years of the 1880s were particularly heavy periods of emigration. From 1863 through 1866, blight and bad weather damaged crops, raising the emigration rate to more than 100,000 a year, and economic distress coupled with agrarian unrest and violence in the early 1880s also motivated large numbers of Irish people to go to America. In 1883, more than 105,000 people left Ireland for the United States. However, remedial land legislation and government aid to the poor significantly reduced the level of emigration after 1883. (These measures will be discussed in greater detail in chapter 7.) In 1901 as a result, only 39,201 Irish immigrants entered the United States.

By the 1880s, however, emigration had become a fixed element in Irish life, a rich subject for folk song and story. Ballads told of peasant lads with kit bags loaded with "Cabbage, spuds and bacon" shipping for "The Shores of Americay" and cities along the East Coast:

> Wid my bundle on my shoulder,
> Faith! there's no man could be boulder;
> I'm lavin' dear old Ireland without warnin'
> For I lately took the notion,
> For to cross the briny ocean,
> And I shtart for Philadelphia in the mornin'.[1]

Despite the quick tempo and jocular lyrics of some of the songs about leaving the Emerald Isle, the ballads also emphasized the hardships waiting for those on the other side of the water who found jobs "working upon the railway, the railway" or

> Sucking up the coal dust into your lungs,
> Underneath the hills where there is no sun
> Try to make a living on a dollar a day,
> Digging bloody coal in Pennsylvania.[2]

While songs about going to America could be exuberant, those about leaving Ireland were inevitably sad. In Percy French's ballad "The Mountains of Mourne," an Irishman in London searching "for gold in the streets" is impressed with the sights and sounds of the great city but longs for his Mary "where dark Mourne sweeps down to the sea." And in French's "Emigrant's Letter," a "long sort of sigh" came from all the passengers on "the grand Allen Liner" when "the last bit of waves hid old Donegal."

If the young men and women sailing away were sad because they were leaving their parents, friends, and the familiarity of easy-going rural Ireland, think of the desolation in the minds and hearts of their mothers and fathers. The young emigrants could look forward to adventure, new experiences, and perhaps fame and fortune in the New World. Their parents were left with memories of sons and daughters whom they probably would never see again and with the knowledge that most of their remaining children would also follow their older siblings to urban America or Britain. A folk custom called the "American wake" symbolized the impact of emigration on Irish family life. On the evening before children left for the New World, families would host large parties filled with food and music. Since the young emigrants would travel distances measured in thousands of miles and culturally would move even further from their families, leaving Ireland meant permanent separation with only an occasional letter to maintain ties with home. On days when ships departed from Irish ports for America, weeping and keening people crowded the docks to wave a permanent farewell to relatives and friends. At such times these port cities resembled cemeteries on a funeral day.

While emigration was an emotional blow for individual families, it was also a major disaster for the Irish nation. Although emigration worked as a safety valve, siphoning off surplus people from a one-dimensional economy and lessening social tensions, it also robbed the country of the brightest, most energetic, and most creative portion of its population. This was particularly true in the last third of the nineteenth century, when the quality of people leaving Ireland obviously was improved over that of the prefamine and immediate postfamine periods.

After 1870, mass education and an improved standard of living coupled with changes in the character and style of Irish Catholicism altered the Irish personality in a positive way. Many of the people who had arrived in the United States before, during, and immediately after the Great Famine of the 1840s were illiterate, and perhaps a third could not speak English well. But by 1870, high-quality elementary education in the controversial Irish national schools had radically reduced illiteracy and increased English language fluency. In 1851, nearly fifty percent of the Irish population over age five could not read or write. By 1901 that figure had decreased to less than fourteen percent with only six percent of persons twelve to forty years of age still considered illiterates. By the beginning of the twentieth century, the literacy rate in Ireland was higher than rates in either Britain or the United States. Irish arrivals at Ellis Island may have been technologically unskilled, but they could read and write and fluently express themselves in English. They had the necessary tools to acquire information that would improve their opportunities for economic and social mobility.

Increased sophistication and self-discipline as well as mass education improved the quality of Irish immigrants. A higher standard of living and a "reformation" in Irish Catholicism contributed to a more refined and controlled Irish personality. The suffering during the Great Famine had shifted the emphasis of popular agitation in Ireland from religious grievances toward agrarian radicalism and attempts to abolish manorialism and the landlord system. The shift was reflected in a rapid increase in tenant right activities, indicating rising expectations derived from improved economic conditions rather than a response to desolate poverty.

In the late nineteenth century, Ireland remained one of the most economically depressed countries in western Europe, but with the exception of Connacht, where the Irish agrarian system continued to follow prefamine patterns—small farms, thick population density, and a predominantly potato diet—between 1851 and the late 1870s the rural standard of living improved considerably. For those who survived, the famine resulted in substantial economic benefits. Death and emigration reduced the 1851 population from its expected nine million to six and a half million, lessening pressure on land resources. Small, uneconomical farms of one to five acres declined from 310,436 in 1841 to 88,083 in 1851. Holdings of between five and fifteen acres also were reduced from 252,799 to 191,854 during the same ten-year period. Larger farms of from fifteen to thirty acres, however, increased from 79,742 to 141,311, and the number of farms with more than thirty acres rose from 49,625 to 149,090. As farms became larger, peasant cottages also improved in size, cleanliness, and comfort. During the famine years approximately 300,000 rural cottages—most of them unsanitary hovels—disappeared, to be replaced by more spacious and healthier homes.

On larger postfamine farms, the change from tillage to grazing agriculture that had started in the eighteenth century continued. Farmers purchased cattle, sheep, pigs, raised chickens, and profited from escalating meat, butter, and egg prices throughout the United Kingdom. Food-producing Ireland became a natural economic partner for urban, industrial Britain. And from 1851 to 1878, agricultural prices rose so much faster than rents that evictions in Ireland became rare. In the twenty-five-year period between 1855 and 1880, only 17,771 families were permanently evicted from their farms, a rate of less than 3 percent of all tenant farmers, and many of these evictees were forced to leave for reasons other than nonpayment of rents. Significant profits from the sale of agricultural products, moderate rents, and the flow of dollars from relatives in the United States all contributed to a rising rural standard of living demonstrated by generous contributions to the construction of Catholic churches, schools, rectories, and convents and by numerous and expanding bank savings accounts.

The church buildings expressed a new kind of Irish Catholicism, one that was even more important to refining the Irish personality and character than either the national schools or a more affluent life-style. Catholicism was the core of Irish life, the essence of Irish identity. The church and her priests were the most powerful molders of Irish opinion and conduct. But prefamine Irish Catholicism had been loosely structured, "racy of the soil," more Irish than Roman in content and style. Irish bishops had been controlled much more by Irish opinion, needs, and interests than they were by Vatican policy. The Irish Catholic hierarchy often foundered over personality conflicts and divided on religious and political issues, and priests did not seem to be overawed by the authority of their bishops. Catholic lay people were pious but were not particularly devout in the official practices of their religion. Because of a shortage of chapels and an indifference to the formalities of organized religion, mass attendance was sparse in many parts of the country.

In postfamine Ireland, Catholicism like other aspects of Irish life changed. There was a rapid and radical transformation in the structure, appearance, discipline, and values of the religion. In addition to the growing affluence of the church—a combined result of the increased prosperity of the Irish laity and British efforts to lure Irish bishops and priests away from nationalism through material gifts to the religious institutions they served —Catholicism in Ireland became significantly more Roman than Irish.

Romanization was the achievement of Paul Cullen, who in 1852 returned to Ireland from Rome where he had been a close friend of Pope Pius IX and had served as director of the Irish College there. From the time he arrived until his death in 1876, Cullen dominated Irish Catholicism, first as archbishop of Armagh, then as cardinal archbishop of Dublin. He reorganized the structure of the church, emphasizing the obedience of laymen to priests, of priests to bishops, and of bishops to Rome. Cullen brought pietism as well as authoritarianism with him from Rome. Novenas, rosaries, forty-hour devotions, and pilgrimages became new and important expressions of Irish Catholicism.[3]

Modern critics who lambast the Irish influence on American Catholicism, describing it as a "Celtic heresy,"[4] do not understand that the Irish personality is both a victim and beneficiary of two kinds of cultural imperialism: Anglicization and Romanization. There really is no type of Catholicism that evolved from a native Irish environment. Catholicism as practiced by the Irish people today contains peasant elements, but religious practices have been shaped, altered, and even distorted by English and Roman influences. The Anglo-Protestant dimension of Irish-Catholic culture is less obvious than the Roman, attitudinal rather than doctrinal or liturgical. This English dimension, however, has made the native Irish more law-and-order-conscious and puritanical than Latin Catholics. While the latter, particularly the men, ignore papal decrees and the instructions of bishops and priests if they find them contradictory or inconvenient to their life-styles, the former are inclined to take authority and rules seriously. While Latin Catholics can shrug their shoulders at regulations they consider stupid or arbitrary, the Irish either insist on living by the rules or changing them. Thus they are at the same time the most rigid and yet the most rebellious Catholics.

Famine memories associated with hunger and death, higher expectations linked to an improved standard of living, and Roman pietism mixed with Anglo-Protestant Evangelicalism and Victorianism all combined to produce a deep, puritanical streak in the Irish personality. Irish Catholics abandoned their devil-may-care attitudes toward marriage and procreation for a hard-headed, materialistic approach. Priests in their sermons constantly emphasized the horrors of sexuality, condemned the transgressions of the flesh, advised men and women to avoid physical and social contact with each other, and extolled the supreme virtue of chastity.[5]

Without doubt, puritanism took much of the zip and flamboyance out of the Irish personality, but the moral austerity of postfamine Irish Catholicism did discipline the Irish character. Irish immigrants who came to the United States after 1870 were not the happy-go-lucky rogues of older days. The Irish crime rate in the United States declined and the Irish-American community began to build a more respectable image.[6] American Catholicism gradually incorporated the pietism and puritanism of the church in Ireland. Irish Catholicism was so effective in its role as the controller of Irish morals and conduct that even anti-Catholic, anti-Irish Anglo-Americans had to reluctantly admit that without the influence of the church the Irish would be more offensive than they already were. In *Poverty and Prog-*

*ress* (1964), Stephan Thernstrom quoted one New England newspaper editor on the subject:

> There is not a reasonable person in the town (New-buryport, Massachusetts), who employs a Catholic girl in his family, who would not prefer one devoted to her religion, constant at church . . . When they deny their religion they seldom accept ours, but that class furnish the night walkers, the drunkards and the criminals.

Did the improved quality of Irish immigrants in postfamine years elevate the economic and social position of Irish-America? In his study of the Irish in one New England town in the late nineteenth century, Thernstrom suggests that it did not. During the 1880s in Newburyport, Massachusetts, the Irish were still holding down the manual-labor positions of their fathers and grandfathers; they were not moving up to the skilled-labor and managerial ranks as fast as native Americans. But they did experience some success: "Through toil and sacrifice they had been able to buy homes, build their church, and obtain a slender margin of economic security."[7] Thernstrom emphasizes the Irish lust to own property—they purchased far more than native Americans of the same class—and their generous contributions to the Catholic church. He argues, however, that the money invested in personal property and in parishes was at the cost of educating Irish children and that the resulting lack of education limited the degree of social mobility.

Although Thernstrom correctly identifies the Irish ambition to possess property and their generosity toward their church, he fails to assess the reasons behind this appetite for property and the need to display Catholic commitments in brick and mortar. To Catholic, peasant immigrants like the Irish, owning property was a symbol of individual freedom and dignity, a natural ambition for people who had been serfs in Europe. Irish generosity to the church was a statement of their devotion to an institution that encompassed both their religious and ethnic loyalties. In Ireland, poverty-stricken and persecuted Catholics maintained their church at great sacrifice, and Irish-Americans were equally magnanimous in responding to the material needs of institutionalized Catholicism. While construction of Catholic parish plants swallowed funds that might have gone in more culturally constructive and economically productive directions, impressive church buildings satisfied psychological needs within Irish ghettos. In addition to demonstrating religious and ethnic loyalties, the structures symbolized a kind of Irish material success. They also provided profits for Irish contractors and jobs for Irish workingmen.

Thernstrom, like numerous historians and social scientists, also places too much weight on Irish experiences in Massachusetts and the rest of New England to the neglect of the Irish in other parts of the United States. They falsely assume that the Irish in places like Boston or Newburyport represented a national ethnic situation. Newburyport was not a particularly good example of Irish success or failure in the United States. At the close of the nineteenth century, only seventeen percent of Irish-American males lived in Massachusetts, Rhode Island, and Connecticut, while nearly as many—fifteen and a half percent—were in Illinois, Iowa, and Missouri. The largest concentration of Irish—thirty-five percent—settled in the Mid-Atlantic states of New York and Pennsylvania. Thus nineteenth-century, Irish New Englanders were as typical of the American Irish as present-day Derry or Belfast Catholics are of the total Catholic population of Ireland. Like contemporary Northern Ireland Catholics, nineteenth-century, Massachusetts Irish Catholics lived in a highly-structured society dominated by a Protestant Ascendancy determined to retain power and the status quo. New England Irishmen started on the basement floor of the American class structure and tended to stay there. Their ghettos were loaded with failure and defeatism, producing a paranoid vision of religion, politics, and other Americans. South Boston's reaction to desegregation and school busing in 1974 and 1975 demonstrates that the paranoia still exists.

While Thernstrom's lack of social mobility thesis is valid for these New England Irish, in other sections of the United States the Irish did advance. When they moved into areas where the social structure was more flexible, varied, and dynamic than it was in New England, the Irish quickly took advantage of opportunities to improve their status. Outside New England, the Irish participated in the optimism and enthusiasm of an expanding nation, losing the defeatist attitudes that plagued them in places like Boston and Newburyport. Newly-arrived Irish immigrants who stayed out of New England were more likely to do well in the United States than third or fourth-generation Boston Irishmen. In the Mid-Atlantic states and in the Midwest and West, they lived with and competed against Anglo-American Protestants and members of other ethnic groups, and the farther west the Irish went, the more confident and competitive they became.[8]

In 1900, although the average Irish-American was a member of a working-class family, many of them had moved into the ranks of skilled labor where they dominated trades like plumbing and plastering. And they had also established a leadership role in the expanding trade union movement. Although few Irishmen were numbered among the country's financial aristocracy, they had a significant middle-class representation. One historian of the American Irish and other Catholic ethnic groups has recently claimed that a larger percentage of Irish-Americans had belonged to the lower middle-class than had German or native Americans, and they were almost as successful in making it into the upper middle-class as were the former. He classifies almost six percent of the American Irish in 1900 as upper and more than fourteen percent as lower middle-class.[9]

As among earlier Irish immigrants, postfamine Irish women often were more vocationally successful than their menfolk. Irish families frequently gave daughters more education than sons to provide the women with a profession like nursing or teaching that would protect them from the harshness of the American urban, industrial environment. Men, on the other hand, were supposed to be tougher and more able to survive rough treatment on their own. Irish women were hard workers and they avoided the addiction to alcohol that destroyed so many Irish men. And in a day when most American women concentrated their talents and energies on taking care of homes and raising children, Irish women were vital administrators and leaders in Catholic social and educational institutions. As nuns, they administered schools and hospitals, teaching children, nursing the sick. Changes in American culture and technology also added new vocations. The daughters and granddaughters of maids and scrubwomen became secretaries, telephone operators, nurses, and teachers in the rapidly developing public school system. By the early twentieth century, Irish-American women dominated the teaching faculties of many urban elementary and secondary schools.

The changing character of urban life and government also opened up vocational opportunities for Irish men. Because of its close affiliation with politics and its promised economic security, the civil service attracted Irish recruits. Mothers and fathers urged their sons to work for the post office, and the danger and excitement of police work and fire fighting appealed to Irish males. The Irish made good policemen; they were tough, physically courageous, loved excitement and comradeship, and were flexible and tolerant of most forms of human frailty except in sexual matters. Unfortunately, this moral tolerance often led to vague and shaky distinctions between honest and dishonest graft. In some ways Irish-American policemen illustrated an apparent contradiction in the Irish personality: how could one man be a rebel, a hater of Peelers in Ireland, and an agent of law and order in the United States?[10] But in the cities of America the Irish cop was defending the laws and institutions of his own country and protecting his own people; he was not imposing alien rule.

Athletics offered Irish-Americans an opportunity to exercise their zest for adventure, excitement, and competition. In the late nineteenth and early twentieth centuries, the Irish, like contemporary blacks, excelled in amateur and professional sports such as boxing, baseball, track and field, and football, winning the dubious title "the fighting Irish." Like members of other minority groups that followed them into urban America, the Irish made first-rate athletes. Ghetto life toughened them for competition, and sports offered fame, fortune, and recognition that they could not garner elsewhere.

Although athletics provided the Irish and other minorities with heroes, diverted physical energies from harmful, socially destructive conduct, and made them competitive in the kind of society where competition was necessary for survival, there were many negative aspects to athletic success. Proficiency at games often confirmed Anglo-American Protestant "racist" stereotypes describing the Irish as belligerent, animal-like people with strong backs but weak minds. Athletic trophies also tended to glorify the wrong values and elevate shallow heroes in ghetto communities. In Irish neighborhoods and Catholic schools too much attention was paid to sports and winning games. This emphasis retarded progress in cultural and intellectual areas, delaying the emergence of an American Catholic intellectual class.

Entertainment also appealed to the Irish urge for money, glory, and to the Irish extroverted personality. In the nineteenth and well into the twentieth century, Irishmen and Jews had the same prominent roles as actors, singers, dancers, and comics as do blacks and Italians today. There seems to be a strong correlation between ghetto backgrounds and show business. Perhaps poverty, persecution, and insecurity encourage people to wear masks to camouflage suffering and to cultivate a sense of humor as a survival technique. As a singer, dancer, composer, playwright, and actor, George M. Cohan (1878–1942) was the epitome of the Irish entertainer. In his songs he demonstrated ethnic pride ("Harrigan"), American patriotism ("It's a Grand Old Flag," "Yankee Doodle Dandy," and "Over There"), Irish-American energy, ambition, cockiness, and enthusiasm.

At the turn of the century, the American Irish were doing a variety of things: mining coal and feeding it into steel mill furnaces, manning railroads, fighting fires, preserving law and order, serving in the armed forces, performing on the stage, pitching curve balls on baseball diamonds, throwing punches in the ring, kicking footballs, nursing patients in hospitals, teaching school, writing newspaper articles, tending bar, practicing law and medicine, saying mass, and managing labor unions and a few businesses. They were slow, however, to contribute significantly to American cultural and intellectual life. Too many of them were too busy caring for large families to think seriously about art, literature, music, and science; too few of them had the kind of liberal arts education that encouraged art or scholarship. Parochial elementary schools concentrated on purging the Irish of their peasant heritage, Anglicizing and Romanizing them in the process, teaching them to read and write, to love God and their country, and to obey the church. They did not emphasize creative thought or imagination. Before World War I few Irish boys and girls went on to secondary schools and before World War II few of them enrolled in college. And Catholic secondary schools and colleges also concentrated more on practical than intellectual educations. In their attempts to preserve the faith in a hostile environment and to civilize the Irish-American community, priests, nuns, and brothers were as much social workers as educators. They wanted their students to get decent jobs and live productive, respectable lives, and Catholic schools indeed were very successful at realizing such goals.

Nor did the old-country heritage inspire Irish-American intellectual or cultural ambitions. In Ireland the national schools, like parochial schools in the United States, were trying to An-

glicize, "civilize" rather than intellectualize the Irish, and sophisticated Anglo-Irish Protestants sent their best talent off to
London to seek fame and fortune. Thus the brightest Protestant
offspring left Ireland while landlords, barristers, bankers, clergymen, and businessmen stayed behind to promote second-rate
imitations of British art and literature rather than encouraging
an original expression of Irish culture.

In the 1890s, the Irish cultural landscape was transformed
when nationalism and Gaelic scholarship combined to inspire
an Anglo-Irish, Protestant-led literary revival, a movement that
made Dublin the literary capital of the Western world. But as
a group, the Irish who came to the United States had no connection with this Irish literary movement. Most of them had left
Ireland before William Butler Yeats and James Joyce began to
publish or before the Abbey Theatre came into existence. Although Irish writers used themes from agrarian folklore and
tradition, they lived in Dublin and wrote for urban audiences.
Most Irish immigrants, who came from peasant stock remote
from the cultural and intellectual life of Dublin, did not appreciate the realism of modern Irish writers, accusing them of
publishing profane attacks on Catholicism, chastity, and the
Irish way of life. When the Abbey Theatre brought John Millington Synge's *Playboy of the Western World* to the United
States, Anglo-Saxon Protestants jammed the theatres while the
Irish stood outside picketing and complaining about the author's paganism and his slurs on the purity of Irish women.

To Irish-Americans, good literature meant the ballad poetry
of Thomas Moore and Young Ireland and the novels of Charles
Kickham. Later generations of better-educated Irish-Americans would look down their noses at Moore, Davis, and Kickham, ridiculing the literary tastes of their peasant predecessors.
But it was better for culturally deprived Irish-Americans to
read second-rate literature than to read no literature at all, and
the romantic writers of the Young Ireland school helped create
Irish pride and dignity and stimulated interest in cultural
things, a prelude to better times.

In the twentieth century, Irish-American literature was inspired by the work of Yeats, Joyce, Synge, Sean O'Casey, Frank O'Connor, and O'Faolain, but in the United States, Irish literature had a journalistic base. Irish-Americans contributed writing ability, imagination, and adventurous personalities to American newspapers. One of them, Finley Peter Dunne (1867–1936) of Chicago, was one of the first Irishmen to bridge the gap between journalism and literature. Martin Dooley, the chief character in Dunne's satirical essays, was an immigrant from Roscommon who operated a saloon on Archey Road (Chicago's Archer Avenue). Every day he and his friend and customer Hennessey discussed local and national affairs, but mostly they talked about their Irish neighbors from Bridgeport and Canaryville: hod carriers, housewives, policemen, firemen, priests, and politicians. Dooley poked fun at Irish vices such as clannishness, volubility, flamboyant American and ethnic patriotisms, the ability to condone political corruption, and their excessive thirst for beer and whiskey. But he also praised virtues like courage, generosity, sentimentality, sense of humor, family solidarity, and hard work. Through Dooley, Dunne satirized Anglo-Saxon Protestants who controlled the country's finances and national affairs, scourging their racist attitudes, militarism, imperialism, and their hypocrisy clothed in reform policies and patriotism. Dunne and another Chicagoan, James T. Farrell (1904– ), pioneered American urban ghetto literature, at the same time initiating a respectable school of Irish-American literature that came to include works by Eugene O'Neill, Edwin O'Connor, J.F. Powers, Jimmy Breslin, Pete Hamill, Joe Flaherty, Elizabeth Cullinan, Tom McHale, Thomas J. Fleming, Frank D. Gilroy, William Gibson, William Alfred, and many others.[11]

# 6

## Communities in Conflict:
## American Nativists and Irish Catholics

❧⟊❧

While immigrant poverty, ignorance, disease, belligerence, alcoholism, and crime frightened and antagonized Anglo-Americans, the establishment of an Irish-American ghetto culture intensified rather than initiated anti-Irish prejudice in the United States. If the Irish had stepped off the boat wearing linen suits and patent leather shoes, waving the American flag in one hand and a university degree in the other, with wallets containing thousand-dollar bills, they might have been considered more respectable. But they still would have been labeled "enemy" aliens, the targets of an American nativism that insisted on a homogeneous society based on Anglo-Saxon, Protestant cultural values.

Despite the American Revolution, the War of 1812, and frequent diplomatic tensions between the United States and England, Americans remained British in language, institutions, tastes, prejudices, and religious preferences. Since anti-Catholicism (no-popery) was the most important ingredient in British nativism, it also served as the ideological foundation for American nativism. Like the English, Anglo-Americans considered the sixteenth, seventeenth, and eighteenth-century wars between England and Catholic Spain and France as crusades against tyranny and ignorance, with Irish Catholics forming a fifth column as agents of papist subversion.

Britain's conflicts with Spain and France and her internal purges of real and imaginary Catholic plots had American dimensions. Most of the original New England Yankees came to America because they believed that the established Anglican church was structurally and liturgically polluted by popery. Their nonconformist friends and relatives in Britain were the elite corps of the parliamentary army that defeated Stuart "despotism" in two seventeenth-century revolutions. And Protestant dissenters on both sides of the Atlantic associated the Stuart monarchy with Catholicism, assuming connections between the Vatican, tyranny, and subversion. Irish Catholics played an important role in the British-Protestant view of history; they rejected English liberty for papist tyranny and fought for James II against the forces of freedom and enlightenment.

In championing the causes of liberty and tolerance, British and Irish-Protestant Whigs insisted that the "glorious revolution" of 1688 was a victory of human rights over authoritarianism, but they excluded Catholics from their demands for freedom of conscience, insisting that Catholicism was an alien ideology whose existence threatened the British constitutional system. Transforming theory into practice, Whig-dominated parliaments in Britain and Ireland adopted the penal laws as expressions of Protestant nativism and as weapons against the dangers of Catholic subversion. Since early American political theory was dominated by British Whig concepts, colonial assemblies also passed laws against Catholics.

No-popery was also a factor in the American Revolution. People in the thirteen colonies passionately protested the Quebec Act (1774), an effort by the British Parliament to pacify French-Catholic opinion in newly conquered Canada. And in the early years of the war against Britain, American soldiers celebrated Guy Fawkes day on 5 November by hanging the pope in effigy.[1] Finally Gen. George Washington ordered an end to such festivities because they offended America's French allies and Catholics in the revolutionary army.

While early, postrevolutionary American nativism was rooted in the British historical experience, local circumstances and situations also played their part. Jeffersonian democracy, which best represented the American liberal tradition, emphasized agrarian virtues, insisting that the small, self-reliant farmer was the ideal citizen. Within this agrarian, populist frame of reference, cities and commerce were tolerated as necessary evils, and Irish immigrants became victims of double jeopardy: they were not only Catholics but also residents of urban dens of iniquity. Irishness, Catholicism, and urban corruption melded in the American mind into a threat to traditional American virtues and values. Irish social vices also intensified the Protestant, agrarian biases of American nativism, provoking fears that were physical, religious, and psychological.

Irish social conduct did place a severe strain on the fabric of urban America, and Catholicism and the American way of life often did appear to be incompatible cultural systems. American institutions nurtured such British, Whig principles as individual liberty and private conscience. European Catholicism, on the other hand, was associated with a reactionary stance; nineteenth-century popes denounced liberalism and democracy, defended authoritarianism, advocated the union of church and state, and condemned freedom of conscience.

American Protestants refused to recognize the differences between Irish and native-American Catholicism and European Catholicism. Irish and American Catholics were the victims, not the instigators, of oppression, bearing the burden of Anglo-Saxon, Protestant tyranny and persecution. They rejected the reactionary political opinions of the Vatican, drawing distinctions between politics and theology. Charles and John Carroll in the United States and Daniel O'Connell in Ireland embraced the principles of Locke and Jefferson in their efforts to liberate American and Irish Catholics from the liabilities of penal legislation.

The difficulties of reconciling loyalty to an absolute religious monarchy with faith in a liberal political system, however, has placed a tremendous strain on the Catholic mind and personality. Although it is possible to draw theoretical boundaries between theology and political theory, in practice many social and economic questions have implications that are impossible to isolate as either secular or spiritual.[2] The effort to adjust and harmonize dual loyalties within the American-Catholic community has often produced schizophrenia, frequently expressed in super-patriotism. In their desire to demonstrate their love of country, Catholic ethnics have been quick to volunteer for military service, but they also at times have zealously supported reactionary causes that profess to be patriotic in origin and goal. American liberals have frequently blasted Catholic ethnic support of irrational anticommunism—Coughlinism in the 1930s and McCarthyism in the 1940s. While this charge is valid, many of these same liberals have also exhibited cloudy political judgment by concentrating criticism on right-wing totalitarianism to the neglect of its left-wing relatives. Liberals have also criticized Catholic interference in the sexual mores of Americans. This is a particularly critical issue now in regard to abortion. But history has yet to judge whether liberals or those Catholics who oppose abortion are doing the most to preserve the dignity of human life.

Following the American Revolution, national and state constitutions destroyed the remnants of official Protestant Ascendancy represented by established churches and penal laws. On the state level the establishment of religious freedom was a slow process: New York did not repeal anti-Catholic legislation until 1806, Connecticut waited until 1818, Massachusetts held out until 1833, and in 1835 North Carolina was the last state to recognize Catholics as first-class citizens. The repeal of state penal laws did not end nativism, but at that time Catholicism was not the main target for postrevolutionary Americanism. In the early years of the new republic, Catholics were too few in number to frighten the Protestant majority. Members of the ruling Federalist Party were far more worried about the radical ideas emanating from the French Revolution, ideas that seemed to be embraced by Thomas Jefferson and his friends. In 1798, Federalists in Congress passed the Alien and Sedition Acts to isolate the United States from the agents of European radicalism, and members of the Society of United Irishmen were included in the Federalist category of undesirable aliens. Promoters of the legislation wanted to protect American values from foreign contamination by demanding a fourteen-year residency requirement for naturalization. Delegates to the 1812–1814 Hartford Convention went even further; they insisted that naturalized citizens should never be eligible for public office.

After 1830, American nativism became more directly associated with anti-Catholicism. Irish immigration fertilized the anti-Catholic roots of American nativism by increasing urban social problems and by making the Catholic church in the United States a larger and more dynamic institution. In 1789, there were only about thirty thousand Catholics in the United States under the authority of one bishop and served by thirty priests. By 1860, the Catholic population had grown to around three million, most of them Irish living in many dioceses and employing many priests, nuns, and brothers. Such massive Catholic expansion exceeded the general rate of population increase in the country.

Before the impact of Irish immigration, American Catholics were culturally Anglo-Saxon, and like their English counterparts they were humble and quiet in their religious observances, tiptoeing about so as not to disturb or antagonize the Protestant majority. English and Anglo-American Catholics also were intent on demonstrating their loyalty to their native countries, anxious to participate in their nation's social, economic, and political life. John Carroll, the first American Catholic bishop, came from an old and respectable American family and was a close personal friend of famous patriots like Benjamin Franklin and George Washington. His brother Charles was one of the signers of the Declaration of Independence. Even as archbishop of Baltimore and as a primate, Carroll kept the Vatican at arm's length, emphasizing the unique qualities of American Catholicism, advocating an English vernacular rather than Latin liturgy.

Many French members of the Society of Priests of St. Sulpice, an order dedicated to the teaching of seminarians, aided the native American clergy in serving the small but widely dispersed Catholic community in postrevolutionary days. Sulpicians were men of culture and dignity who sympathized with Carroll's desire for a distinctly American-Catholic church, one that would merge into the mainstream of Anglo-Saxon culture. But Irish immigration shattered the hopes for an Anglo-Saxon, American-Catholic church. Early Irish immigrants were obviously not Anglo-Saxons; perhaps a third of them could not even speak adequate English, and their manners and life-style repulsed native Americans. Irish priests lacked the learning and sophistication of the native and French Catholic clergy and, like their parishoners, were aggressive rather than passive Catholics. Since Irish immigrants came to the United States to escape British, Anglo-Saxon, Protestant religious, political, and economic oppression, they were not interested in courting or pleasing American Anglo-Saxon Protestants. They were not going to be humble about their religious and cultural values in a land that promised them freedom.

Archbishop Ambrose Marechal, Carroll's French successor as head of the American church was determined to prevent the Irish clergy from gaining control. He disliked their crude peasant manners and lack of sophistication which limited their ability to raise the cultural level of their turbulent parishioners. And the archbishop feared that the coarse and aggressive Irish would alienate American nativists, causing persecution of Catholics. Marechal's anxieties were justified. Irish priests were as culturally and intellectually unpolished as the people they served. And many of them were men who had had disciplinary problems with their original Irish bishops or who were too fond of the bottle. When they arrived in the United States, they continued to indulge their vices and resist the authority of the American hierarchy. Some Irish priests encouraged lay boards of trustees to declare their independence from the control of American bishops. Marechal complained to Rome that priests from Ireland were unreliable and sources of scandal. After the Irish finally gained control of the American church, Irish bishops like John England from Charleston, South Carolina, took steps to improve the quality of the clergy. They built seminaries to educate the priests and they insisted that bishops in Ireland send only good men to the American mission.

The vast numbers of Irish immigrants, their concentration in cities, and their demand for Irish priests eventually did transfer control of the Catholic church in the United States from a native and French to an Irish clergy and made it an urban rather than a rural institution. American Catholicism became and for a long time remained part of an Irish-Catholic religious empire that dominated the English-speaking world, and the old, Anglo-Saxon Protestant versus Irish-Catholic conflict was extended to a new arena. In the old country Anglo-Saxons invaded Ireland; in the New World the Irish repaid the visit.

Education provided a persistent, fundamental, and highly emotional issue in the many conflicts between nativists and Catholics. Using the King James Version of the Bible, state-supported public schools provided religious and moral training. Remembering bitter experiences in the old country, Irish-American Catholics were convinced that religious education in public schools was a cover for Protestant proselytism, so they established their own denominational schools and demanded state aid.

During the late 1830s and early 1840s, New York was the scene of intense emotional conflicts between nativists and Catholics over the school question. Concerned about the education of immigrant children, Gov. William Seward was sympathetic to Catholic requests for public funds, but other politicians preferred a second solution. In 1842, the New York state legislature secularized public schools, setting a precedent which led to the national principle of separation of church and state in tax-supported, educational institutions.

At the time, neither Catholics nor Protestants were satisfied with secularization as a compromise solution to their conflicting positions. Catholics continued to expand the parochial school system as a defense against proselytism and secularism and futilely continued to demand state funds; Protestants denounced Catholic opposition to Bible reading in public schools as a clear example of the difference between the high moral tone and truths of scriptural Protestant Christianity and the ignorance and pretensions of popery. They also criticized parochial schools as the purveyors of alien ideas and values and as barriers preventing the assimilation of immigrants into the American cultural system.

Without a doubt, anti-Catholicism was the leading American neurosis in the 1830s, 1840s, and 1850s. During the 1830s, probably a majority of Americans actually believed that an international conspiracy directed by European despots was using Catholicism as an instrument to smother the American beacon of freedom. Prominent people like Lyman Beecher and Samuel F.B. Morse warned the public that the Hapsburg empire, under the evil influence of von Metternich, and the Vatican wanted to destroy the United States. They warned that Catholic Europe had picked the Mississippi Valley as the most vulnerable point and planned to flood the area with immigrants. Jesuits disguised as farmers, tinkers, and medicine men were already scouting the region as a prelude to invasion, it was claimed. Protestant newspapers concentrated on the Mississippi Valley Catholic conspiracy, and Protestants from all over the United States contributed large sums of money to the crusade to save the West from popery.

No-popery also served as a stimulant to American publishing businesses. Hungry Protestant readers devoured anti-Catholic books, pamphlets, and newspapers. Much of the nativist propaganda had originated in England during the controversy over Catholic Emancipation in the 1820s. Pornography was an important anti-Catholic element, as many books, pamphlets, and platform speakers described the sexual depravity associated with Catholic religious practices. Both alleged and real ex-priests and nuns moved around the American lecture circuit with stories of orgies behind convent walls and seductions in the confessional.

Maria Monk was the heroine of the Protestant, anti-Catholic crusade. Her *Awful Disclosures of the Hotel Dieu in Montreal* (1836) was anti-Catholic nativism's equivalent of the anti-Semitic *Protocols of the Elders of Zion.* Maria Monk was a mentally-retarded and deranged Protestant girl who ended her days as a prostitute. Her only contact with Catholicism was as a patient in a Catholic hospital, but she claimed to be an escaped nun, and anti-Catholics decided to exploit her story. In her account of convent life in Montreal, Maria Monk told of seductions by priests in the confessional and of frequent sexual encounters between priests and nuns. She described tunnels connecting the rectory and convent which were used as passages to lust and as burial grounds for babies resulting from the illicit unions between priests and nuns. According to Monk, the unfortunate infants were baptized and then murdered so that the secrets of the convent would never leak to the outside world. Maria Monk's revelations became an immediate best-seller and led to a number of convent inspections, all disproving her allegations. But the truth was irrelevant to anti-Catholics. Protestants wanted to believe the most gruesome stories of Catholic depravity, so Maria Monk's tale of horror and lechery continued to anger and stimulate American nativists. It was even unearthed in 1960 as an argument against the election of John F. Kennedy to the Presidency.

The no-popery crusade was violent as well as pornographic. In August 1831, the burning of an Ursuline convent in Charlestown, Massachusetts, started a wave of shootings, hangings, and burnings that did not subside until the 1860s. Irish-Catholic ghettos and churches were the main targets of Anglo-Saxon Protestant, nativist violence. In 1844, when Francis Kendrick, bishop of Philadelphia, insisted on the right of parochial schools to public financing, a Protestant mob invaded the Irish ghetto, burning homes and dynamiting Catholic churches. Mob leaders justified their foray by claiming that the Irish were storing arms in church basements as a prelude to a Catholic revolution. Events in Philadelphia encouraged New York nativists to attack the Irish. While the nativists were busy planning their offensive, Archbishop John Hughes surrounded Catholic churches with armed Irish guards and threatened to turn New York into another blazing Moscow if one Catholic church was desecrated. City officials and nativist leaders got the message, and the Philadelphia atrocity story did not have a New York addendum. But anti-Irish violence in Boston, New York, Louisville, and New Orleans continued to disturb the calm of urban America. In the early 1850s, a Protestant mob attacked and burned the Irish section of Lawrence, Massachusetts, and in 1855, Boston's older families (Brahmins) dismissed their Irish servants after hearing a rumor that the women were Vatican agents in a plot to poison the Protestant leadership of Massachusetts.

No-popery also had its political dimensions. Many American politicians campaigned on nativist platforms and slogans, and both the Federalist and Whig parties were willing to express anti-Catholic sentiments to win votes. Local nativist parties enjoyed election successes, and by 1854 an anti-Catholic, secret society, the Order of the Star Spangled Banner, had evolved into the native American Party. Members took Masonic-style oaths and used a variety of countersigns. When asked about their party goals, principles, and symbols, members feigned ignorance, earning for the group the popular name Know-Nothing Party.

By advocating laws that would restrict immigration, make it difficult to become a citizen, and disqualify naturalized citizens for public office, Know-Nothings were determined to keep political power in native-American hands. Although the objectives of the party were directed against foreign influences, Know-Nothings concentrated their energies on the war against Catholics, particularly the Irish.[3] Membership in the American Party did not necessarily imply ignorance or a reactionary point of view. Many respectable American reformers were attracted to nativism as a method of controlling and reversing the Irish urban blight.

Know-Nothing candidates had spectacular successes in the 1854 and 1855 local, state, and national elections, winning victories in Massachusetts, Delaware, Pennsylvania, Rhode Island, New Hampshire, Connecticut, Maryland, Kentucky, New York, and California, and they lost by only small margins in a number of other states. Massachusetts, where Know-Nothings captured the governor's mansion and both houses of the legislature, became the symbol of nativist success. They immediately formed a state legislative committee to investigate convents and placed a strict residency requirement for naturalization on the statute books. Exhilarated by their election successes in 1854 and 1855, American Party leaders fully expected to capture the White House in 1856. Boston's Irish-Catholic newspaper *The Pilot* conceded such a grim possibility.

In the 1856 presidential election, Americans gave 800,000 votes to the Know-Nothing candidate, former Whig President Millard Fillmore, but he lost the election. By 1856 anti-Catholicism had receded as a public passion, taking a subordinate position to the sectional tensions between North and South that were bringing the country to the edge of civil war.

When tension erupted into conflict in 1861, the war gave Irish-Americans an opportunity to prove their patriotism. In addition to the many thousands of first and second-generation American Irish who fought in the Union army, 144,221 natives of Ireland served the cause. The Irish left many dead on the battlefields. At Fredericksburg, the Irish Brigade under the command of Young Irelander Thomas Meagher kept attacking a well-fortified Confederate position until one of the brigade's regiments lost 550 of its 700 men. And after the battle of Chancellorsville only 520 men survived out of the brigade's entire five regiments.

Irish-Catholic chaplains brought spiritual consolation to men in combat, and Irish-Catholic nuns tended the wounded in hospitals. While Irish-American soldiers acquired reputations for insubordination and sloppy discipline, they also earned compliments for their courage. Many Confederate officers considered the Irish the best soldiers in the Union army. And Irishmen, including 40,000 from Ireland, also served the South. After the Irish contribution to the war effort, it was very difficult for nativist politicians or journalists on either side of the Mason-Dixon Line to criticize Irish devotion to the United States. Through the sacrifice of war, Irish-Americans gained a brief respite from prejudice.

Nativism rooted in Anglo-American Protestantism did not fade away, but immediately after the Civil War public attention and energy were focused on Reconstruction in the South and industrialism in the North. With the beginnings of the extensive Industrial Revolution in the United States, factories, mills, and railroads needed immigrant laborers. Italians, Poles, and Jews from eastern Europe joined the Irish and Germans as ethnic members of the urban, industrial proletariat.

Since nativism could not triumph in the face of the nation's rising labor needs, American leaders were forced to adopt a new vision of the country to accommodate the immigrant newcomers. The melting pot thesis replaced nativism as the new philosophy of the American spirit. Oliver Wendell Holmes announced that the United States was the new Rome, a nation that could and would assimilate the vitality and intelligence of many people while maintaining unity and consensus. Emma Lazarus' statement on the Statue of Liberty, erected in New York harbor in 1886, expressed the new American attitude toward European immigrants:

Give me your tired, your poor,
Your huddled masses yearning to breathe free,
The wretched refuse of your teeming shore,
Send these, the homeless, tempest-tossed to me:
I lift my lamp beside the golden door.

Although Lazarus's description of the immigrants was distorted—they were the most vital and intelligent members of Europe's peasant and working classes, not refuse—the sentiment was humane, promising that the United States would provide an environment of tolerance and opportunity.

With its spirit of freedom and encouragement of pluralism and diversity, the melting pot thesis encouraged liberal-minded members of the American Catholic hierarchy to move their church into an accommodation with American life and culture. During the 1880s and 1890s many prelates, among them James Cardinal Gibbons, primate and archbishop of Baltimore; John Ireland, archbishop of St. Paul; John Lancaster Spalding, bishop of Peoria; John Keane, bishop of Richmond, then rector of the Catholic University in Washington, D.C., and finally archbishop of Dubuque; and Denis O'Connell, who served as rector of both the American College in Rome and Catholic University before becoming bishop of Richmond, insisted that the Catholic church in the United States must adjust to the American political, cultural, and social climate. Spalding came from Anglo-American, Catholic stock, but Ireland, Keane, and O'Connell were born in Ireland while Gibbons as a child lived and attended elementary school there. Spalding and Ireland gave the new movement in the Catholic church a midwestern tone. The former was the most intellectual of the liberal bishops, the latter the most dynamic and articulate. Catholics in both Europe and the United States considered Ireland to be the leader of American progressive Catholicism.

Ireland and his friends denied any real or theoretical conflict between American liberal democracy and Catholicism. They emphasized the melting pot similarities between the United States and the Roman Catholic church, and predicted that American freedom and the principle of a free church in a free state—Daniel O'Connellism—would promote the growth and influence of American Catholicism. Ireland and his associates described American democracy as the perfect political system, engaged in friendly ecumenical dialogues with Protestant leaders, and spoke before predominantly Protestant audiences. They even championed the public school system as a powerful instrument of culture and freedom. Archbishop Ireland went so far in this direction as to work out a shared-time experiment involving parochial and public schools in Faribault, Minnesota.

In addition to blessing American democracy, Gibbons, Ireland, Spalding, Keane, and O'Connell were harsh critics of *laissez faire* capitalism and champions of social justice. They encouraged the development of the American labor movement, defending the Knights of Labor against a threatened papal condemnation urged by some conservative members of the American hierarchy. They demanded quality schools to produce a sophisticated and intellectual laity, and they were the force behind the founding of the Catholic University, expecting it to become a first-rate academic institution, a model of Christian excellence. Liberal bishops and priests also unsuccessfully resisted the appointment of a Papal Nuncio to the United States, fearing that a Vatican ambassador would be insensitive to the nuances of the American church functioning within a liberal, democratic environment.

Convinced that American Catholicism must continue to reflect and preserve the integrity of ethnic cultures to keep alive Catholic loyalties in a secular environment, midwestern German bishops opposed the liberal efforts of the midwestern Irish to Americanize the church. Led by Bernard McQuaid, bishop of Rochester, and Michael Corrigan, archbishop of New York, many eastern Irish bishops joined the Germans in defending ethnicity as a Catholic shield. Corrigan and McQuaid also opposed the social and economic opinions of the liberal Midwest priests and prelates, supporting the *laissez faire* capitalist system, denouncing labor unions as a source of social unrest, and preaching the redemptive role of poverty. The two bishops shared papal hostilities to liberalism and modernism and argued in favor of the Roman position urging the union of church and state. Conservative prelates like Corrigan and McQuaid frowned on the notion of lay leadership or devotion to intellectual pursuits, insisting that Catholic education must concentrate on preserving the faith. Their opposition to liberalism and intellectualism subsequently prevented the Catholic University from reaching the academic heights expected by Keane, Spalding, Gibbons, Ireland, and O'Connell.

Religious orders became involved in the controversy between liberal Americanizers and conservative Romanists. Paulists and Holy Cross fathers at Notre Dame, at that time a small college near South Bend, Indiana, argued that Catholicism in the United States must accommodate itself to the American situation. Founded in 1858 by Isaac Hecker, a New Englander who converted from transcendentalism to Catholicism, the Paulists may have been the most talented and intellectual body of men in the late nineteenth-century American church. In their stylish, intelligent, and articulate periodical *The Catholic World,* they attempted to explain Catholicism to Protestant America. The Jesuits, who operated a number of secondary schools and colleges for the sons of upper middle-class Catholic families, opposed the liberal views of the Americanizers, not out of a sense of ethnicity, but because their order was strongly committed to Roman power and conservatism.

Americanization became a European as well as an American controversy within the Catholic church. In France, liberal Catholics used American ideas to defend their positions in debates against conservative opponents, and in the process they distorted liberal, American-Catholic political and social theories into a modernist theology. Conservative French bishops supported by American Bishop Sebastian Messmer of Green Bay, who represented midwestern German interests, and by

McQuaid and Corrigan, who spoke for the eastern Irish, urged Pope Leo XIII to officially brand Americanization a heresy. In January 1899 the pope wrote Cardinal Gibbons labeling the following opinions as heresy: action is more important than contemplation, natural virtues take precedence over supernatural virtues, and instructions of private conscience are superior to those of a Catholic one guided by the Holy Spirit through the offices of the church.[4] Although Gibbons and other liberal bishops correctly replied that their Americanization policy had never advocated what the pope condemned, they had been censured and humiliated, and their conservative opponents were ecstatic and arrogant in victory. During the subsequent reign of Pope Pius X, the situation worsened for Catholic liberals in the United States and Europe as the Vatican purged suspected modernists from the fold. The atmosphere of oppression created a spiritual reign of terror and made liberals very cautious about expressing their opinions.

Despite the conservative, midwestern German and eastern Irish victory at Rome and the antiliberal attitude in the universal church which lasted until the time of John XXIII in the late 1950s and early 1960s, the liberal, midwestern Irish tradition survived in the American church. Monsignor John Ryan, Archbishop Bernard Sheil of Chicago, John Courtney Murray, S.J., and Sen. Eugene McCarthy of Minnesota are a few examples of its persistence and vitality. And American, liberal Catholicism did win victories in 1962 at Vatican II when the Council accepted the principles of ecumenism, religious freedom, and private conscience and admitted the validity of a separation of church and state.

The melting pot thesis survived as an almost-official doctrine in response to the diversity of the American ethnic and racial structure, but in the 1880s economic depression and the closing of the western frontier diminished American zeal for pluralism and the assimilation of immigrants. As factories, mines, and mills shut down, banks closed, and the stock market plummeted, many Americans concluded that their country's potential had reached maximum limits. They began to suggest that the nation's resources and opportunities had to be rationed and bestowed on native-born Americans. They said that there was no more room for strangers, who would only compete with Anglo-Americans for employment and strain the country's social fabric to the danger point.

American xenophobia had a multiclass foundation. While laboring men feared job competition from immigrants, members of the middle class doubted that the capitalist system could survive the combined impact of depression and immigration. They worried that the expanding labor movement was permeated with European socialist ideology. These anxieties seemed to be confirmed by increasing numbers of strikes, some of them violent, in response to economic depression. Chicago was the scene of two sensational confrontations between proletarian discontent and capitalist intransigence. In 1886, eleven people were killed and a hundred were wounded in a riot in Chicago's Haymarket Square. Eight years later, Pres. Grover Cleveland called out troops to smash a strike at the Pullman Company. A jury convicted eleven anarchists as inciters of the Haymarket Square violence, and the state of Illinois executed four of them. After the Pullman strike, the government sent Eugene V. Debs, the socialist railway union leader, to prison.

Terrorized by strikes and general labor unrest, wealthy, property-owning Americans demanded restrictions on immigration as a method of protecting the United States from influxes of Marxism, syndicalism, and anarchism. Although the protests against proletarian radicalism and foreign influences were largely anti-Semitic in nature, the Irish were included in the list of dangerous aliens. While it was true that most Irish labor leaders were associated with the more conservative craft unions, some of them leaned farther to the left. And the violence of the Molly Maguires in the Pennsylvania coal fields encouraged many nativists to link the Irish to anticapitalist, antiproperty violence.[5] In addition to radicalism, there was always the old issue of religion. The Irish were Catholic and

Catholicism was obviously subversive. How could a real American serve a foreign ruler like the pope?[6]

The Industrial Revolution affected rural as well as urban America, effecting dramatic changes in agricultural technology and forcing farmers to purchase expensive machinery, often on credit. Rural people felt themselves at the mercy of bankers as well as the weather, and recessions and depressions determined food prices and the ability to pay loans and interest. Populist ideology appealed to frustrated agrarian and small-town America; it was a rural citizen's revolt against the financial power of urban capitalism. Populism as a distinct brand of American radicalism now has a popular image—many contemporary politicians describe themselves as new populists—but in the 1880s and 1890s it was saturated with anti-Catholic and anti-Semitic bigotry. According to populist mythology, Jews and Catholics represented urban aliens exploiting native Americans on the farms and in the small towns.[7]

Although working and lower middle-class people and farmers continued to express nativism in an Evangelical Protestant style, upper and professional middle-class sophisticates began to abandon "crude" religious bigotry and to rationalize their nativism in pseudoscientific terms, condemning inferior races rather than alien creeds. American racists borrowed most of their ideas and arguments from English intellectual sources. In British universities, respected historians like John R. Green, Edward A. Freeman, James A. Froude, Thomas Macaulay, and William Stubbs argued that Angles, Saxons, and Jutes had carried the seeds of liberty with them from the forests of Germany in the fifth century, planting them in English soil where they flowered into the British system of constitutional government and free institutions.

Late nineteenth-century English scholars and intellectuals liked to contrast Anglo-Saxon qualities with those of the Celtic or Irish personality, describing the English as masculine, rational, industrious, thrifty with resources, and committed to individual freedom and the Irish as feminine, emotional, lazy, improvident, and dependent. They concluded that Anglo-Saxons were natural masters, Celts natural slaves, and that the Irish were fortunate to find benevolent English leaders to protect them from their faulty natures. The April 1868 issue of the Whig journal *Edinburgh Review* criticized the Irish from the perspective of Anglo-Saxon racism, reasoning that they functioned best within the controls of the free yet disciplined British political system:

> They possess, no doubt, qualities of a very serviceable kind, but these qualities require the example and power of another race, more highly endowed, to bring them to perfection and turn them to full account . . . The Irish are deficient in that unquiet energy, that talent for accumulation, those indefinite desires which are the mainsprings of successful colonization, and they are deficient too in that faculty of self-government without which free institutions can neither flourish nor be permanently maintained.

Such historical explanations for Anglo-Saxon superiority and Celtic inferiority were bolstered by anthropological, ethnological, and biological arguments. Scholars measured skulls, jawbones, and other portions of human skeletons and then constructed a primate scale which placed Anglo-Saxons next to God on top, the Irish just above apes, and blacks on the very bottom.

Respectable, well-educated Liberals as well as reactionary Tories accepted Anglo-Saxon racism. For example, in 1881 English historian Edward Augustus Freeman sent back this observation from a visit to the United States:

> This would be a grand land if only every Irishman would kill a negro, and be hanged for it. I find this sentiment generally approved—sometimes with the qualification

that they want Irish and negroes for servants, not being able to get any other. This looks like the ancient weakness of craving for a subject race.

And in 1892, Sidney and Beatrice Webb, parents of the Fabian Society, the intellectual arm of the Labour Party, visited Ireland where they found the natives charming, "but we detest them, as we should the hottentots—for their very virtues." Their Irish journey convinced the Webbs that Britain must give Ireland Home Rule in order to get rid "of this detestable race."[8]

Comparing the Irish to black African Hottentots was a fashionable English intellectual exercise. Lord Salisbury, leader of the Unionist Party and prime minister, was an inflexible opponent of any self-government concessions to Irish nationalist agitation. He believed that the Irish were as incompetent to manage their own affairs as the Hottentots.

In the closing years of the nineteenth and the early part of the twentieth centuries, Anglo-Saxon racism was very chic in American universities, drawing rooms, and private clubs. It was often expressed in the vocabulary of another English import, Social Darwinism. Americans used Anglo-Saxon racism and "survival of the fittest" sociology as propaganda weapons in the war against Latin Spaniards and to justify imperialistic ventures in South America and the Far East, claiming that they were bringing the advantages of a superior civilization to the deprived savages of the underdeveloped world.

American nativists also used Anglo-Saxon racist themes at home in their campaign for legislation to restrict immigration and to make it more difficult for aliens to become naturalized American citizens. New England Brahmins like historian Henry Adams and Cabot Lodge, Republican senator from Massachusetts, were among the founders of the Immigrant Restriction League in 1894. Franklin Walker, president of the Massachusetts Institute of Technology, described the American immigration and naturalization process as "the survival of the unfit," and two popular authors, William Z. Ripley, *The Races of Europe* (1899), and Madison Grant, *The Passing of a Great Race* (1916) warned that Anglo-Saxon culture and racial purity in the United States were threatened by the inferior hordes entering the country.

Since Jews, Italians, Poles, and blacks presented more obvious physical, cultural, and linguistic contrasts to Anglo-Americans than did light-skinned, mostly blue-eyed, English-speaking Irishmen, the American Irish were not the main targets of Anglo-Saxon racism in the United States. They remained, however, American nativism's leading Catholic, ethnic opponent. The Irish had been the first ethnic group to arrive in the United States; they controlled the Catholic church, still the principal irritant to nativist sensibilities; they dominated urban politics in the North, challenging Anglo-American Protestant ascendancy; they organized other ethnics in the Democratic Party and the labor movement. And there was, of course, the ancient rivalry planted in the old country. While the Irish might resemble Anglos, they were less anxious to associate with them than were many other ethnics. Jews and many non-Irish Catholics often were obsequious in their relations with Anglo-America. They were hungry to belong. But because they had long been the victims of Anglo-Saxon Protestant prejudice, the Irish distrusted the honor and integrity of the Anglo-American community. They knew Anglo-Saxon Protestants better than other minority groups did, and Anglo-Saxon Protestants were well aware of the fact.

The 1880s revival of nativism with its religious, economic, and racist dimensions encouraged the creation of a number of organizations designed to protect the United States from alien pollution. In 1887, the American Protective Association began in Clinton, Iowa, enlisted more than a million members from throughout the country, and began mouthing the old lies—the pornography of Maria Monk and stories of guns stored in the basements of Catholic churches. Before it faded away in the late

1890s, the APA did succeed in influencing local politics and in discouraging some employers from hiring Catholics.

Following the official demise of the APA in 1911, other organizations carried on the Protestant, Anglo-Saxon, racist crusade against the malignant influences of Catholicism and racial inferiority: the Guardians of Liberty, the American Minute Men, Covenanters, and the Knights of Luther. But none of them was as powerful as the Ku Klux Klan. The KKK originated in the South during Reconstruction as a terrorist organization to intimidate newly freed blacks and carpetbaggers from the North. After southern state legislatures enacted Jim Crow segregation laws and the United States Supreme Court accepted the principle of apartheid, the KKK, its task accomplished, ceased operation in 1871.

In 1915, a Georgia preacher named William J. Simmons revived the Klan, and in the 1920s it became so powerful that its membership may have reached four million. The new KKK was a major force in southern and midwestern states, particularly Indiana, enlisting politicians, lawyers, doctors, businessmen, and Protestant clergymen in its causes. The KKK of the 1920s was more of a nativist organization than its Reconstruction predecessor, concentrating its hate on Catholics and Jews as well as on blacks. During the Presidential election of 1928, the KKK militantly campaigned against Democratic candidate Al Smith, labeling him a symbol of urban minority groups. Mobs of men in white sheets marched down streets throughout the South, Border States, and Midwest and burned crosses on Catholic lawns. No doubt, Smith would have lost the election regardless of the ethnic religious issue, but his Irish-Catholic, urban background fanned the flames of bigotry, significantly reducing the Democratic vote.

# 7

## Irish-America and the
## Course of Irish Nationalism

In response to the pressures, hostility, and prejudices of Anglo-American Protestant nativism, Irish nationalism jelled and flourished in the ghettos of urban America as a search for identity, an expression of vengeance, and a quest for respectability. Before the Great Famine rapidly expanded the communities of the Diaspora, Irish nationalism was more hope and aspiration than reality. While O'Connell's Catholic and repeal associations helped the Irish to develop skill in manipulating public opinion, helped them unite and mobilize for agitation, and helped to lay the structural foundations of Irish nationalism, there was much to be done before the Irish people could think of themselves as distinctly Irish and before they could realize the implications of that conceptual identity.

As an eighteenth-century, cosmopolitan, Whig patriot, O'Connell did not understand the significance of cultural identity as a dimension of nationalism. When Young Irelanders in the 1840s began to push beyond the frontiers outlined by O'Connell, in the process creating an Irish cultural nationalism, most of the Irish population were illiterate peasants unable to comprehend the complete message of the Young Ireland newspaper, the *Nation*. And priests, fearing that Young Irelanders were the Paracletes of Continental secularism, radicalism, and anticlericalism, remained loyal to the memory, message, and tactics of O'Connell.

Geography and the manorial economy also obstructed the advance of Irish nationalism. Although a little country, Ireland is divided by a number of small mountain ranges, and in the early nineteenth century primitive transportation facilities strengthened regional boundaries. "Ireland" meant less than terms like townland, parish, county, or province. And Irish tenant farmers functioned as serfs within a primitive social and economic system, existing without adequate legal rights or weapons to protect them from exorbitant rents or arbitrary evictions. The tension between Protestant landlords and Catholic tenant farmers was only one aspect of class divisions and conflicts. Catholic agricultural laborers in turn were as much exploited by their Catholic tenant-farmer employers as they were by agents of the landlord system. Among the rural Irish masses, the major concern was survival rather than national freedom. Tradition, fear-induced allegiances to landlords, and land hunger diluted much of the Catholic unity and patriotism that O'Connell had forged.

When the Irish came to the United States they brought their townland, parish, county, regional, and clan loyalties with them, but the common ghetto experience and Anglo-American Protestant hatred contributed to the creation of a larger Irish identity. Men from all parts of Ireland worshipped together in the same Catholic churches, voted as a bloc for Democratic Party machines, and worked side by side on the railroads and in the mines and factories. Anglo-American contempt for all things Irish deepened an already festering Irish inferiority complex, necessitating a search for pride through identity. Irish-Americans soon cultivated their own "racial" myths to match those of their persecutors, rejecting what they considered to be O'Connell's "West British" patriotism and turning to the poems, essays, and doctrines of Young Ireland as the source of their cultural and revolutionary nationalism. Young Ireland refugees from the 1848 comic-opera, cabbage patch revolution left Ireland as dismal failures; they arrived in America as heroes. Emigration and the development of an Irish identity among American immigrants speeded the progress of Irish nationalism on both sides of the Atlantic.

Throughout the nineteenth century Irish-Americans read literature that created and sustained cultural and revolutionary nationalism. In the immediate postfamine period, Thomas Davis, Charles Gavan Duffy, James Clarence Mangan, and John Mitchel were the evangelists of cultural nationalism. Late in the nineteenth century, T. D. Sullivan's edited collection *Speeches from the Dock* inspired the American Irish with the eloquence so many Irish rebels seem to express on the way to the gallows. Many a second-generation Irish-American lad (dubbed a "narrowback" by native Irishmen) listened in awe, reverence, and pulsing anger as his Irish-born father or grandfather recited Robert Emmet's defiant speech from the dock.

In the United States the American Irish formed societies to study and preserve the Irish language, and in Catholic parish halls they attended concerts featuring Thomas Moore's *Irish Melodies.* They read and memorized passages from Charles Kickham's *Knocknagow* (1879), a novel that reinforced their romantic image of Ireland and the courage, generosity, spirituality, and purity of her people. They cheered Kickham's noble Celtic hero Matt "the Thrasher" Donovan when he threw the sledge farther than Captain French, a representative and champion of the Tipperary Protestant Ascendancy, and they wept when beautiful Nora Lacy faced a painful death with saintly joy and stoicism. In another Kickham novel, *Sally Cavanagh* (1869), Neddy Shea expressed the Irish-American messianic determination to liberate Ireland from British tyranny. As a one-armed veteran of the American Civil War, Neddy returned to Ireland to mark the grave of his mother, a victim of landlord greed and cruelty. With eyes flashing anger, he shouted out his hatred of English and landlord oppression, proclaiming that although he was maimed fighting for the United States, he still had one "arm left for Ireland."

Irish-American nationalism was saturated with hate; many Irishmen harbored a deeper hatred of England than love for Ireland. Despising England was a catharsis for Irish-American tensions and frustrations, a way of expressing and explaining Irish failure, a way of striking out at real and imaginary enemies. Britain had to be punished and humiliated, not only as a step toward Irish freedom but as an atonement for her sins against the Irish. British laws, cruelty, religious bigotry, insensitivity, and indifference to Irish needs had contributed to the deaths and exile of millions of Irish people.

To the American Irish, Britain was the source of Irish disgrace and humiliation at home and abroad. In one of his poems, "Remorse for Intemperate Speech," William Butler Yeats described how the Irish left their country with maimed personalities, full of "great hatred," carrying from their "mother's womb a fanatic heart." And during his American exile, John Mitchel, the most passionate and unforgiving of the Young Irelanders, analyzed the motives underlying his nationalism:

> I have found that there was perhaps less of love in it than of hate—less of filial affection to my country than of scornful impatience at the thought that I had the misfortune, I and my children, to be born in a country which suffered itself to be oppressed and humiliated by another . . . And hatred being the thing I chiefly cherished and cultivated, the thing which I specially hated was the British system . . . wishing always that I could strike it between wind and water, and shiver its timbers.[1]

There were those who never reconciled themselves to physical or spiritual exile from Ireland or whose need for a scapegoat to explain their lack of success in the United States formed the core of a paranoid Irish nationalism. But other Irish-Americans, people who had achieved social and economic mobility, worked for an Irish nation-state that could earn them respectability in the general American community. They believed that an independent Ireland would help them be assimilated in the United States. These searchers for status and respectability argued that an Ireland wearing the British collar and leash was a symbol of Irish inferiority and degradation, encouraging the contempt of Anglo-Americans. But a free Ireland "numbered among the nations of the earth" would elevate her exiled children in the eyes of other Americans. The Irish may have been the first but they were certainly not the last minority group in the United States to link their destiny to the sovereignty of their homeland. Contemporary Jews, blacks, and Slavs insist respectively on the continued existence of Israel, African freedom, and the independence of Poland and other countries in eastern Europe for the same reasons that nineteenth-century Irish-Americans became involved in Irish nationalism.

Because respectability was such a strong motivation in Irish-American nationalism, the middle class tended to be more active in Irish freedom movements than the lower class. The latter group was more concerned with the bread-and-butter issues of American politics. With the tremendous improvement in the quality of Irish immigrants after 1870 and the rapid occupational and economic mobility of first, second and third-generation Irish-Americans, increasing psychological needs for recognition and social status aided the forces of nationalism.

* * *

The beginnings of Irish-American nationalism already were evident during the Catholic Emancipation agitation in the 1820s, when American Irish-Catholics, with some Protestant support, vocalized their interest in Catholic civil rights in Ireland. But the repeal movement in the 1840s actually initiated

Irish-American nationalism. Almost every Irish community in the United States had a local repeal club which sent dollars to swell the treasury of the organization in Dublin. In his speeches, O'Connell emphasized that the Irish of the Diaspora had joined with their kinsmen back home in the repeal movement, warning the British that Irish nationalism had international implications.[2] Pro-repeal speeches and statements from prominent Americans like Gov. William Seward of New York and Pres. John Tyler indicated the potential importance of Irish nationalism as a factor in the American political arena.

In order to consolidate the energies of Irish-American nationalism and publicize its cause and aims, American-Irish leaders organized two national repeal conventions in the 1840s, but the conclaves revealed dissension in Irish-American ranks. Many American proponents of repeal, particularly from the South, criticized O'Connell's attacks on slavery and his demands that Irish-Americans remain true to the liberal, democratic values that they learned at home and to the basic principles of the American *Declaration of Independence.* O'Connell encouraged them to empathize with the slaves, another group that had suffered from cruelty and enslavement, to join the abolitionist crusade, and to demand full civil rights for blacks once they were free. O'Connell went so far in his denunciation of black slavery that he would not accept donations from repeal clubs in the South, insisting that dollars stained with the blood of black suffering could never be used to free slaves in Ireland. Irish-American rejection of O'Connell's stand on slavery revealed their commitment to American institutions and values and their sensitivity to outside attacks, even from Ireland, on the American way of life.

Famine and revolution in Ireland escalated the development of Irish-American nationalism. The many deaths from hunger and fever and the mass exodus from Ireland convinced many of the Irish at home and abroad that the British were attempting to solve the Irish Question through a policy of extermination. The 1848 rebellion sent Young Irelanders fleeing to the United States, providing the leadership and rhetoric to mobilize Irish discontent in a counteroffensive against Anglo-Saxon, Protestant nativism.

In developing a rationale for a war on British imperialism, Irish-American nationalist propagandists emphasized their Americanism, praising the United States as the cradle of human liberty, in contrast to aristocratic and imperialistic Britain. They insisted that the United States had a moral obligation to lift the burden of oppression from Ireland. The Irish were the first Americans to use ethnicity as a political tool to manipulate American foreign policy in support of a European freedom movement, a precedent to be followed later by a large number of minority groups.

After the revolutionary fiasco of 1848, nationalist agitation in Ireland returned to its constitutional channels. Charles Gavan Duffy resurrected the two conflicting strategies—agrarian and political—debated in the Irish Confederation in 1847, fusing them into one movement. Along with two other newspapermen, Dr. John Gray and Frederick Lucas, proprietors and editors of the *Freeman's Journal* and *Tablet,* and with William Sharman Crawford, Ulster Protestant M.P. and champion of tenant right, Duffy created an independent Irish party dedicated to the achievement of secure tenures at fair rents for Irish tenant farmers. Duffy and his friends hoped that a coalition between Protestant tenant farmers from Ulster and Catholic farmers from throughout Ireland could eventually break down sectarian animosities and lead to an ecumenical nationalist movement.

Unfortunately, the Independent Irish Party that emerged from the general election of 1852 with forty-eight seats in the British House of Commons was more than an agrarian, issue-oriented "League of the North and South." Duffy, Gray, Lucas, and Crawford had also accepted the collaboration of the Irish Brigade. George Henry Moore, M.P., had organized the brigade to mobilize Catholic opinion in the United Kingdom against anti-Catholicism as expressed in the Whig government's Ecclesiastical Titles Bill.[3] Duffy admired Moore and respected his integrity, but he suspected that many members of the "Pope's Brass Band"—a popular nickname for the brigade —were unscrupulous opportunists using popular Irish causes to get elected to Parliament where they could intrigue for place and preferment.

Duffy's suspicions were quickly confirmed when, after the general election, two brigade members of the Irish party, John Sadleir and William Keogh, accepted positions in Lord Aberdeen's Peelite-Whig coalition government. Some Catholic bishops approved of Keogh and Sadleir breaking their pledges of independent opposition, arguing that it was good for the church to have friends and champions in high places. The conflict between the principle of independent opposition and the machinations of clerical politics led to bitter words and feelings between Duffy and Dublin's Archbishop Cullen, who considered the editor of the *Nation* an Irish Mazzini. In disgust, Duffy sold the *Nation,* quit Irish politics, and departed for a successful career in Australian politics.

While clerical politics was the most dramatic issue in the 1859 collapse of the new party, it was not necessarily the decisive factor in its dissolution. From the time of O'Connell's entry into the British House of Commons in 1829 until Charles Stewart Parnell took over the helm of constitutional nationalism in the 1880s, the Irish cause at Westminster suffered from shabby parliamentary representation. Since candidates in parliamentary elections paid their own expenses and, if elected, served without salary, British politics was a hobby for the aristocracy and gentry. In Ireland, members of the large, land-owning classes were almost always committed to the Union with Britain as a guarantee of their property rights, political and social influence, and Protestant Ascendancy. Many of those who declared themselves nationalist candidates at general and by-elections in Ireland were men on the make who quickly betrayed their cause and constituencies once safely entrenched at West- minster. People like Sadleir and Keogh were more the symp- toms than the cause of the malaise that affected parliamentary nationalism.

In addition to the animosity between Duffy and Cullen and the shady and shabby quality of Irish nationalist M.P.s, changes in the climate of tenant right opinion in the 1850s also damaged the Irish party. The famine had encouraged a coalition between Protestant and Catholic tenant farmers, but the agricultural prosperity of the 1850s, 1860s, and early 1870s resurrected sec- tarian differences at the expense of peasant solidarity. It was always difficult for Ulster Protestants of any class to remain in long association with Catholics or to emphasize their Irish over their British identities. In Ireland conflict was more cultural than class, and religion continued to designate cultural commit- ments.

In 1864, after the failure of the party, Cullen threw his sup- port behind the National Association which George Henry Moore, John Francis Maguire, and John Blake Dillon had organized to agitate for the disestablishment of the Protestant church in Ireland and to promote tenants' rights. Cullen and other Irish bishops were far from social or economic reactionar- ies. They were interested in tenant right as a way of improving the rural economy so that the peasant masses would not have to emigrate to the cruel, secular environments of urban Britain and America.

The National Association formed an alliance with British radicals and nonconformists in the Liberation Society, an orga- nization dedicated to the complete separation of church and state in the United Kingdom. These British leftist enemies of the established church wanted to attack it first in Catholic Ireland where it was most vulnerable to criticism. While this alliance between Irish Catholicism and British nonconformity was not always ideologically harmonious, it did succeed in impressing W. E. Gladstone and other Liberal politicians with the need to solve the religious dimensions of the Irish Question.

In 1869, Gladstone and the Liberal majority in the House of Commons disestablished the Protestant church in Ireland. Pope Pius IX, who hated the principle of separation of church and state, would have preferred that his old friend Cardinal Cullen had favored dual establishment of both Protestant and Catholic churches rather than the disestablishment of the former. But the cardinal was influenced by the spirit of O'Connell's liberal nationalism. He, like other Irish Catholics, knew from the Catholic experience in Ireland that a church free from entanglements with the state was more likely to be a healthy institution. Irish Catholicism was certainly more vital than either Irish or British Protestantism. They also realized that Irish Catholicism had much more vigor than Catholicism in Latin countries where there was church-state unity.

A year after the Disestablishment Act, Gladstone gave Ireland land legislation preventing evictions except for the non-payment of rent and offering government loans to encourage Irish farmers to buy their farms from landlords. The Irish Land Act did not work, however, because an escape clause permitted landlords to raise rents and then evict when their tenants could not meet the new charges, and the land purchase provisions did not offer the kind of interest-rate terms that would encourage tenants to buy their farms. However, the legislation was an important precedent, a harbinger of things to come; it was the first time that a British government had tacitly agreed that property rights were not absolute, that they were limited by obligations to social justice. Ireland had forced a change in direction of British social and economic thought, one that would eventually lead to a welfare state.

Irish-American nationalist leaders were not interested in the tactics and manipulations of parliamentarians back in Ireland. The collapse of the Independent Irish Party only confirmed their suspicions that Ireland could not sever its painful ties with

Britain without violence. They were convinced that the British so hated Ireland and the Irish that they could not be persuaded that Ireland merited self-government.

During the 1850s, Irish-American nationalists worked out a revolutionary strategy that remained consistent for much of the nineteenth and twentieth centuries. They decided to use the United States as an arsenal for Irish freedom by providing money and guns for liberation movements in Ireland and by using Irish political power to shape American foreign policy in an anti-British context. During the 1844–1846 dispute between America and Britain over the Oregon boundary, the American Irish were in the front ranks of the war hawks. They constantly tried to promote armed conflicts between Britain and her Continental enemies, emphasizing the slogan "England's difficulty is Ireland's opportunity." For example, during the Crimean War of 1853–1856, Irish-American agents tried to persuade the czar to ally Russia with the forces of Irish nationalism. And they offered their support to Spanish government efforts to recover Gibraltar from Britain, hoping in turn to win a pledge from Spain to aid revolution in Ireland. Throughout the 1850s and 1860s, Irish-Americans hoped and prayed that Napoleon III would dispatch an army of liberation to Ireland.

While most Irish-American nationalist plans had a fantasy-land quality, Fenianism was something more; it was a tough, hard-nosed commitment to revolution. Fenianism emerged in 1858 from the Emmet Monument Association, a New York-based organization dedicated to fulfilling an obligation to nationalist Robert Emmet: they wanted to write his epitaph in an Irish nation-state. Two Young Ireland veterans of 1848, John O'Mahony and Michael Doheny, the latter the author of *The Felon's Track* (1849), were directors of the Emmet Monument Association. They, along with another rebel, James Stephens, escaped a British dragnet in 1848 and managed to get to Paris. Doheny then crossed over to New York, but O'Mahony and Stephens, working as a translator and an English teacher respectively, stayed on in the French capital, absorbing revolutionary conspiracy tactics from a variety of political refugees. In 1851 they both manned the barricades in a futile effort to resist Louis Napoleon's coup-d'etat against the Second Republic.

In Paris, Stephens and O'Mahony formulated plans to launch an Irish revolutionary movement designed to achieve a democratic republic. Ideologically they were socialists, but they decided to play down economic issues, still entertaining the Irish-nationalist fantasy that Protestant property owners could be persuaded to support Irish freedom. As a result of this unrealistic concept of a nonsectarian Irish nationalism, Stephens and O'Mahony, like Irish patriots before and after them, deprived their movement of a significant economic dimension.

Responding to an appeal from Doheny, O'Mahony left Paris in 1854 for New York to enlist Irish-Americans in revolutionary conspiracy. Stephens, on the other hand, decided to concentrate his recruiting efforts on the Irish in the United Kingdom. In 1858 he launched the Irish Republican Brotherhood (IRB), absorbing the Cork-centered, literary-political club, the Phoenix Society, which Jeremiah O'Donovan Rossa had founded in 1856. O'Donovan Rossa, a dashing, romantic, Gaelic-speaking nationalist who played a leading role in Irish liberation movements on both sides of the Atlantic, like other Irish patriots, used the legendary phoenix as a symbol of his country's determination to rise from the ashes of British conquest. The same year that Stephens organized the IRB in the United Kingdom, O'Mahony transformed the Emmet Monument Association into its American wing. But since he was a Gaelic scholar who admired the "Fianna" sagas of ancient Irish literature, O'Mahony decided to name the American organization the Fenian Brotherhood. Because of its romantic allusions to the Gaelic past, Fenianism became the popular designation for republicanism in Ireland, Britain, and America.

In order to preserve a maximum of secrecy and security, O'Mahony and Stephens employed Continental conspiracy tactics, organizing the Fenians into "circles" commanded by a "centre," and each circle was divided into smaller cells led by "captains," who had authority over "sergeants," who supervised the work of "privates." Republicans in the lower ranks knew only their immediate cell comrades. Stephens was head centre for the United Kingdom; O'Mahony held that post in the United States. Recruits took oaths of secrecy, obedience to officers, and loyalty to the Irish republic. One Fenian leader, John Devoy, concentrated on enlisting Irish soldiers already in the British army, hoping to create a fifth column in the ranks of the enemy.

Most of the leaders of the 1848 Young Ireland revolution refused to endorse revolutionary republicanism, and next to the British government, the Catholic church in Ireland was the leading foe of Fenianism. Bishops denounced the IRB as a secret, oath-bound society, denying its members the consolation of the sacraments. Dr. David Moriarty, bishop of Kerry and the most outspoken clerical enemy of the republicans, described them as "swindlers" and "criminals" deserving damnation, claiming that for their kind "eternity is not long enough, nor hell hot enough." But oaths and secrecy were only minor issues in the confrontation between bishops and Fenians; political considerations were far more important. Revolutionary conspiracy threatened to wreck the prospects for an alliance that Cardinal Cullen, through the National Association, was negotiating with British Liberals, a compact that promised the disestablishment of the Protestant church and government money for Catholic education. And Cullen and his fellow prelates were also frightened by the violent rhetoric and strategy of the IRB, believing that the group's inspiration came from Continental, anti-Catholic, radical nationalism (Garibaldi) and the violent tones of urban America. Irish bishops were worried that Fenianism might produce a revolution that would destroy Irish lives and property without bringing either freedom or prosperity to compensate for the sacrifice.[4]

In 1861 Fenians engineered a patriot funeral to challenge Cullen in a contest for the approval of Irish nationalist opinion. Terence Belew McManus, another Young Ireland veteran of 1848 and also an escapee from Van Dieman's Land, settled in San Francisco and died there in poor straits. American Fenians decided to ship his body back to Ireland for proper tribute and burial. As the coffin traveled across the United States, Irish-Americans paid tribute to McManus's memory along the way. Placing loyalty to a fellow Ulsterman and empathy for nationalist sentiments above episcopal solidarity, Archbishop John Hughes of New York said a funeral mass for McManus in St. Patrick's Cathedral. But while the coffin was crossing the Atlantic on the last stage of McManus's voyage home, Cardinal Cullen decreed that no Catholic church in his archdiocese could be used for any religious ceremony that might be construed as a tribute to revolutionary nationalism.

Deprived of a religious setting, the IRB waked McManus in the Mechanic's Institute (later the Abbey Theatre). Fifty thousand people followed the coffin through the streets of Dublin on its way to Glasnevin Cemetery, while hundreds of thousands lined the funeral route. At the graveside, Stephens and other IRB leaders eulogized McManus with fiery Fenian propaganda, and Father Patrick Lavelle, a radical cleric from Mayo, defied Cullen by blessing the coffin before it was lowered into Irish soil.

The McManus funeral was a great psychological victory for Fenianism, perhaps the high point of the movement. But then the American Civil War interrupted the normal evolution of the IRB. Republican emotions were divided over the sectional conflict between North and South. Many feared that the war would divert the attention of Irish-America from its main goal of Irish freedom, but most Fenians enthusiastically supported the

Union because they wanted a strong, unified American foe of British power and imperialism. A number of Irish-Americans hoped, even believed, that pro-Southern, British opinion would result in a military confrontation between Britain and the United States, resulting in Irish freedom. Many Irish-Americans took advantage of the war to enlist in either the Union or Confederate armies as a means of acquiring military expertise which they hoped someday to use against British imperialism. In addition, Fenian recruiters were busy in both camps enlisting talent for the republican cause. During national Fenian conventions, a large number of delegates appeared in uniforms of Union blue.

Following the Confederate surrender at Appomattox, republicans in Ireland and America began to plan for revolution. By then there were almost 50,000 Irish-Americans enrolled in the brotherhood, and thousands more contributed dollars to the effort. In 1865, the American Irish provided the Fenian treasury with $228,000; the next year they increased their contributions to almost $500,000. According to the revolutionary blueprint, Irish-Americans would participate in an Irish insurrection and would provide money and equipment for the venture. Once the fighting started, republicans in the British army would mutiny, paralyzing British efforts to crush the Fenians.

Immediately after the conclusion of the Civil War in their own country, combat-trained Irish-Americans began to drift over to Ireland to begin drilling the Irish for rebellion. But before a revolution could begin, dissension and factionalism split the ranks of American Fenians, halting plans to attack British power in Ireland. In 1865, a national convention of the Fenian Brotherhood in Philadelphia had adopted a new constitution changing the organizational structure of the American branch to harmonize with the country's political system. The constitution abolished the head centre, substituting a president responsible to a general congress, itself divided into a senate and house of delegates.

Disagreement over this new structure was only one aspect of dissension within the republican movement. Col. William R. Roberts, the dominant personality in the Fenian senate, disagreed with the Stephens-O'Mahony strategy for revolution. He insisted that Irish-Americans should strike at British imperialism in Canada rather than concentrate their resources on revolution in Ireland. Roberts reasoned that a captured Canada could be held as hostage for a free Ireland. This conflict in strategy between Pres. O'Mahony and the senate prevented the shipment of an adequate supply of guns and ammunition to Ireland. Faced with a shortage of weapons and the split in the American Fenian organization, Stephens postponed revolution in Ireland, refusing to reenact the farce of 1848.

While Fenians were quarreling over leadership and strategy, British agents were successfully penetrating the leaky IRB structure on both sides of the Atlantic. After a spy in the office of the Fenian newspaper in Dublin, *The Irish People,* provided the government with incriminating documents, officials shut down the paper and arrested its staff, along with Stephens, the international head centre. At the same time that British agents infiltrated the IRB, however, Fenians were operating within the ranks of the police. Through the efforts of John Devoy and republicans in the police, Stephens managed to escape from prison and immediately left for the United States to patch up the quarrel between O'Mahony and Roberts. But by the time he landed in New York, the senate had already deposed the president, and Stephens's abrasive personality irritated rather than smoothed the troubled waters of Irish-American nationalism.

In May 1866, American Fenians invaded Canada with a force of about six hundred men, defeated a company of Canadian volunteers and then retreated before the regular army advanced on them. Instead of discouraging raids across the borders of a friendly neighbor, the United States government used the Fenian threat against Canada as a diplomatic weapon in negotiations with the British. The United States at that time was insisting that Britain pay millions of dollars in reparation for the damage to Union shipping inflicted by the Alabama, a Confederate cruiser built in British shipyards. And the United States also wanted Britain to accept the naturalization process when applied to former citizens of the United Kingdom. Fenianism could particularly benefit from the last demand. Many Fenians captured and imprisoned by the British were naturalized American citizens and appealed to the United States for support. Links between United States government officials and Fenians are evidenced by the fact that the Irish republicans invading Canada were equipped with American army surplus guns and ammunition, and the government arranged the transportation home of those Fenians who retreated south of the Canadian border after the attack in 1866.

With Irish-Americans involved in incursions into Canada and thus increasingly reluctant to commit supplies to Ireland, Stephens again decided to delay an Irish revolution. For this prudent decision, American Fenians branded him a coward and deposed him as international head centre. Early in 1867, a humiliated and frustrated Stephens sailed from New York on his way to a second Paris exile. Never again would he play a decisive role in Irish nationalism.

While Stephens was busy conspiring in the United States, the British government once more caught the IRB napping. It transferred Irish soldiers stationed in their own country to other parts of the United Kingdom and empire, suspended habeas corpus, and arrested prominent Fenian leaders. In a futile gesture of defiance, outnumbered, poorly-trained and equipped IRB companies in Kerry, Cork, Tipperary, Limerick, Dublin, and Clare attacked the barracks of the Royal Irish Constabulary and other symbols of British rule. During the snowy months of February and March 1867, the constabulary, assisted by the army, easily smashed and routed the small bands of brave but incompetent rebels.

Fenian violence in the United Kingdom was not restricted to Ireland. In September 1867, a republican rescue party attacked a police van in Manchester, England, freeing two Irish-Americans—Thomas J. Kelly, successor to Stephens as head centre, and Capt. Timothy Deasy—but in doing so accidentally killed a police sergeant. In response to this act of violence, the police arrested Fenians W. P. Allen, Michael Larkin, Michael O'Brien, and Edward Condon, charging them with murder. While all four had been members of the rescue party, there was no solid evidence that any of them had fired the fatal shot. After a trial held in an atmosphere of anti-Irish hatred and vengeance, a jury found all of the accused guilty and a judge sentenced them to death by hanging. Shortly before the scheduled execution, the government reprieved Condon because he was an American citizen. O'Brien claimed the same privilege, but he had earlier avoided a stiff sentence because he was an American, and the government had no intention of repeating such a lenient act. The remaining three were hanged.

Later in 1867, another Fenian-connected incident occurred in England. When republicans attempted to liberate some of their comrades from Clerkenwell Prison by dynamiting a wall, they killed twelve innocent people and wounded more than a hundred others. Such acts intensified anti-Irish prejudices in Britain, but the disintegration of the Fenian movement in Ireland and the arrest of many of its members brought the IRB a large measure of public respect and sympathy in Ireland. Prominent people, including Catholic bishops and priests and constitutional nationalist politicians, joined an Amnesty Association which petitioned the British government for the release of jailed Fenians. In Ireland, Allen, Larkin, and O'Brien became known as the Manchester Martyrs, victims of British hatred masquerading as justice. T. D. Sullivan of the *Nation* wrote a poem inspired by Allen's last words and put it to the tune of an American Union army song, "Tramp, Tramp, Tramp the Boys are Marching." Titled "God Save Ireland," it became the anthem of Irish nationalism until replaced by "The Soldier's Song" during the 1919–1921 Anglo-Irish War. It went in part:

> God save Ireland cried the heroes,
> God save Ireland said they all,
> Whether on the scaffold high
> Or on the battlefield we die,
> Oh what matter where for Ireland dear we fall.

With Fenians enshrined as martyrs for Irish freedom, Cardinal Cullen found it difficult to sustain clerical animosity to republicanism. Prayers for the souls of Allen, Larkin, and O'Brien and for the pardon of Fenian prisoners flowed from the Catholic altars of Ireland. Some members of the hierarchy and clergy justified their empathy for republicans by arguing that the split between Irish and American Fenianism purged the former of secularism and violence. When the pope in 1870 explicitly condemned the IRB as a dangerous, anti-Catholic secret society, nationalist opinion made it clear that Irish Catholics resented the move.

Perhaps Fenians became popular in Catholic Ireland because they no longer constituted a serious threat to either clerical authority or law and order. The tides of Irish nationalism were flowing back into the constitutional mainstream. In 1870, Isaac Butt, a former Protestant conservative who had become an active Irish nationalist and served as president of the Amnesty Association, established the Home Government Association. Butt hoped to use the HGA to persuade British and Irish Protestants that a federal contract between Ireland and Britain would be a conservative and lasting solution to the Irish Question. Irish electors endorsed the Home Rule movement and its candidates at by- and general elections. In 1874, Irish constituencies elected fifty-nine Home Rule M.P.s to the British House of Commons and they promptly organized the Irish Parliamentary Party with Butt as chairman. Most of the Irish in Britain, including ex-Fenians, respected Butt for his commitment to Irish nationalism. They formed the Home Rule Confederation of Great Britain, with branches all over England and Scotland, to encourage the federalist effort by using the Irish vote in British politics.

In the United States, the hysteria of revived nativism canceled out some of the efforts of Catholic Americanizers and sustained Irish-American nationalism as one expression of ethnic identity. But by the mid-1870s the Fenian Brotherhood no longer represented the Irish freedom cause in the United States. In 1870, after the British government conceded the Alabama claims and recognized the validity of American naturalization of former United Kingdom citizens, Pres. Ulysses S. Grant made it clear that his administration would no longer tolerate a professed Irish nationalist government-in-exile using America as a base to attack British territory in Canada.

Following Grant's statement, a large number of the American Irish abandoned Fenianism to join the Clan na Gael. Jerome J. Collins founded the clan in 1867, but John Devoy, arriving in the United States in 1871 following his release from a British prison, quickly dominated the new revolutionary republican organization. In 1877, the clan concluded a formal alliance with the Irish Republican Brotherhood in the United Kingdom, establishing a joint Revolutionary Directory to plot the liberation of Ireland. More disciplined and secretive than Fenians, the clan attracted the allegiance of prominent Irish-American politicians, businessmen, and other professional people. Among them were Terence V. Powderly, grand master workman of the Knights of Labor and former mayor of Scranton, Pennsylvania; S. B. Conover, U. S. senator from Florida; and John W. Goff, who became a New York State Supreme Court justice. Local government politicians were also clansmen, and from 1876 through 1881, the clan's central executive spent $60,000 financing the efforts of fellow Irishman John Holland to invent a submarine to sweep the British navy from the seas. Holland's invention eventually became the model for the first successful U. S. Navy submarine.

In the late 1870s, John Devoy was pondering ways to bring the American Clan na Gael into contact with the masses in Ireland, who were becoming dissatisfied with the political and economic climate. By summer 1876, Isaac Butt's gentle but apathetic leadership and the inactivity and opportunism of many Home Rule M.P.s created cynicism about the possibilities of parliamentary nationalism. In 1877, a large portion of Irish nationalists in both Ireland and Britain deserted Butt to follow Charles Stewart Parnell, a young Protestant landlord from Wicklow who had rejected the policy of conciliation in the House of Commons in favor of one of obstruction. Obstruction as practiced by Parnell, his colleague Joseph Biggar, and a few other Home Rule M.P.s antagonized British politicians and journalists. But the more British party leaders and newspapers attacked Parnell and his friends as barbarians, the more popular they became among nationalists in Ireland and Britain.

Despite his growing prestige among the Irish in the United Kingdom, however, Parnell preferred not to challenge Butt for the leadership of the bankrupt Home Rule League or the demoralized Irish party. Instead, he ousted Butt as president of the Home Rule Confederation of Great Britain and continued to build constituent support in Ireland, waiting for a new general election to return a braver, bolder body of Irish M.P.s to Westminster. Parnell was also interested in enlisting the enthusiasm and dollars of the most important wing of the Diaspora, the American Irish.

At the same time that Parnell was emerging from the back benches of the Irish party as the new hero of Irish nationalism, Ireland's agrarian economy was experiencing a massive depression. In 1877, after many years of abundant harvests and rising agricultural prices, bad weather destroyed the potato crop, recalling memories of the Great Famine. And in the late 1870s, inexpensively cultivated and harvested American and

Canadian grain began to flood the United Kingdom, bringing a sharp reduction in agricultural prices.

While John Devoy was trying to combine elements of Irish-American power, Parnell's parliamentary obstruction policy, rural economic depression in Ireland, and British-Russian confrontation over the collapsing Turkish empire into a situation ripe for Irish revolution, Irish-American journalist Patrick Ford, populist editor of the New York-based *Irish World,* argued that the agrarian question was the key to Irish freedom. Ford considered American capitalism and the Irish landlord system to be twin evils exploiting the Irish poor on both sides of the Atlantic. He advised Devoy to mobilize all the Irish, at home and abroad, against the landlord system in Ireland in the same way O'Connell had organized them around the issue of Catholic Emancipation.

In collaboration with Ford and other Irish-American leaders, Devoy wove the strands of agrarian radicalism and revolutionary nationalism into a comprehensive strategy. According to this plan, called the New Departure, Parnell and his colleagues in the "active wing" of the parliamentary party would continue to argue for Home Rule in the British House of Commons, and while public attention was focused on them, republicans would be quietly preparing the Irish people for a war of liberation. They would recruit and radicalize the peasant masses by agitating for stable tenures at fair rents and for the tenant's right to sell his interest in a farm if he left or was evicted. Tenant right was to be the prelude to an even more radical demand: the complete abolition of the landlord system and the establishment of peasant proprietorship.[5] When the peasantry was emotionally aroused and disciplined for combat, Parnell would then issue an ultimatum to the British Parliament: Home Rule or else. If British leaders rejected the ultimatum, Parnell and his associates would withdraw from Westminster and establish an Irish parliament in Dublin, defended by guns provided by Irish-America. Calling on the traditions and mythology of Irish nationalism, the New Departure projected that by 1882, the centenary anniversary of Grattan's victory over British imperialism, the revolutionary strategy would have called forth the beginnings of the Irish nation-state. When Clan na Gael leaders wired Parnell the terms of a New Departure alliance, he cautiously responded without being specific. He wanted and needed Irish-American support and money, but not at the price of his independence; Parnell had no intention of becoming a mere cog in Clan na Gael strategy. He also feared that an open alliance with revolutionary republicanism would antagonize the Catholic hierarchy, hurting his chances to become the acknowledged leader of parliamentary nationalism. Parnell was always polite to clan envoys, indicating his interest in an American alliance, but he kept his options open by never making any firm commitments. He did, however, identify with the agrarian phase of the New Departure, cooperating with its emissary, Michael Davitt.

After serving seven years in a British prison for Fenian activities, Davitt had become a New Departure disciple while visiting the United States. In 1879, under instructions from Ford and Devoy, he returned to Ireland to mobilize the Irish peasantry. Davitt created the Land League of Mayo, which later evolved into the National Land League. Demanding the end of the landlord system, the Land League attracted massive support, absorbing the secret terrorist societies that had resurfaced during the depression period of the late 1870s. Parnell, Joseph Biggar, O'Connor Power, and other obstructionist, Home Rule M.P.s appeared on Land League platforms reiterating the old James Fintan Lalor slogan, "The land of Ireland for the people of Ireland." Parnell was most impressive when he told an audience in Ennis, County Clare, "to keep a firm grip on their homesteads." His advice later was applied to a Mayo estate managed by Capt. Charles Cunningham Boycott, and "boycotting" became a successful tactic in the war against manorialism and a new word in the English language.

Collected and distributed through a Clan na Gael front—the Irish National and Industrial League of the United States— Irish-American money financed the land war in Ireland, making it possible for Irish tenant farmers to hold out against eviction threats. Davitt described Irish-America as "the avenging wolfhound of Irish nationalism," and Land League meetings displayed posters praising the American republic as the enemy of British tyranny.

Davitt was a dedicated and unselfish leader. When he realized that Parnell possessed more charisma, he resigned as president of the National Land League and persuaded the Home Ruler to take his place. In that capacity, Parnell toured the United States in 1880 to meet the leaders of Irish-America and to solicit funds for the Land League. He was in demand as a speaker and even addressed a joint session of Congress. After returning to Ireland, Parnell contested and won three Irish seats in a general election, finally deciding to represent Cork in the House of Commons. Shortly after the election, a majority of Home Rule M.P.s elected Parnell as party chairman. He replaced William Shaw, a Cork banker who had become Home Rule leader in Parliament when Butt died in 1879.

Although Parnell was chairman of the Home Ruler M.P.s, he continued to give most of his attention to Land League duties, directing agrarian protests that bordered on the fringes of revolution. Not since the glorious days of repeal in 1843 had an Irish movement so captured public enthusiasm and support. The American Irish continued to contribute dollars to aid evicted tenants, purchase legal aid for embattled farmers, and publicize the antilandlord cause. Despite passionate rhetoric, Land League officials tried to restrain and direct dissatisfaction into passive resistance to manorialism and constitutional demands for land reform. But the old traditions of secret-society violence were difficult to restrain. Dangerous men maimed cattle, burned hayricks, and assaulted landlord agents and those peasants who cooperated with landlords. Although Parnell and his lieutenants might have lost all control over the movement, they did manage to keep violence isolated and to a minimum, preventing the situation from deteriorating into a bloody class war.

Finally, the agitation forced Prime Minister Gladstone into major concessions to Irish rural discontent. In 1881, he steered legislation through Parliament which guaranteed Irish farmers stable tenure at fair rents. This Land Act destroyed manorialism in Ireland and set the stage for peasant land purchase and proprietorship. But since Irish-Americans supported the Land League as only one phase of a grand strategy leading to Irish freedom, Parnell could not afford to offend his constituents by being grateful to the British Liberals. Instead, he insisted that the Land Act be extended to include tenants in arrears and cautioned the Irish public not to trust Gladstone until the new legislation had been tested in the land courts. His haughtiness forced the British government to send Parnell to Kilmainham Prison, but at that time he reasoned it was a good place for him to be. Parnell feared that extremist elements in the Land League would take Gladstone's concession to tenant right as an admission of Liberal weakness and would push for insurrection. He preferred that the British prime minister, rather than the leader of parliamentary Irish nationalism, deal with the hotheads. In prison Parnell would be a martyred hero while Gladstone was doing his work for him.

Finally, with Parnell restless in his prison cell and Gladstone keen on soothing the Irish mood by coming to terms with the popular nationalist leader, an agreement was reached between the two men: the famous Kilmainham Treaty. For Parnell's promise to support the Liberal government's Irish policy, the administration released him from prison and promised an amendment to the Land Act that would extend its benefits to tenants in arrears and would end coercion.

When Parnell walked out of Kilmainham in May 1882, the Land League had been outlawed and rural Ireland was relatively calm. Since the vast majority of tenant farmers seemed contented with the Land Act, Parnell could turn Irish energy and Irish-American money away from agrarian protest and apply them to the Home Rule issue. Using Irish-American money to pay the election expenses and living costs of Home Rule M.P.s, he solved a financial problem troubling parliamentary nationalism since O'Connell's time. Parnell recruited young, fervent, and talented nationalists into the Irish party and turned it into the most effective party in the British Parliament. The third Reform Bill, which extended suffrage to peasant class males in the rural areas of the United Kingdom, also aided parliamentary nationalism by enabling the Irish party to increase its strength to eighty-five M.P.s. With a large Irish party in the House of Commons supported by a strong constituency organization in Ireland—the National League—Parnell changed the strategy of Home Rule agitation at Westminster from obstruction to working for the balance of power. This new tactic, applied in 1885, persuaded Gladstone to lead the Liberals into an alliance with Irish nationalists. Although an 1886 split in the Liberal, Whig, and Radical coalition defeated the first Home Rule Bill and the Conservative House of Lords vetoed the second in 1893, the Irish and Liberal British parties were joined in an often uneasy marriage which could only be torn asunder by death or divorce.

In the early 1880s, Parnell had cleverly outflanked the American Clan na Gael. Using the agrarian phase of the New Departure strategy, he gained control of Irish peasant loyalty and Irish-American financial resources. When tenant right triumphed in Ireland, Parnell was the leader of the Irish, and the Irish at home and abroad were both committed to constitutional nationalism in the form of Home Rule. While the clan was isolated, futilely financing stupid bombing campaigns in Britain, naively hoping to intimidate British politicians into conceding Irish self-government, most Irish-Americans were contributing their dollars to the Parnell-dominated American National League.

In early December 1890, however, after a messy, uncontested court case in which Capt. William O'Shea successfully sued his wife Katharine for divorce, naming Parnell as her lover, Gladstone convinced a majority of the Irish party to vote to replace Parnell as chairman with Justin McCarthy. Gladstone's conduct was determined by the necessities of British politics. Nonconformist Protestants, the core of the Liberal constituency, told the prime minister that they could no longer support him unless he severed his connection with Parnell the adulterer. The Irish party had no choice but to concede to Gladstone's request; Home Rule was more important than Parnell, and its achievement depended on the Irish-Liberal alliance.

Parnell, however, refused to accept the decision of his party colleagues, appealing over their heads to the ultimate source of his strength, the Irish people. This brought Catholic bishops and priests into the conflict. They could not afford to appear more tolerant toward adultery and divorce than British Protestants, and their influence over the value system of Catholic Ireland was the crucial element in the defeat of Parnell and his constituent candidates in a number of subsequent Irish by-elections. The strain of campaigning in the cold, damp countryside destroyed Parnell's health. On 6 October 1891 he died in Brighton of rheumatic fever.

Parnell's death did not end the division in parliamentary nationalism. Bitter disputes and by-election contests between the Parnellite minority and the anti-Parnellite majority intensified the cynicism and apathy that had invaded Home Rule ranks with the divorce scandal and the conflict over party leadership. This plummeting nationalist morale affected the Irish both at home and abroad, reducing the funds of the fragmented party.

The need to restore confidence in the ranks of Irish nationalism, particularly in the affluent Irish-American wing, forced a reunification of the Irish party. In 1900, John Dillon, who had replaced Justin McCarthy as chairman of the anti-Parnellite faction, graciously stepped aside and consented to the election of Parnellite leader John Redmond as chairman of a united party. Because when traveling in the United States Home Rulers disguised the British constitutional mentality of their party, and tailored their comments to the militantly anti-British sentiments of Irish-American audiences, Americans continued to bankroll parliamentary nationalism as an effective path to Irish freedom.

While the American branch of the United Irish League—the successor to the National League—continued to collect funds for the Irish party, Irish-American leaders pressured American politicians to work against British interests. According to one student of Irish-American nationalism, Irish-American opinion and politics helped prevent Anglo-American trade agreements and foreign policy accommodations.[6] The American Irish opposed any free trade agreements that might benefit British commerce, and during the 1895–1896 Venezuelan boundary dispute they agitated for a showdown between the United States and Britain.

In 1911, the Irish Parliamentary Party, taking advantage of an even balance between Liberal and Unionist (Conservative) M.P.s in the House of Commons, forced the Liberal government to curb the absolute veto power of the House of Lords to a three-session, two-year duration as a prelude to Home Rule. And in 1912, British Prime Minister Herbert Asquith introduced the third Home Rule Bill, guaranteed by the constitutional process of victory in 1914. After almost a century of effort Irish nationalists, playing by British parliamentary rules, had nearly grasped the ultimate victory. But when that victory seemed inevitable, the British suddenly changed the rules.

While Irish nationalists prepared to inaugurate an Irish parliament in Dublin, Ulster Protestants, supported by British

Conservatives, threatened civil war to prevent their participation in a united Irish nation. The threat intimidated British liberals into compromising Home Rule by suggesting a partition of Ireland. Responding to British Liberal pressure to make some concession, Redmond said that he was prepared to concede an exclusion of the four northeastern counties (except for the cities of Newry and Derry), where anti-Home Rule Protestants comprised a majority. But Ulster Orangemen, their Dublin Protestant leader Sir Edward Carson, and some of their British Tory allies demanded that all or at least six of the nine Ulster counties be excluded from the settlement. With the tones of political debate becoming more shrill and with Protestant Orange and Catholic Green volunteer forces parading with rifles in Belfast and Dublin, World War I rescued the United Kingdom from perhaps an even worse catastrophe, civil war.

When the war began, many Irish-Americans and some of the Irish in Ireland objected to Redmond's decision to support the British war effort as a democratic crusade against German authoritarianism and in defense of the sovereignty of small nations like Belgium. Redmond also believed that if Irishmen did their duty then the British might limit the extent of Ulster exclusion from Home Rule after the war. Irish-Americans and extreme nationalists in Ireland viewed World War I as nothing more than a conflict between militaristic empires and resented an Irish leader advising Irishmen to shed their blood to maintain British imperialism. Clan na Gael leaders joined with German-Americans in demanding that the United States remain neutral. In 1916, John Devoy and his associates helped plan the Easter Week Rebellion in Dublin, seeking the support of the German government for Irish revolution.[7]

Once the United States entered the war in April 1917 on the side of Britain and France, the overwhelming majority of Irish-Americans placed their loyalty to the United States over any commitment to Irish nationalism. As in previous wars, they rushed to the colors and enthusiastically purchased victory bonds. Irish-American George M. Cohan wrote the songs that best captured the spirit of American patriotism. And Irish-American regiments like the New York "Fighting 69th" proved Irish courage on the battlefield. But once the war in Europe was over, Irish-Americans resumed their interest in the Irish freedom movement.

The British government's intimidation by Ulster Protestant and British Conservative demands that Ulster counties be excluded from Home Rule, the execution of leaders of the Easter Week "blood sacrifice," the imprisonment of thousands of Irish nationalists without legal due process, and the slaughter of Irish soldiers on the western front and in the ill-fated Gallipoli venture all combined to destroy the credibility of the Irish Parliamentary Party and the brand of constitutional nationalism it represented. In the December 1918 United Kingdom general election, Irish voters returned seventy-three Sinn Fein Party candidates pledged to an independent Irish republic.[8] They refused to sit in the British House of Commons, stayed in Dublin, and organized an Irish parliament, the Dail, which was defended by the Irish Volunteers, rechristened the Irish Republican Army. During 1919, engagements between IRA guerrilla companies and the Royal Irish Constabulary escalated into the Anglo-Irish War, which continued until a truce was called in the summer of 1921.

Following the armistice which concluded World War I, the American Irish contributed money and guns to the Sinn Fein effort in Ireland, and they pressured the United States government to recognize the Irish Republic. President Wilson's pro-British biases and his refusal to include Ireland in his principle of self-determination cost the Democratic Party many Irish votes in the presidential election of 1920. In 1921, Irish-America contributed to the international public opinion that finally pressured the British government into concluding a treaty with Irish rebels giving dominion status to an Irish Free State which included twenty-six of the thirty-two Irish counties.[9]

In the course of the Anglo-Irish War, Irish-Americans re-vealed that they were essentially more anti-British than pro-Irish independence. When American-born Eamon de Valera, Easter Week hero and president of the Dail, visited the United States in 1919–1920 to collect funds for the war of liberation and to recruit American political support for the Irish Republic, a number of Clan na Gael leaders considered him too tepid in his hostility to Britain. Realizing that history, economics, and geography required close ties between Ireland and Britain, de Valera said that he would be willing to accept a relationship analagous to the one between the United States and Cuba at the time. Considering the Irish president's "Cuban Proposal" a surrender of Irish sovereignty, Daniel F. Cohalan, a New York judge and friend of Devoy, furiously censured the Irish leader:

If Ireland were to change her position, and to seek a measure of self-government that would align her in the future with England as an ally, in what I regard as the inevitable struggle for freedom of the seas that must shortly come between America and England, every loyal American will, without hesitation, take a position un-reservedly upon the side of America.[10]

Cohalan's statement emphasized the fact that much of Irish-American nationalism was more a search for respectability in the United States and a hatred for England than a love of Ireland.

# 8

## Irish-American Politics

✻✦✻

At the same time the American Irish were responding to American nativism by cultivating Irish nationalism as an expression of identity and as part of a search for respectability, they were using politics to achieve power. And they had the skills to operate the machinery of the American political system. The Irish may have arrived in the United States technologically impoverished, but they came politically experienced. Before crossing the Atlantic, they had already confronted Anglo-Saxon political, social, and economic ascendancy in the United Kingdom. Using the existing avenues of the British constitutional system and creating the tactics of modern democratic pressure politics, Daniel O'Connell, the first Irish machine boss, had mobilized his people for political action. Since necessity forced Irish agitators to operate within the context of Anglo-Saxon Protestant political traditions, the Irish arrived in the United States already familiar with the rules of the Anglo-American political game and with considerable confidence in their ability to manipulate such rules to achieve power and influence. The consolidation of the Irish-American community around the standard of Catholicism helped provide a focal point for political as well as ethnic organization. And the gregarious character of the Irish personality also contributed to their political skills. Despite a reputation for aggressiveness and pugnacity, the Irish like, enjoy and are interested in people, preferring to convince by argument and persuasion rather than force. Irish violence is usually more verbal than physical.

Since the beginnings of the American republic, the Irish have been so closely associated with the Democratic Party that Irish-Catholic-Democrat seems almost a natural trinity. For a long time the Irish-Catholic Democratic alliance satisfied mutual interests and needs. While Jeffersonian democrats in the late 1700s and early 1800s were winning Irish loyalty with a welcome to America and an egalitarian political philosophy, the Federalist authors of the anti-immigrant Alien and Sedition Acts reminded the Irish of the Tory, Protestant Ascendancy in the old country. Because the Whig successors to the Federalists also identified their party with wealth, property, and Anglo-Saxon Protestant nativism, Jeffersonian and Jacksonian democracy continued to attract and maintain Irish support. Since Andrew Jackson's parents had emigrated from Ulster and he had humbled the British at New Orleans, Irish-Americans were particularly fond and proud of the rough-mannered, outspoken Tennessean. In the 1850s, when the Republican Party began to challenge the Democrats, the Irish refused to desert the memory of Jefferson and Jackson. To them, the new party was just another expression of anti-Irish, anti-Catholic prejudice, and Republicans did appeal to and inherit the nativist vote.

When the Irish arrived in urban America, Democratic machines controlled most cities. Local party leaders saw to it that the newcomers were quickly naturalized and registered as voters. Democratic bosses recruited the Irish as shock troops, and the Irish did their duty by voting—often more than once—and their street gangs protected party candidates and intimidated opposition forces. But they had no intention of remaining buck privates in the Democratic army. Slowly but surely the Irish began to take control of their own ghettos, building mini-machines within the general party structure, and began to move up the leadership ladder from block captains to district or precinct leaders to aldermen. In their political quest for power, Irish politicians used Catholic solidarity as a voting base, saloons as political clubs, and police and fire department appointments as patronage sources to recruit votes and party workers.

The increase in the numbers and the quality of Irish immigration in the post-Civil War period aided the expansion of Irish political power in urban America. By 1900, Irish politicians had moved up from the lower ranks to leadership levels of Democratic organizations in most of the large cities in the United States, but the methods of control varied from place to place. In the early 1870s, after the Tweed Ring scandals had almost ruined the Democratic machine, "Honest" John Kelly assumed command of New York's Tammany Hall. He consolidated a loosely structured feudal system into a centralized monarchy, very much in the image of his beloved Catholic church. The Irish made Tammany the most effective political organization in the United States, but few Irish machines could duplicate the efficiency or discipline of the New York operation. In Boston, particularly after 1900, Irish politics resembled the clan rather than the monarchical system with a number of bosses controlling pockets of power in the city and jealously guarding their fiefs. And until the reign of the Kelly-Nash machine of the 1930s, later perfected by Richard J. Daley in the 1950s, 1960s, and 1970s, Irish politics in Chicago resembled Boston politics more than it did the New York system.

Many Americans, not only nativists but also some Irish people, have accused the Irish of lowering the moral tone of politics in the United States. They charge them with allowing graft and corruption and with cynically exploiting the acquisitive side of human nature as a method of gaining and holding power. Critics of the Irish also blame them for introducing a politics of revenge into American life, claiming that they employed political power to settle old scores with Anglo-American Protestants. In his novel, *The Governor* (1970), a fictionalized account of modern urban politics in Massachusetts, Edward R. F. Sheehan emphasized the revenge theme with Francis Xavier Cassidy, commissioner of public works, as the Irish sword of retribution:

> There, in those deep and misty bogs of his mind, he inexorably relived all the nightmares of his race, even the nightmares he never dreamed. There, in the most wretched hovels of his soul, he felt the pangs of potato hunger and the British lash against his back, only to take flight across a hostile sea to meaner hovels still and horrid Yankee mills whose owners paid him pennies and then posted notices at their gates NO IRISH NEED APPLY.

Sheehan described James Michael Curley, Boston mayor and local Irish champion in the struggle against Anglo-America, as another "tribal hero who squandered his remarkable talents and devoted a lifetime to settling old scores, a crippled warrior egging on an amused mob of shanty Irish in the sacking of the Yankee Troy."

Curley inspired the creation of Edwin O'Connor's Frank Skeffington in *The Last Hurrah* (1956), one of the most popular of Irish-American political novels. On occasion, Skeffington practiced the politics of revenge. He explained to his nephew and confidant, Adam, that the bitter feud between himself and Amos Force, the Yankee newspaper publisher, started when Amos's father fired Skeffington's immigrant mother from her job as a house servant when she was caught taking food scraps home to her hungry children:

> "As for Amos, he's never been able to forget that the son of the servant who committed this crime against his purse became mayor of his city and governor of his state, and in the course of doing so managed to make life just a little

more difficult for him. Amos's life hasn't exactly been a bed of pain, but I think I can say with all modesty that it's been considerably more painful than if I hadn't been around. In any case, that's how it all started, and that's why your paper, even today, continues its splendid crusade for better government. Which is to say, government without me. Amos has a long memory, you see. I may add," he said impassively, "that so have I."

Although the American Irish have not done much to raise the standards of political conduct in the United States, it is a considerable distortion of historical reality to blame them for all of the seamy aspects of urban government. Irish-American politicians and their machines were and still are guilty of graft and the use of clout, but their political ethics do not vary dramatically from traditional, Anglo-American, Protestant practices in business and politics. While it is not an adequate defense to argue that two wrongs make a right, Irish politicians have a point when they brand attacks on their ethics as jealous hypocrisy, when they argue that the proceeds they earned from graft were less magnificent and less immoral than the profits of American business enterprises. They have asked: What right do men who exploit the working class through high prices and low wages have to demand urban reform to smash Irish power, particularly when that power provides food, clothing, shelter, and jobs to people made poor by the businessman's greed?

Political machines and party bosses existed in rural and urban America long before the Irish arrived, and the politics of revenge also preceded them to the "shores of Americay." When Irish politicians won elections, appointed their friends to office, and then raided the public treasury for public works projects that provided both graft and jobs, they were following an old American political tradition: "To the victor belong the spoils." Irish hostility to political reform was not a defense of corruption so much as it was a response to nativism. As a group, reformers were much more interested in driving Irish Catholics from office than they were in improving the economic status of the urban poor. Reformism's emphasis on temperance was one expression of the middle-class, Anglo-American, Protestant core of the movement and its hostility to Catholic ethnicity. To the Irish and other Catholics, reformism was an attack on their life-styles, threatening the few pleasures enjoyed by the ghetto poor.

Irish politicians could and did argue with some justice that the difference between their machines and the Anglo-American ones they replaced was a higher degree of efficiency and compassion rather than more corruption. The Anglo-American machines took; the Irish took as well, but they also gave, distinguishing between honest and dishonest graft.[1] They employed the power of political organization to provide coal, food, jobs, and bail for their troubled constituents. They erected mini-welfare states not only to win votes but also because they were concerned with their people's struggles against a cold, urban environment. And "their people" frequently meant more than just the Irish. Irish politicians, particularly in Chicago and New York where ethnic patterns were very complex and varied, formed coalitions among minority groups. They protected Poles, Jews, and Italians as well as the Irish. The diary of Tammany stalwart George Washington Plunkett best describes the busy, multi-ethnic schedule of an urban Irish politician of the late nineteenth century:

2 A.M. Wakened by a boy with message from bartender to bail him out of jail. 3 A.M. Back to bed. 6 A.M. Fire engines, up and off to the scene to see my election district captains tending the burnt-out tenants. Got names for new homes. 8:30 to police court. Six drunken constituents on hand. Got four released by a timely word to the judge. Paid the other's (sic) fines. Nine o'clock to Municipal court. Told an election district captain to act as lawyer for

a widow threatened with dispossession. 11 to 3 P.M. Found jobs for four constituents. 3 P.M. an Italian funeral, sat conspicuously up front. 4 P.M. A Jewish funeral—up front again, in the synagogue. 7 P.M. Meeting of district captains and reviewed the list of all voters, who's for us, who's agin. 8 P.M. Church fair. Bought ice cream for the girls; took fathers for a little something around the corner. 9 P.M. Back in club-house. Heard complaints of a dozen push cart pedlars. 10:30 A Jewish wedding. Had sent handsome present to the bride. Midnight—to bed.

Irish politics also confronted the hostility of Irish nationalism, although in many instances it was difficult to separate the two. This was particularly true in Chicago where, during the 1880s, the Irish members of the Democratic machine were also prominent in the Clan na Gael, as was well-known Republican A. M. Sullivan. But many nationalists like John Devoy, editor of the *Gaelic American* in New York and enemy of Sullivan within the clan, were purists who did not want to besmirch Irish nationalism with the stench of politics. They compared politics in America with parliamentarianism in Ireland, claiming both were corrupt and self-serving.

Nationalists like Devoy described politicians as shifty vote hustlers who were indifferent to Irish freedom, and they resented the fanatic loyalty of the American Irish to the Democratic Party. If the Irish had to engage in politics, they argued, their vote should go to the highest bidder, the party most willing to lean in the direction of a pro-Irish nationalist, anti-British foreign policy. In 1884, Devoy and his friends asked the Irish to vote for James G. Blaine, the Republican opposing Grover Cleveland in the presidential election, and in 1888 and 1892 they pleaded with them to cast ballots for Benjamin Harrison rather than Cleveland. When Woodrow Wilson ran for a second term in 1916, Irish-American nationalists joined with some Catholic priests in asking the American Irish to reject the

Democrat for the Republican candidate, Charles Evans Hughes. The priests thought Wilson too friendly toward anti-Catholic revolutionaries in Mexico; nationalists considered his reaction to World War I too pro-British. On each of these occasions, the Irish working class ignored the recommendations of nationalists and clerics and followed the advice of their Democratic politicians. In the polling booth, they voted as American, working-class people, not as Irish nationalists. They consulted their economic interests and remained steadfast Democrats.

\* \* \*

Even among the many Americans who dislike the Irish because they believe they are agents of Catholic ignorance and authoritarianism or who find them crude, arrogant, and aggressive, there are those who concede them a kind of political genius. Frequently this admission has been made more in a spirit of fear than of admiration. In January 1916, Sir Cecil Spring-Rice, United Kingdom ambassador to the United States, wrote to his foreign secretary, Sir Edward Grey, about the difficulty of persuading the United States to support Britain in her war against the Central Powers. He attributed many of his problems to the Irish, who had "unequaled power of political organization" and were the "best politicians in the country."[2] Anglo-American Protestants had watched with a mixture of amazement and anguish as the Irish had proceeded to gain political control over urban America. In the April 1894 issue of *The Forum,* John Paul Bocock discussed "The Irish Conquest of Our Cities," claiming that Irish oligarchies dominated New York, Brooklyn, Jersey City, Hoboken, Boston, Chicago, Buffalo, Albany, Troy, Pittsburgh, St. Paul, St. Louis, Kansas City, Omaha, New Orleans, and San Francisco. He asked

What do the majorities of the citizens of American municipalities think of themselves? How has it come about that the system of government so admirably conceived by the fathers has worked out so perfectly in national affairs and so poorly in municipal affairs? Philadelphia, Boston and New York were once governed by the Quakers, the Puritans, and the Knickerbockers. Are they better governed now, since from the turbulence of municipal politics the Irish-Americans have plucked both wealth and power?

Some contemporary Irish-American scholars and intellectuals seem as concerned about the dark side of Irish politics as Bocock was back in the 1890s. In his essay "The Irish" in *Beyond the Melting Pot* (1963), Daniel Patrick Moynihan, an adviser to both Kennedy and Nixon, former ambassador to India, and currently envoy to the United Nations, leveled a devastating attack on the Irish role in urban affairs, insisting that the Irish political style lacked purpose beyond the acquisition of power:

> The Irish were uncommonly successful in politics. They ran the city. But the very parochialism and bureaucracy that enabled them to succeed in politics prevented them from doing much with government. In a sense the Irish did not know what to do with power once they got it. They never thought of politics as an instrument of social change.

According to Moynihan, Irish-American political perspectives never really advanced beyond the rural-parish, old-country value system; Irish attitudes were static and thus essentially conservative. Although their political genius was directed at the seizure and maintenance of power, he argues, it lacked the idealism and social conscience that translates power into constructive change. American urban problems created by rapid industrialization and population growth demanded reform, says Moynihan, but Irish power paralyzed the responses of city governments, frustrating social improvement, and serving as a negative rather than a positive force for urban development. Before *Beyond the Melting Pot* reached the reading public, Thomas J. Fleming anticipated the Moynihan thesis in *All Good Men* (1961), one of a series of novels he has written about the Irish in a New Jersey city. The book presents the theme in the words of Larry Donahue, an ambitious, unstable, bitter young politician critical of the local Irish boss and machine:

> This city is a living testimonial to the ineptitude and rotten morals of the Irish who are running it . . . I'm serious. Thirty years of absolute power. What would a Jew have done with it? Or a New England Yank? We'd be living in a dream city with equal housing and equal opportunity and equal justice for everybody.

More recently, in a revisionist lecture, "The Irish in United States Politics," delivered before the April 1975 American Committee for Irish Studies meeting at Stonehill College in Easton, Massachusetts, Thomas N. Brown argued that historians, social scientists, creative writers, and journalists have exaggerated the existence of a unique Irish political style and approach to the American political process. He insisted that the techniques of Irish-American politics have varied from city to city and from generation to generation, responding to local issues, values, and challenges. Brown offered evidence indicating that Irish-American politics in Boston traditionally have been more "Boston" than "Irish" and suggested that the same would hold true for other cities like New York or Chicago.

If Brown meant that there is more than one Irish-American approach to urban problems and more than one type of Irish political personality, he is obviously correct. There is no universal Irish politician; the American Irish did take on the tones and colors of regional values. And while the Irish did arrive in the

United States with considerable experience in the art of political organization, rough-and-tumble, urban American politics did shape their approaches to government. Although scholars, intellectuals, and the literati have exaggerated the uniqueness of and have overly romanticized Irish-American politics, it does have its distinct attributes. In fact, the flexibility that Brown emphasized is one of its main components.

Anglicization and Romanization, both tempered by the trials and tribulations of nationalist movements, have strongly influenced Irish politics. This book repeatedly has emphasized that the Irish are both the victims and the beneficiaries of two kinds of cultural imperialisms. Anglicization and Romanization, added to the fading memories of a defeated Gaelic culture, fashioned the values of the Irish at home and abroad, and all dimensions of the Irish personality have been as apparent in politics as in religion and literature. Political Anglicization was nurtured in the long struggle for Irish freedom, imparting to Irish nationalism an emphasis on the defense of natural and individual rights as the purpose of good government. In the early decades of the nineteenth century, Daniel O'Connell organized the Irish masses for political action and impregnated Irish nationalism with a firm commitment to liberal democracy.

O'Connell did more than just borrow principles and methods of British constitutionalism and pass them on to his Irish followers; he also developed protest tactics that contributed to the advance of liberty throughout the Western world. In his campaigns to emancipate Catholics and to repeal the Union, he created the first modern political party in the United Kingdom, one that rested on constituent support as well as on activity in the British House of Commons. And O'Connell was the first European politician to achieve significant victories for individual freedom in the oppressive Age of Metternich by applying the "moral force" of disciplined public opinion. As he worked with British Whig and Radical politicians for reform in Irish government, he taught his people that the success of democratic politics depended on compromise, the notion that some improvement was better than none at all.

Later in the nineteenth century, Charles Stewart Parnell built on the foundations that O'Connell had so firmly laid. Although less charismatic than the Kerry Catholic, the Wicklow Protestant also helped Anglicize Irish politics. His obstruction policy in the House of Commons, his energetic leadership of the Land League attack on the landlord system, and his masterful employment of balance-of-power politics to force Liberals to adopt Home Rule taught the Irish how to manipulate the weaknesses and strength of parliamentary government to achieve power.

While it employed the liberal principles of the British system, the Irish political perspective was also colored by the Catholic experience, and this Romanization gave the Irish a profoundly different point of view than Anglo-Saxon and Anglo-American liberal democrats, a difference not detected by Moynihan and other critics of the Irish political style. Moynihan, in fact, seems to have accepted a rather prejudiced view among historians that American social reform is the achievement of Protestant, middle-class progressivism accomplished despite conservative, Catholic, ethnic opposition.

Throughout the nineteenth century, however, it was American Protestants who insisted on a conservative, self-help social ethic, a *laissez faire* creed, while Irish politicians tried to improve the standard of living of the urban poor through government intervention. Dispensing buckets of coal, food baskets, public works, and other forms of patronage employment was often an inefficient and graft-ridden system of social justice, but the Irish approach rather than that of Anglo-Saxon Protestants was the precursor of welfare state liberalism in the United States.

The Irish-Catholic sense of community encourages a collectivist rather than an atomistic approach to the social order; thus they have no emotional or intellectual antipathy to a welfare state. In contrast, Anglo-Saxon and Anglo-American Protestant liberalism draws its sustenance from an individualistic religious and economic ideology which emphasizes the rights of the person against the "oppression" of the community. The Protestant conscience and value system find it much more difficult to deal with urban industrial social questions than does the Catholic, community-centered point of view.

Thus when they advocate or support social reform, the Irish are not functioning as liberals in the Anglo-Saxon or Anglo-American Protestant sense of the word. Irish and other Catholic ethnics cannot emotionally or intellectually accept the tenets of the eighteenth-century Enlightenment, which comprises the framework of the value system of the United States, a nation conceived and born in the "Age of Reason"; they cannot accept a dogmatic faith in the perfectibility of human nature and in the inevitability of progress. Philosophically, the Irish view of the human condition is much closer to Burkean conservatism than to Lockean, Jeffersonian, or Benthamite liberalism. They believe in the dark side of human nature, the existence of objective evil, and the influence of irrational forces on the human personality and the historical process.

Paradoxically, this conservative, skeptical, often cynical attitude toward man and his environment has made the Irish more successful as practical reformers than ideological liberals have been. The Irish strive for improvement rather than perfection, always conscious of the importance of blending change with traditions.

In the twentieth century, following a major economic depression that shook confidence in *laissez faire* capitalism, a majority of American citizens concluded that social security was an essential foundation for human freedom. When they decided that government had an obligation to guarantee that social security, it was Irish politicians in cities, not Anglo-American Protestant leaders in suburban or rural America, who served as the core of minority group coalitions that made possible the New Deal, Fair Deal, New Frontier, and the Great Society.[3]

In Ireland and the United States, the Irish have blended the methodology and principles of Anglo-Saxon and Anglo-American, Protestant, liberal politics, a Catholic sense of community, and their own tolerant and gregarious personalities into a unique brand of politics. And because they bridged the gulf between Roman Catholic and Anglo-Saxon Protestant cultures, the Irish were the only European ethnics who could have led the American Catholic community into an accommodation with the dominant, Anglo-American Protestant ethos.[4]

While Irish-Americans were helping other Catholic ethnics to adjust to the American system and pushing a reluctant United States along the road to the welfare state, Irish politicians were quietly achieving a successful social revolution in the status and condition of their own people. In little more than a hundred years, the American Irish moved from the basements, attics, and shacks of Boston, Philadelphia, New York, Chicago, and New Orleans ghettos to the front ranks of American social, political, and intellectual society, including a brief residency in that very famous mansion on Pennsylvania Avenue in Washington, D.C.

# 9

## From Ghetto to Suburbs:
## From Someplace to No Place?

From the time of the Great Famine in the mid-1840s until the conclusion of the Anglo-Irish War, Irish-American fanaticism and money sustained Irish nationalism. But after the 1921 treaty ending the war between Britain and Ireland, most of the American Irish gradually disassociated themselves from Irish affairs. To them the establishment of the Irish Free State seemed a major concession to the objectives of Irish nationalism. They agreed with Michael Collins that dominion status was a firm foundation for the continued expansion of Irish sovereignty, a prediction that was gradually fulfilled in the 1920s, 1930s, and 1940s until Ireland became a republic outside the Commonwealth in 1948. A year of brutal civil war between defenders of the Irish Free State and die-hard Republicans in Ireland following the treaty disgusted many Irish-Americans.

A decrease in physical and cultural contacts between the Irish in Ireland and those in the United States also weakened the concept of an international, unified Irish community. Nativist-inspired legislation in 1921 and 1924 restricting immigration and the Great Depression of the late 1920s and early 1930s reduced the number of Irish emigrating to the United States.

Most of the Irish who left their country for employment opportunities abroad went to Britain where the cultural and emotional break with Ireland seemed less severe than in America. Inexpensive ship and air fares have made it easy for Irish exiles to return home from England and Scotland for Christmas and summer holidays.

In addition to the decline in Irish emigration to the United States, the decision of posttreaty Ireland to promote a more exclusive brand of nationalism, and, more recently, the Irish government's emphasis on the Irish as a European rather than a Diasporic people has widened the communication gap between the Irish at home and in America. Contemporary nationalism with its paradoxical combination of provincial Gaelic and cosmopolitan common market and European community dimensions neglects the rich, cultural potential of uniting the Irish at home with sophisticated, intellectual Irish colonies in the United States and in the British Commonwealth.

But the separation between the Irish in Ireland and their kinsmen in the United States is a mutual rather than one-sided decision to move in different cultural spheres. In the course of the twentieth century the American Irish passed through an identity crisis and in doing so lost their psychological dependence on Irish nationalism. In "The Bent Twig—A Note on Nationalism," *Foreign Affairs,* October 1972, Isaiah Berlin defines nationalism as an expression of "the inflamed desire of the insufficiently regarded to count for something among the cultures of the world." During the nineteenth and early twentieth centuries, Irish-Americans were certainly among the "insufficiently regarded," yearning for respectability, blaming their low status in the United States on the British conquest of their homeland, and insisting that a free Ireland would emancipate them from the humiliation of Anglo-Saxon contempt. However, following World War I, they rapidly achieved prosperity and gained respectability, and their dependence on nationality decreased.

Irish-America's response to the contemporary crisis in Northern Ireland perhaps most clearly reveals the passing of nationalistic dependence. After the British Parliament partitioned Ireland in the 1920 Government of Ireland Bill, the leadership of the Protestant majority in six-county Northern Ireland, which gained a measure of self-government under Home Rule, immediately converted the territory into "a Protestant nation for a Protestant people." For all practical purposes this meant apartheid. Gerrymandering, a house-occupancy franchise, and double votes for business properties denied Catholics a proportionate share of power in local government, even in places where they were in the majority. Catholics retreated into their ghettos, rejecting the concept of a Protestant, British Northern Ireland and remaining loyal to the Irish nation represented first by the Irish Free State and then by the Irish Republic in the South. Some of them unleashed their frustrations by joining the Irish Republican Army and participating in terrorist attacks on the symbols of British authority in the six counties.

After World War II, many northern Catholics wearied of their suffering and their depressed ghetto conditions. They also became wary of promises of rescue by politicians in the South and realized that, instead of destroying apartheid, IRA violence only served to escalate Protestant counter-terrorism and made existence even more miserable for them in the North. In their own effort to obtain a fair share of the British welfare state, a large and influential section of the six-county Catholic community formed the Northern Ireland Civil Rights Association in 1967 and decided to imitate black protest tactics in the United States. In 1968, singing "We Shall Overcome," large numbers of northern Catholics, joined by Protestant and Catholic students from Queen's University in Belfast, marched for minority civil rights.

Peaceful marches and demonstrations confused Northern Ireland police and government officials. They preferred to deal with the IRA, whose terrorism justified the Special Powers Act, legislation permitting the jailing of suspected republican nationalists without charge or trial and creating a gestapo-like, "B Special" police force to intimidate the Catholic minority. Despite the constitutional methods of the Northern Ireland Civil Rights Association, policemen beat up peaceful demonstrators and joined politicians in looking the other way when Protestant mobs assaulted marchers and threatened to invade Catholic ghettos. The failure of peaceful protest, the refusal of Northern Ireland politicians and policemen to protect Catholic liberties, and Protestant violence revived the then moribund IRA as a Catholic defense force.[1] And the restoration of the IRA meant that Irish nationalism rather than civil rights became the vital issue in the Ulster crisis.

Suppression of civil rights demonstrations and violent confrontations between Catholics and Protestants, covered by television crews from all over the world, made public the semifascist character of Northern Ireland. Embarrassed by their dirty linen, British politicians pressured the Northern Ireland government to make some concessions to civil rights demands. Paralyzed by their ties to the ultra-Protestant Orange lodges, however, Northern Ireland leaders procrastinated while their country marched toward civil war. In August 1969, confronting the probability of a sectarian massacre in the Six Counties, the British government sent troops to Northern Ireland. At first, Catholics welcomed them as protectors. But since the army was there to preserve law and order as well as to prevent sectarian strife, it supported the existing Protestant Unionist government, disarming Catholics and jailing suspected IRA members and friends.

Finally, in March 1972, the British suspended the Northern Ireland government, temporarily incorporated the Six Counties into the rest of the United Kingdom political system, and began to plan a reformed Northern Ireland that would bestow civil rights on all of its citizens and perhaps pave the way to a united Ireland. But Protestant hostility to such concepts as Catholic equality, power sharing, and the prospect of a United Ireland, Catholic wariness of British integrity, and the continued terrorism of the Provisional IRA and Unionist gangs have prevented a final solution to the Ulster crisis. Perhaps there are no satisfactory alternatives. Meanwhile, the violence goes on with the death toll, as of mid-1975, in excess of 1,200.[2]

The crisis in the Six Counties has telescoped centuries of Irish history into a few short years: Protestant bigotry challenging Irish Catholic nationalism; the irresponsibility, insensitivity, and ignorance of British politicians dealing with Ireland; British soldiers shooting Irish civilians; Irish revolutionaries ambushing British soldiers; curfews, coercion, and internment. And the social and economic conditions of the large Catholic minority in the North are reminiscent of those in the Irish ghettos in nineteenth-century, urban America. The Ulster Orangeman bears a striking resemblance to the Know-Nothing Party member or the Ku Kluxer. If Irish-American nationalism were still a vital force, then seven years of such conditions in Northern Ireland should have triggered it into massive action. But the American Irish seem to have lost their historical memories. The connection between the situation in Northern Ireland and the experience of their ancestors here and in Ireland has not touched the hearts or minds of most of them.

In pubs in Boston, New York, Chicago, and San Francisco, Irish-American college students do sing nationalist ballads, demanding that Britain return the fourth green field to Cathleen ni Houlihan.[3] And a number of Irish-Americans contribute money to IRA front groups, who in turn purchase the bullets and bombs that kill innocent people in Britain and Ireland. Many of the young, middle-class pub balladeers are ignorant of Irish history, untouched by Irish culture, and are only romantically reacting to the enthusiasm of youth, the Irishness of their names, the beat of the music, and the need for a cause. Their elders who support IRA violence by contributing money seem to represent the residue of Irish-American ghetto paranoia;

most of them are still seeking an identity through the old slogans and hatreds of Irish nationalism.[4]

But only a minority of Irish-Americans are deeply involved with the situation in Northern Ireland. Most of the American Irish are apathetic or puzzled about the situation in the six counties. They are unable to see that the issues in the North are culture and nationality rather than religion, that religion is only a symbol of cultural identities—Protestant equals British while Catholic means Irish—and that this conflict between cultures is the essence of the Irish historical process. Such ignorance is most unfortunate, because an historically and culturally aware Irish community in the United States could balance the lunacy of those who support the IRA. It could bring legitimate and rational pressure to bear on both the British and United States governments to defend Catholic civil rights in Northern Ireland.

Most Irish-Americans have become too successful in the United States to think much about events in Ireland. Except for a few isolated pockets of failure like South Boston, Irish-America, freed from the burden of assimilating large numbers of new immigrants, has evolved from an essentially working to a middle-class community. Irish vaudeville song-and-dance men and actors from the legitimate theatre, for example, have been joined in the entertainment field by Academy Award winners like Spencer Tracy, Gene Kelly, Bing Crosby, and motion picture director John Ford.

Although the Irish today are prominent among the executives, coaches, and managers of athletic teams, they are not as numerous among the athletes themselves. Since James J. Braddock lost the heavyweight championship to Joe Louis in Commiskey Park in June 1937 and Billy Conn narrowly failed to win it back for the Irish four years later, few Irishmen have made their careers in boxing rings around the country. And the "Fighting Irish" of Notre Dame today are more often Poles, Italians, or blacks. Young Irish students enter colleges and universities with goals other than athletic championships or trophies. Instead, they want to become business executives, lawyers, doctors, professors, or poets.

The American Irish took their biggest leap forward in social and occupational mobility after World War II with education providing the springboard. Immediately following their discharges from the armed forces, hundreds of thousands of Irish-Americans took advantage of the G. I. Bill of Rights by enrolling in colleges and universities at government expense. Of all the Catholic ethnics, the Irish were in the best position to take advantage of the government's generosity; they had the secondary school educational backgrounds to succeed on the university level. In contrast to other Catholic groups, the American Irish could afford the high tuitions at Catholic high schools, they had reached the point in the American assimilation process where they realized the importance of education for mobility, and they still closely associated their Irish and Catholic identities, insisting that both could best be preserved in a Catholic environment. So they sent their children to Catholic secondary schools, which were much more effective as college preparatory institutions than their urban public school counterparts. In the 1940s, parochial schools in American cities were dominated by Irish clerical and lay faculties teaching mostly Irish students. In Chicago, for example, before World War II the quality Catholic secondary schools were predominantly Irish, more than 90 percent in some instances. Because Irish-Americans were in such an excellent position to take advantage of college educational opportunities which the G. I. Bill offered, Irish ex-servicemen skipped one, sometimes two generations on the mobility ladder, in a number of instances moving from peasant father to professor, lawyer, or doctor son. A majority of Americans at the top of the business and professional worlds in the 1970s are products of United States government educational opportunities, and the American Irish are prominent in both groups.

Education thus helped change the life-style and geography of Irish-America and along with World War II started the dissolution of the Irish physical ghetto. Travel and new experiences broadened the perspectives of many Irish-American servicemen. A number of them never returned to their home neighborhoods; some even married outside the ethnic group. And in the 1950s more Irish-Americans began to leave the urban ghettos. College-educated people moved to what they hoped would be a more comfortable, affluent, and cosmopolitan world in suburbia. Such moves were hastened by the increasing migration of blacks from the rural South to find jobs in the urban North. As the surplus population in the black ghettos began to spill over into Irish neighborhoods, the Irish started to migrate themselves. Black movement into and Irish exodus out of the cities weakened the structure of and financial support for the Irish-dominated, urban-centered Catholic church, forcing painful and difficult readjustments in religious goals and tasks.[5]

Social and educational mobility also expanded the political influence of the American Irish. For a brief time, the anti-Catholic propaganda and Ku Klux Klan terrorism that disgraced the presidential election of 1928 and helped bring about Smith's defeat increased Irish defensiveness, adding bricks to the psychological walls of the ghetto. But after 1928, Anglo-Saxon Protestant nativism, which had remained a vital, emotional force in rural and small-town America, seemed to lose much of its potency. The Great Depression brought all nationalities together to fight a common cause—poverty. If Smith had won the Democratic nomination in 1932, a majority of Americans probably would have elected him president, regardless of his Catholicism.

International problems also weakened American nativism. During the 1940s, 1950s, and 1960s, Americans from all religions, ethnic groups, and races pulled together to combat fascism and communism in hot and cold wars. In Europe, on islands all over the South Pacific, in Korea, and Vietnam, Catholic ethnics continued to serve their country. At home, they joined operations like the Federal Bureau of Investigation and the Central Intelligence Agency to seek out and destroy enemies of American freedom.[6] Military service, particularly during World War II, brought varieties of Americans together in common discomfort, danger, and purpose. This experience promoted mutual understanding and lessened cultural prejudices and hostilities.

Irish influence in politics began to take on significant national dimensions during the 1930s. Franklin D. Roosevelt rewarded the Irish for their contribution to the minority-group coalition which made up the Democratic Party by selecting Irishmen James J. Farley and Frank Walsh as members of his cabinet and appointing Frank Murphy to the U.S. Supreme Court. He also placed Catholics, most of them Irish, in one out of every four government positions open for appointment. Some political commentators, however, seem to think that while the New Deal opened up national opportunities for the Irish political genius, its massive welfare state programs undermined the power of their urban machines. In *The Last Hurrah,* Edwin O'Connor blamed the failure of Frank Skeffington to win his last big campaign for mayor on the inroads of the New Deal:

> All over the country the bosses have been dying for the last twenty years, thanks to Roosevelt . . . The old boss was strong simply because he held all the cards. If anybody wanted anything—jobs, favors, cash—he could only go to the boss, the local leader. What Roosevelt did was to take the handouts out of local hands. A few little things like Social Security, Unemployment Insurance, and the like— that's what shifted the gears, sport. No need now to depend on the boss for everything; the Federal Government was getting into the act. Otherwise known as the social revolution.

O'Connor's explanation for the eventual downfall of the Irish urban, political machine was premature, however. At the same time that his novel was a best-seller, Mayor Richard J. Daley of Chicago was constructing the most powerful, efficient, and successful political machine in the history of urban America. Daley perfected his machine by using the federal funds that O'Connor said were destroying Irish urban political power. The mayor persuaded Washington to channel federal money through his organization to the people, thus increasing the power and influence of the Cook County Democratic machine. Other local leaders have followed Daley's example.

While urban Democratic machines still exist, the Irish role in them is diminishing. Daley indeed may be "the last hurrah," the end of a line of great Irish bosses. Successful in business and the professions, most of the Irish have left the cities for the suburbs, transferring control of the machines to blacks or other Catholic ethnics still residing in the inner cities. But the Irish have not completely abandoned their love of politics. Their positions as leaders in the U. S. Congress, as residents of governor's mansions, and their attractiveness as presidential candidates have replaced their fading presence in city halls. John Fitzgerald Kennedy's victory in the 1960 presidential election symbolized the Irish-Catholic climb from the murky bogs of ward politics to the heights of national power.

Kennedy caught the presidential virus when he narrowly lost an open race for vice-president on the Democratic ticket at the 1956 convention. For the next four years he applied a considerable amount of his family fortune, political skills, charm, and good looks to building an effective campaign organization and acquiring public popularity to win the presidential nomination in 1960. At first, both liberal supporters of presidential hopeful Adlai E. Stevenson II and tough, pragmatic, Catholic politicians tried to resist the Kennedy onslaught. The latter group feared that a Kennedy nomination could revive anti-Catholic, anti-ethnic nativism, retarding the progress of their people in the United States. But in the long run they had to submit to the reality of Kennedy power, which was demonstrated in primary victories over Minnesota Sen. Hubert Humphrey in Wisconsin and in rural, Protestant West Virginia.

After a first-ballot victory at the Democratic convention in Los Angeles, Kennedy began a vigorous campaign, insisting that he was not the "Catholic candidate." Before an assembly of Protestant clergymen in Houston in 1960, he emphasized his commitment to the basic principles of the American constitutional system:

> I believe in an America where the separation of Church and State is absolute—where no Catholic prelate would tell the President (should he be a Catholic) how to act, and no Protestant minister would tell his parishoners for whom to vote—where no church or church school is granted any public funds or political preference—and where no man is denied public office merely because his religion differs from the President who might appoint him or the people who might elect him.

Kennedy went on to insist that his private religious convictions would not interfere with his public obligations to the presidency:

> If my church attempted to influence me in a way which was improper or which affected adversely my responsibilities as a public servant, sworn to uphold the Constitution, then I would reply to them that this was an improper action on their part, that it was one to which I could not subscribe, that I was opposed to it, and that it would be an unfortunate breach—an interference with the American political system. I am confident there would be no such interference.[7]

Although Kennedy sincerely maintained his political independence from Catholic pressure groups, he also went all out for the Catholic ethnic vote, concentrating his campaign in states where it could influence victory—New York, Pennsylvania, Illinois, New Jersey, Massachusetts, Connecticut, California, Michigan, Minnesota, Ohio, Wisconsin, and Maryland.[8] Altogether, Kennedy attracted somewhere between 61 (IBM computer calculations) and 78 (Gallup Poll) percent of the Catholic vote. Actually, that was probably a smaller percentage of the Catholic constituency than Roosevelt won in 1936, but it represented a significant reversal of the Catholic drift to Dwight D. Eisenhower, the Republican candidate, in 1956.

Jews and blacks also joined the Catholics and voted in large majorities for Kennedy, restoring the minority group Democratic coalition of the 1940s and 1950s. A substantial majority of Protestants, on the other hand, voted against him, many because he was a Catholic ethnic but most because they were Republicans, and Protestants usually vote Republican. And since the Catholic ethnic-black-Jewish minority-group alliance cannot win a presidential election on its own strength, a significant number of Protestants must also have voted for Kennedy. In fact, the size of the Catholic vote in the Democratic column disappointed the Kennedy people. Obviously, many Catholics did not consider the election a decisive factor in the future of American Catholicism. Probably only about fifty percent of German Catholics voted for the Democratic candidate—this hurt in Wisconsin and Ohio—and many middle-class Irish Catholics in the Middle Atlantic states, who became more conservative as they grew wealthier, voted Republican. The election was uncomfortably close for the Democrats with a Kennedy margin of only slightly more than a hundred thousand votes. Apparently the residue of nativism and some unexpected Catholic defections to the Republican side helped turn the election into an early-morning cliff-hanger.

John F. Kennedy might not have been the most intellectually, religiously, or culturally Irish of Catholic political leaders in the early 1960s, but this rather secular, very pragmatic, Harvard-educated Irish-American was the right person to be the first Catholic president of the United States; he was the least offensive to Protestants still suspicious of the Americanization of their Catholic fellow citizens.[9] American Catholics like to speak of the era of the two Johns: John XXIII, the pope who tried to revitalize their church, and John F. Kennedy, the politician who smashed an important discriminatory barrier.

The climate of opinion, religion, and politics has changed since the mid-1960s. Paul VI has negated much of the work of John XXIII, disillusioning many liberal Catholics; time, events, and the critical pens of revisionist journalists and historians have dimmed the luster of the Kennedy years. In retrospect, Kennedy does seem to have had more style than substance; his rhetoric promised more than he delivered. His words often encouraged a dangerous American chauvinism and arrogance in tense, cold-war situations. He certainly bears much responsibility for that contemporary American foreign policy and military disaster, Vietnam. But the photographs of Kennedy in the homes of poor black and ethnic Americans, the terrible sense of loss and grief—particularly among the young—following his assassination in 1963, and the weeping people who still visit his grave at Arlington indicate that Kennedy was able to communicate a sense of compassion and hope that no president since has been able to match.

In contrast with the Johnson and Nixon years, the Kennedy era seems one of enthusiasm and idealism, a time when it was a joy to be alive and to be an American. The president's exuberance, intelligence, and self-deprecating wit lifted the spirits of the nation. When a cumbersome, eighteenth-century American political system deals with the problems of a twentieth-century world, solutions are often impossible. In these circumstances a leader with style and grace, one who inspires confidence, energy, and idealism contributes more than can be measured in quantitative terms. Kennedy may not have been able to repair the sagging American body, but he comforted and revitalized the American soul.

Kennedy as president had much more significance for ethnic Catholics than for Anglo-American Protestants. If he had lost his bid for the White House, Catholic America might have retreated into the bitterness and defensiveness that followed Smith's defeat in 1928. Many of them would have complained that they would always be second-class citizens in the United States. Such an attitude could have led to serious group neuroses, frustrating the intellectual and creative talents of the Catholic community. And the entire nation would have been poorer for the loss of Catholic energy and ability. But Kennedy's triumph over Nixon and his subsequent popularity with the American public diminished Catholic anxieties about their place in America, unleashing a flurry of endeavor, producing an abundant harvest of excellence.

In his essay on the New York Irish in *Beyond the Melting Pot,* Daniel Patrick Moynihan suggested that the influence of the Irish in American national politics peaked with Kennedy.

But he is gone, and there is none like him. Although he may yet emerge as the first of a new breed, all that is certain is that he was the last of an old one. The era of the Irish politician culminated in Kennedy. He was born to the work and was at every stage in his life a "pro." He rose on the willing backs of three generations of district leaders and county chairmen who, like Barabbas himself, may in the end have been saved for their one moment of recognition that something special had appeared among them. That moment was in 1960 when the Irish party chieftains of the great Eastern and Midwestern cities, for reasons they could probably even now not fully explain, came together to nominate for President the grandson of Honey Fitz . . . It was the last hurrah. He the youngest and newest, served in a final moment of ascendancy. On the day he died, the President of the United States, the Speaker of the House of Representatives, the Majority Leader of the United States Senate, the Chairman of the National Committee were all Irish, all Catholic, all Democrats. It will not come again.

Moynihan's pessimistic estimate of the future of Irish-American politics may have been more a product of grief over the assassination than of shrewd judgment. Five years after Kennedy died from bullet wounds in Dallas his brother Robert, a senator from New York, and another Irish-American liberal, Sen. Eugene McCarthy, were campaigning for the presidency. Today President Kennedy's youngest brother Teddy, a senator from Massachusetts, ranks as the most popular Democratic politician in public opinion polls. Mike Mansfield is still senate majority leader, and Thomas P. (Tip) O'Neill from Massachusetts leads Democratic forces in the U.S. House of Representatives. The November 1974 general election saw Edmund G. Brown, Jr. and Hugh L. Carey elected governors of the two most populous states in the union, California and New York respectively, providing the Democratic party with two more Irish presidential possibilities.

Despite economic and political successes, there are a number of intellectuals and literati in the Irish-American community who have been skeptical of the progress of their coethnics in twentieth-century America, arguing that in one important aspect of life—intellectualism—the result has been more tinsel than gold. In *American Catholics and the Intellectual Life* (1955), Monsignor John Tracy Ellis, then distinguished professor of church history at the Catholic University of America, criticized the failure of American Catholics to place as much emphasis on learning as they do on material success. He quoted from a 1941 comment by Denis W. Brogan, the British American-studies scholar: "In no Western society is the intellectual prestige of Catholicism lower than in the country where, in such respects as wealth, numbers, and strength of organization it is so powerful." Ellis's censure of the low standard of American Catholic intellectualism was for all practical purposes a criticism of the Irish who have dominated the educational and administrative structure of the church in the United States.

In assigning blame for the poverty of the collective Catholic intellect, Ellis accused both the Catholic and general American environments. He argued that Catholic colleges and universities reflected the interests and needs of a church serving ethnic communities with few intellectual resources. Catholic education adjusted to the peasant mentalities of its constituency rather than attempting to lift the cultural level of its students. And Ellis said that Catholic intellectualism was frustrated by the adoption of the anti-intellectual, materialistic values of American life and by the challenge of American nativism. American Catholics tried to achieve success in American terms, which meant amassing wealth, not knowledge. And their response to anti-Catholicism in turn created a ghetto mentality that emphasized Catholic apologetics rather than creative thought.[10]

Ellis and his many allies were correct; despite their improving financial and social statuses, American Catholics had not proven themselves intellectually. But perhaps the critics place too much blame on the schools for the failure to inspire art and scholarship. Actually, the elementary and secondary parochial schools in most urban centers are and have been much better than their public school counterparts. While it is true that Catholic colleges and universities have nurtured authoritarian teachers and teaching methods and a medieval intellectual perspective, they have improved somewhat since World War II, and an increasing number of Catholics attend state-supported and non-Catholic, private colleges and universities.

Lack of confidence and opportunity more than inadequate educational institutions retarded the advance of Catholic intel-

lectualism. When Ellis published his indictment of Catholic
schools in the 1950s, the impact of the G.I. Bill of Rights was
not yet apparent. Since that time the Irish and, to a lesser
extent, other Catholic ethnics have produced an abundant supply of professionals, artists, businessmen, and housewives with
sophisticated cultural tastes. In "Making it in America: Ethnic
Groups and Social Status," *Social Policy,* September/October
1973, Andrew M. Greeley offers evidence to suggest that the
Irish are anything but anti-intellectual. Next to the Jews, they
send a larger proportion of their young people to colleges and
universities than any other group in the United States.

To many Irish-American writers, fancy suburban homes,
influential economic and social positions, important political
offices, and fat incomes have not fundamentally changed the
personality of the American Irish. Such writers continue to
describe Irish-America in the same way as did James T. Farrell
in the 1930s: as a narrow-minded, provincial community saturated with paranoia, puritanism, bigotry, and anti-intellectualism. In *Moon Gaffney* (1947), Harry Sylvester scrutinized the
lace-curtain Brooklyn Irish. He found them ultra-conservative
on social and political issues, sexually ignorant and prudish,
chauvinistically Irish, arrogant toward other Catholic ethnics,
and prejudiced against blacks and Jews. Their clerics were
particularly reactionary and stupid. Father Malone belonged to
the anti-Semitic Christian Front, which had a significant following among the Boston and New York Irish, and he preached
a fascist creed in his Sunday sermons. Father O'Driscoll, who
taught Catholic dogma at a girls' college, thought it great fun
to purposely give false information about the rhythm method
of birth control so that his students would become pregnant
on their honeymoons. O'Driscoll and Father Rhatigan, another parish priest, tried to persuade bright, sensitive Ellen
Doarn that she should marry Peter Callahan, an alcoholic
lout, arguing that he came from a good Irish-Catholic family,
the love of a good woman would reform him, and that

there were many worse vices than a manly addiction to drink. Although *Moon Gaffney* created a minor sensation in Catholic intellectual circles during the late 1940s, it was more sociological opinion than good literature. But its stereotyped characters persisted in the work of artists more talented than Sylvester. In *Principatio* (1970), a novel of real comic and satirical brilliance, Tom McHale dissects the Philadelphia Corrigans, a family of funeral directors and saloon owners, hypocrites who make money selling liquor to the blacks they hate. And in *Farragan's Retreat* (1971) an even more polished novel than *Principatio,* McHale revisits the Philadelphia Irish in the form of the Farragans, a right-wing, racist, super-patriotic, puritan clan. Arthur Farragan, who must cover religious statues in his bedroom before he can make love to his wife, receives orders from a family conclave to execute his son Simon because the young man opposed the war in Vietnam and avoided the draft by escaping to Canada.

Well-known journalist Jimmy Breslin is also a sharp critic of Irish-America. In *World Without End Amen* (1973), Irish cops who live in the New York borough of Queens suffer the whole range of Irish literary vices and neuroses. Their warped sexual attitudes prevent love and communication with wives and encourage adultery and deviant behavior. The cops manifest fear, social insecurity, racism, and ignorance by beating up blacks and homosexuals; they demonstrate their patriotism by standing at attention and singing along with jukebox recordings of Kate Smith's versions of "God Bless America" and "The Star Spangled Banner" and by supporting the political ambitions of anti-black, anti-intellectual George Wallace.

Although the Irish writers' word war against what they consider suffocating mores of the American Irish-Catholic community has produced first-rate literature, it has also confirmed some anti-Irish, anti-Catholic prejudices and has exaggerated and distorted the reality of Irish-America. The stereotypes that appear in contemporary Irish-American literature are not typical Irish-American men and women; they represent aberrations rather than normality.

Unfortunately, the residue of ghetto neuroses has led some Irish-Americans into right-wing, paranoid politics, providing ammunition for those who insist that the Irish are congenitally reactionary. Until recently, American Catholics have been obsessively and uncritically loyal to the papacy. Accepted by non-Catholics as representative of the mind of the American church, prelates like Francis Cardinal Spellman gave an ultraconservative sheen to Catholicism in the United States. Many Catholic clerics and journalists praised totalitarian regimes in other countries, portraying Mussolini, Franco, Perón, and Salazar as bulwarks against atheistic communism. In the 1930s, millions of Catholics and other Americans listened on Sunday afternoons to the "radio priest," Father Coughlin, as he shifted from being a populist supporter of Roosevelt to an anti-Semitic advocate of fascism. A generation later, priests and Catholic newspapers and periodicals exalted Jesuit-educated (Marquette University) Sen. Joseph McCarthy of Wisconsin as the new anticommunist hero, even though he cruelly destroyed the reputations of decent men and women in his chase of phantom security risks in government.[11] And more recently, many Irish Catholics are attracted to the right-wing extremism of the John Birch Society.

But reactionary newspapers, clergy, and politicians represent only one element—mostly eastern—of Irish-American Catholicism. *Commonweal* and the *Davenport Messenger* have been as politically left as *Our Sunday Visitor* and the *Brooklyn Tablet* have been right, Archbishop Bernard Sheil was as liberal as Spellman was conservative, and Sen. Eugene McCarthy defended civil liberties with as much energy as Joseph McCarthy expended trying to destroy them. Most Irish-American supporters of Father Coughlin rejected him when he championed Mussolini, libeled Jews, and insulted F.D.R., and they did not endorse Franco's destruction of the Spanish Republic.[12]

As has been emphasized in other parts of this book, Irish and other American ethnic-Catholics have been an essential constituency for liberal, welfare-state politics in the United States. And since 1945, increased educational opportunities have made Irish Catholics even more liberal and sophisticated in their attitudes. According to Andrew M. Greeley and his colleague William McCready at the National Opinion Research Center in Chicago, public opinion samples indicate that, next to American Jews, the Irish are the most liberal group in the United States on such issues as civil rights, religious and racial tolerance, social reform, and peace. Harris and Gallup polls concur with Greeley's findings.[13] Many people are wary of using the results of opinion polls and quantitative methodology as a basis for historical analysis, but the conduct of numerous Irish-Americans who have marched for racial equality and against genocide in Southeast Asia, often risking their lives and freedom to do so, and the efforts of numerous Irish-American politicians to end the war in Vietnam and to make America a land of liberty and equality of opportunity testifies to the depths of Irish-American humanism and liberal idealism.

\* \* \*

Contradicting Tom McHale's Philadelphia Corrigans and Farragans and Jimmy Breslin's New York cops, America's urban Irish Catholics have come a long way since James T. Farrell's Studs Lonigan and Danny O'Neill played baseball in Chicago's Washington Park. Irish-America still contains its share of racists, reactionaries, and pious prudes, but they are in the minority, even on a regional basis. With the exception of Jews, the Irish are climbing the ladder of success faster than any other segment of the American population, flocking into colleges, universities, professional and graduate schools, swelling the ranks of the nation's leaders. At the same time they retain their political skills, displaying them on national as well as local stages, and they are in the front lines of protests demanding civil liberties, peace, social, and interracial justice. The Irish are even numbered among the so-called beautiful people—part of the Kennedy heritage. On television handsome men, women, and children wearing Irish knit sweaters and with Irish names like Kevin, Brian, Sean, Sheila, and Maureen sell cars, soap, and toothpaste.

Achievement, success, and respectability are the pleasant aspect of the contemporary Irish-American condition, but there is also something sad and disturbing about the present status of the American Irish. Just when they have become a significant force for justice and compassion and important contributors to literature and the intellectual environment, the Irish seem to be disappearing as a unique piece of the nation's social mosaic. The American Irish have either lost or are losing their ethnic identity. Very few Americans who consider themselves Irish—even those who have attended colleges or universities—know much about Irish history or literature.[14] In a generation or two there might not even be a definable Irish-American community.

What happened to Irish identity in the United States? Did it vanish with economic success, social mobility, and the migration to the suburbs? Perhaps, but the dissolution of the physical ghettos and the Irish ascent in American society seem to be inadequate explanations. Ghettos are states of mind as well as places. American Jews, for example, have managed to retain their cultural uniqueness in suburbia. Perhaps the American Irish identity is too linked to the fate of Catholicism to survive on its own.

Continental and English Catholics do not understand the significance of inseparable Irish and Catholic identities. With the possible exception of the Poles, most other Catholics distinguish between their national, religious, even cultural heritages.[15] Historical experience, however, has denied the Irish this option. With the exception of Northern Ireland, where a Catholic minority has been victimized by a Protestant majority, the connection between the Irish and Catholicism has been more important in the United States than in Ireland. In addition to historical memories of Anglo-Saxon persecution, Anglo-American nativism, poverty, and alienation combined to enhance Catholic loyalties among Irish-Americans. Catholicism was the glue holding the ghetto together, the one familiar institution bridging Old and New World experiences. It assuaged Irish misery, disciplined Irish conduct, and drew people from different parishes and counties in Ireland into an Irish-American community. Catholic schools trained teachers, lawyers, doctors, physicians, small businessmen, politicians, priests, nuns, and brothers to serve the needs of self-sufficient Irish neighborhoods.

But beginning in the late nineteenth century, the Catholic church in America began to undermine the Irish identity that it had forged. Although Irish-American Catholicism retained old country puritan, devotional, and peasant ideals, liberal bishops, mainly from the Midwest, insisted on Americanization while their conservative colleagues in the East demanded Romanization. In America as in Ireland, the two cultural systems, Romanization and Anglicization, continued to modify the original Gaelic personality, and the Catholic church and its educational system literally became the agents of anti-Irish cultural imperialism.

In the 1970s, at a time when ethnicity has become a matter of pride and concern, it is difficult to understand why Irish-American Catholic educators have rejected their own cultural heritage and insist that their students do the same. The rural origins of Irish immigrants and the value systems of seminary and convent educations seem to provide some explanation for this puzzle. Irish administrators and faculty members have been ashamed of their peasant roots. In seeking respectability for themselves, their church and their students, they have emphasized a Catholic culture that is pseudomedieval in spirit, Continental or British in content and location. They have both encouraged and required Irish-American students to read and admire Aquinas, Dante, Chaucer—in expurgated editions—and Shakespeare. When it comes to modern Catholic thought, students in Catholic schools study Newman, Chesterton, Belloc, Knox, Waugh, Greene, Bernanos, Mauriac, Péguy, Maritain, and Gilson. While no one can dispute the artistic and intellectual merit of these distinguished writers and philosophers, modern Ireland has also inspired genius: Yeats, Synge, Joyce, O'Faolain, O'Connor, O'Casey, Beckett, Friel, Moore (Brian), Kinsella, Montague, Nolan, Kiely, Heaney, and many others.

But Catholic secondary schools, colleges, and universities have largely ignored Irish writers or have distorted their works by presenting them as examples of British regional literature. Instead of building an appreciation in Irish-American students for literary excellence and intellectualism through highly-regarded writing by Irishmen, Catholic education has exalted traditions and values external to its constituency.

When Monsignor John Tracy Ellis and others criticized the inadequacy of American Catholic education in the 1950s, they missed the fundamental weakness of Catholic schools: the institutions are imitative rather than unique. If Catholic schools had emphasized the cultural traditions of the Irish and other Catholic ethnics, they perhaps would have been more successful at producing intellectuals, artists, and scholars. Pseudomedievalism, Anglicization, and Romanization have not stimulated young minds or imaginations; instead they have encouraged intellectual mediocrity, antiquarianism, aridity, and second or third-rate imitations of British and Continental philosophy, art, and literature.[16] In the 1970s, American Catholic colleges and universities still emphasize the history of Western civilization with stress on the medieval period as the "Age of Faith"; they also offer English history but ignore its Irish dimensions.

All American students, including Catholic ethnics, should be aware of their European and American heritages and Anglo-Saxon contributions to their culture. But Irish, Polish, and

Italian-American students, as well as other ethnic groups, also should have some understanding of their unique cultural heritages. Irish-Americans should know that while Ireland participated in the evolution of Western civilization, she also previewed many of the experiences of contemporary, underdeveloped countries emerging from colonial status. And they should understand that their ancestors not only pioneered the urban ghetto in the United States but also were the "blacks" of the United Kingdom, victims of imperialism, racism, and manorialism.

What can the traditional Western civilization course, as taught in an American, Catholic college or university, say to the Irish? Irishmen never shared in the richness of medieval, aristocratic culture. Ireland missed many of the more glorious phases of Western history, mainly the latter part of the Middle Ages and the Renaissance. Many aspects of Western civilization were imposed on the Irish from the outside by their conquerors. Ancestors of contemporary Irish-Americans participated in Western civilization as serfs rather than masters. Unlike the brilliant triumphs of British history, the Irish past is a sad narrative of poverty and oppression. The Irish story was a struggle against slavery, hunger, and ignorance, an effort frequently interrupted by defeat, famine, and exile to lands where they were despised and unwanted.

In the 1970s, however, Irish history may be more relevant than either English or Continental history. In this era of disintegrating empires, guerrilla wars of liberation, emerging nations, racial pride, and ethnic consciousness, the Irish experience—Zion and Diaspora—is rich in example and insight. Unfortunately, the vast majority of American Irish have been severed from their historical roots by Catholic education. They are ignorant of who they are and know little of the influences that shaped their personalities. They are unable to look into their own backgrounds to understand the problems of other groups attempting to achieve status and security in urban America.

Irish-Americans are not equipped to use the abundant resources of Irish history and literature to expand their cultural and intellectual perspectives.

The emphasis in Catholic education on Catholic, Continental, and Anglo-Saxon histories at the expense of Irish culture has created a situation where people who live in Irish neighborhoods remain religiously, perhaps emotionally, but certainly not culturally Irish. Emerging from the ghetto, the American Irish find their Catholicism tested and eroded by the process of assimilation into suburban melting pots. Catholicism was an Irish identity badge, but the passing of the physical ghetto lessened confidence in the church as the ultimate institution. Suburban Irish-Americans began to question an authoritarian, institutional structure that conflicted with their liberal, middle-class American values. They also rejected an intellectually and culturally impoverished medievalism unable to address itself to contemporary social problems.

Irish identity is going, going, and soon it will be gone. And it will be difficult—probably impossible—for the American Irish to recover something that has almost disappeared. Their commitment to Catholicism is ambiguous, and their experience in Catholic schools has deprived them of an Irish cultural heritage and awareness that might have withstood the collapse of the old neighborhoods. Many of them see no value in continuing to support a parochial school system which is merely a well-disciplined imitation of its public school counterpart, both emphasizing Anglo-Saxon Protestant cultural values. They say, "If you want a first-rate WASP education, go to the WASPS and get it."[17]

Few Catholic leaders or educators in the United States comprehend the consequences of the loss of Irish and other ethnic identities. They do realize that attendance at Catholic religious services is rapidly declining, reflecting a dissipating confidence in the church and her clergy, but they cannot see the connection between this decline in Catholic loyalty and diminishing ethnicity.[18] Scholars have offered a variety of reasons for the vacant pews at Sunday mass and the indifference—sometimes hostility —among Catholics toward the authority of the church. Some say that the papacy and the American Catholic hierarchy have been unresponsive to the social, economic, and intellectual challenges of the time. Others believe that the reforms that came out of Vatican II have disturbed the faith of many Catholics. Liberals argue that Paul VI's refusal to approve birth control has created a crisis of authority in the church. Many conservatives insist that the new Protestant-style liturgy and a search for relevance have alienated a large number of Catholics who prefer a church which emphasizes continuity and tradition.

There is a certain amount of credibility in all of these analyses. No doubt theological, liturgical, and social value changes in the church came too fast for some, too slow for others. But there is another reason for the current malaise in American Catholicism, simpler than the conflicts between liberal and conservative outlooks. For many people, when they cease to be ethnic there is no longer any strong reason for them to remain Catholic. When Irish-America lost its ethnicity, Catholicism lost relevance as a symbol of Irish identity. When one reflects on the American Catholic past, Archbishop John Ireland and his liberal friends seem to have been the good guys in their fight against conservative, Old-World types, but on one point history has proved conservative bishops like McQuaid and Corrigan right. The destruction of ethnicity has endangered Catholicism.

But many intelligent and sophisticated people argue that the collapse of Irish identity and Irish assimilation into the greater American community has been a desirable thing, the culmination of a great success story, a promise that other minority groups can also make it in American society. They insist that ethnicity is divisive both in the church and the nation, that American Catholics should abandon their Old-World allegiances and think of themselves as American Roman Catholics.

This may be a fashionable but it is also a provincial point of view. Although consensus is necessary for the operation of a successful liberal democracy, the strength, uniqueness, vitality, and genius of both the American nation and the Catholic church come from the tensions between unity and diversity. Declining racial and ethnic identities have encouraged conformity rather than consensus.

Although it is probably too late to matter, Irish-America should ask whether the price of assimilation and abandoned ethnic identity has been too high. After Vietnam and Watergate, many Irish-Americans have come to realize that they probably gave up a great deal for very little; the American mainstream has the stench of an open sewer. Irish-America exists in a cultural nowhere. The trip from the old city neighborhoods to the suburbs has been a journey from someplace to no place. It is probably too late to save the Irish, but their experience may help other ethnics to learn to cherish cultural heritages that are priceless and irreplaceable.

# Recommended Reading

*Although this list is not a definitive bibliography of Irish-America, these are the books that have influenced my interpretation of Irish-America. Most of the articles that I consider important to an understanding of the American Irish have been cited either in the text of the book or in the footnotes.*

## IRISH HERITAGE

There are a number of books that provide useful, general information about the Irish background of the Irish-American experience. J.C. Beckett's *A Short History of Ireland,* 3d ed. (New York: Hutchinson's University Library, 1966); Edmund Curtis's *A History of Ireland,* paperback ed. (New York: Barnes and Noble Books, 1968); and T.W. Moody's and F.X. Martin's *The Course of Irish History* (New York: Weybright and Talley, Inc., 1967) are general surveys of Irish history. *A History of Modern Ireland* by Giovanni Costigan (New York: Pegasus, 1969) has introductory material but concentrates on Irish history from the sixteenth century to the present. J.C. Beckett's *The Making of Modern Ireland, 1603–1923* (New York: Alfred A. Knopf, Inc., 1966) and Patrick O'Farrell's *Ireland's English Question,* paperback ed. (New York: Schocken Books Inc., 1972) also emphasize the period from the Tudors to the twentieth century. Beckett's strong point is the eighteenth century; O'Farrell concentrates on the link between Catholic and Irish identities. *The Irish Question, 1800–1922* by Lawrence J. McCaffrey, paperback ed. (Lexington, Ky.: University of Kentucky Press, 1968) discusses Ireland during the period of union with England, emphasizing the interaction between Irish and British history, using Ireland as an example of colonialism, nationalism in an underdeveloped country, and as a testing ground for British liberalism. Oliver MacDonagh's *Ireland,* paperback ed. (Englewood Cliffs, N.J.: Prentice-Hall, Inc., 1968) is both an intelligent and well-written interpretation of Irish history, particularly the post-treaty period. *Ireland Since the Famine* by F. S. L. Lyons (New York: Charles Scribner's Sons, 1971) is a model combination of fact and interpretation and an essential volume to an Irish-studies library.

Recently Gill & Macmillan have published an eleven-volume paperback history of Ireland, edited by Margaret MacCurtain and James Lydon. All the volumes in The Gill History of Ireland series (Dublin: Gill & Macmillan Ltd.) are brief and informative; some of them are excellent. The series includes Gearóid Mac Niocaill, *Ireland Before the Vikings* (1972); Donncha Ó Corráin, *Ireland Before the Normans* (1972); Michael Dolley, *Anglo-Norman Ireland* (1972); Kenneth Nicholls, *Gaelic and Gaelicized Ireland in the Middle Ages* (1972); John Watt, *The Church in Medieval Ireland* (1972); James Lydon, *Ireland in the Later Middle Ages* (1972); Margaret MacCurtain, *Tudor and Stuart Ireland* (1972); Edith Mary Johnston, *Ireland in the Eighteenth Century* (1974); Gearóid Ó Tuathaigh, *Ireland Before the Famine, 1798–1848* (1972); Joseph Lee, *The Modernization of Irish Society, 1848–1918* (1973); and John A. Murphy, *Ireland in the Twentieth Century* (1975).

K.H. Connell's *The Population of Ireland, 1750–1845* (London: Oxford University Press, 1950) is the most important secondary-source analysis of the Irish social and economic systems that produced famine and emigration. Conrad Arensberg's *The Irish Countryman: An Anthropological Study,* paperback ed. (Garden City, N.Y.: Natural History Press, 1968) and Emyr Estyn Evan's *Irish Heritage* (Dundalk, Ireland: W. Tempest, Dundalgan Press, 1945) both provide information about peasant customs and values. Sean O'Faolain's *The Irish,* paperback ed. (Harmondsworth, Middlesex, England: Penguin, 1969) is a perceptive discussion of the complexities within the Irish personality and the Celtic, Anglo-Saxon, Anglo-Irish, and Roman Catholic contributions to Irishness. *The Politics of Irish Literature* by Malcolm Brown, paperback ed. (Seattle: University of Washington Press, 1973), which deals with the relationships between Irish literature, politics, and nationalism, is the closest thing in print to a survey of Irish intellectual history since 1800. Robert Kee's *The Green Flag* (New York: The Delacorte Press, 1972) is an extensive, well written, and thoughtful history of Irish nationalism from its beginnings through the present.

## The American Irish

A great deal of spade work in quantitative history using parish records and election results needs to be done before a satisfactory, detailed study of Irish-American history can appear. Perhaps this work will never be completed. Unfortunately, when the Irish broke down the nativist barriers that excluded them from full participation in academic life, ethnicity was not fashionable, and their cautiousness and inferiority complexes kept them aloof from Irish studies. Only Irish-Americans can fully appreciate the nuances of the American-Irish experience, and since the Irish are disappearing as a unique ethnic group, there may not be a sufficient number of scholars available to probe the Irish-American past.

John B. Duff's *The Irish in America,* paperback ed. (Belmont, Cal.: Wadsworth Publishing Co. Inc., 1971); Andrew M. Greeley's *That Most Distressful Nation,* paperback ed. (Chicago: Quadrangle Books, Inc., 1973); Joseph P. O'Grady's *How the Irish Became American,* paperback ed. (New York: Twayne Publishers, Inc., 1973); William V. Shannon's *The American Irish,* paperback ed. (New York: The Macmillan Company, 1974); and Carl Wittke's *The Irish in America* (New York: Russell & Russell Publishers, 1970) are all surveys in Irish-American history available to readers. Wittke is rich in detail. Shannon's study is more than narrative history; it has solid and perceptive essays on the Irish-American political style, literature, Irish athletic prowess, and religious values. Greeley combines sociological and historical perspectives, insisting that Irish-America has emerged as a progressive, intellectual, and liberal community. He is convinced that there still is a unique Irish identity in the United States. O'Grady and Duff present brief examinations of the Irish-American experience that make their books useful texts in ethnic history courses. The problem with all of the above surveys is that they are not critical enough of the assimilation process, and none of them adequately discusses old-country elements in the Irish-American personality.

Terry Coleman's *Going to America,* paperback ed. (New York: Doubleday & Company, Inc., Anchor, 1973) and Philip Taylor's *The Distant Magnet,* paperback ed. (New York: Harper & Row Publishers, 1971) detail the process of emigration. Coleman concentrates on the departure from Liverpool and the hardships of the long transatlantic crossing. Most of the emigrants he discusses were Irish. Taylor examines the entire scope of European emigration, describing the voyage to America but also discussing the problems that newcomers found in their new homeland.

John F. Maguire was the proprietor of the *Cork Examiner* and a prominent nationalist M.P. in the British Parliament. His *The Irish in America* (New York: Arno Press, Inc., 1974), originally published in 1868, is still a valuable source on the conditions and attitudes of early immigrants. W.F. Adams's *Ireland and Irish Immigration to the New World from 1815 to the Famine* (New York: Russell & Russell Publishers, 1967) reflects some Anglo-American Protestant antipathies to Irish-Catholic culture, but it is an excellent study of the character of Irish emigration before the Great Famine. *To the Golden Door* by George W. Potter (Westport, Conn.: Greenwood Press, Inc., 1974) also deals with the prefamine immigrants. While it is a gold mine of information, Potter is too concerned with and probably exaggerates Irish economic and social success. Unfortunately, the author died before the completion of his work and the reader is left in the dark concerning the sources for much of his information and conclusions.

Arnold Schrier's *Ireland and The American Emigration* (New York: Russell & Russell Publishers, 1970) describes the Irish reaction to the United States through immigrant letters back home. *Boston's Immigrants: A Study in Acculturation* by Oscar Handlin, paperback ed. (New York: Atheneum Publishers, 1968) is a well-regarded case study of the first Irish ghetto in the United States. Stephan Thernstrom's *Poverty and Progress* (Cambridge: Harvard University Press, 1964) discusses the failure of Irish economic and social mobility in Newburyport, Mass., from 1850 to 1880. In a more recent book, *The Other Bostonians: Poverty and Progress in the American Metropolis, 1860–1970* (Cambridge: Harvard University Press, 1973), Thernstrom shows that the Irish in Boston were no more successful in moving up the American success ladder than those in Newburyport. Instead of

*Ireland* (London: Geoffrey Chapman Ltd., 1968), argues that the authoritarianism, clericalism, puritanism, and anti-intellectualism associated with Irish Catholicism were imported from Rome and Britain. John Whyte's *Church and State in Modern Ireland, 1923–1970* (New York: Barnes & Noble Books, 1971) is an examination of the relationship between the Catholic church and the Irish state since 1923.

Information about the American branch of the Irish-Catholic spiritual empire can be found in Thomas N. Brown's and Thomas McAvoy's *The United States of America,* volume 6 of the series A History of Irish Catholicism, edited by Patrick J. Corish (Dublin: Gill & Macmillan Ltd., 1970); John Cogley's *Catholic America* (New York: The Dial Press, 1973); Robert D. Cross's *The Emergence of Catholic Liberalism in America,* paperback ed. (Chicago: Quadrangle Books, Inc., 1967); John Tracy Ellis's *American Catholicism,* paperback ed. (Chicago: University of Chicago Press, 1957); *Catholicism in America,* edited by Philip Gleason, paperback ed. (New York: Harper & Row Publishers, 1970); Andrew M. Greeley's *The Catholic Experience,* paperback ed. (New York: Doubleday & Company, Inc., Image Books, 1967); Thomas T. McAvoy's *History of the Catholic Church in the United States* (South Bend, Ind.: University of Notre Dame Press, 1969); and Garry Wills's *Bare Ruined Choirs* (Garden City, N.Y.: Doubleday & Company, Inc., 1972). John Tracy Ellis's *American Catholics and the Intellectual Life* (Chicago: The Heritage Foundation, 1956) and *American Catholic Dilemma* by Thomas O'Dea, paperback ed. (New York: The New American Library Inc., 1962) both touched off a major controversy within American Catholic circles by criticizing the failure of Catholics in the United States to make a significant cultural contribution to the nation and by blaming Catholic education for this failure.

Among the many volumes on Irish-American politics, Daniel P. Moynihan's essay "The Irish" in *Beyond the Melting Pot* by Nathan Glazer and Moynihan, paperback ed. (Cambridge: M.I.T. Press, 1963) is a distortion of reality, but it is well written, provocative, and often quoted. Edward M. Levine's *The Irish and Irish Politicans* (South Bend, Ind.: University of Notre Dame Press, 1966) concentrates on Irish politicians in Chicago. Abigail McCarthy's autobiographical

creating a kind of national Irish-American stereotype—which som
people claim that he does—Thernstrom's findings prove that the Ma
sachusetts Irish are historical fossils rather than typical members
the American-Irish community. Other recommended studies of Iris
communities are Dennis Clark's *The Irish in Philadelphia: Ten Gene
ations of Urban Experience* (Philadelphia: Temple University Pres
1974); Earl F. Niehaus's *The Irish in New Orleans, 1800–1860* (Bat
Rouge: Louisiana State University Press, 1965); and Justille McDo
ald's *History of the Irish in Wisconsin in the Nineteenth Centu.
(Washington, D.C.: Catholic University Press, 1954). In *Catho*
*Colonization on the Western Frontier* (New Haven: Yale Universi
Press, 1957), James P. Shannon tells the story of Archbishop Jol
Ireland's futile effort to plant an Irish colony in rural Minnesot
indicating that in America the Irish were primarily urban dwelle

Readers interested in comparing and contrasting the urban Irish
Britain and America can consult John Archer Jackson's *The Irish*
*Britain* (Cleveland: The Press of Western Reserve University, 196
Kevin O'Connor's *The Irish in Britain* (London: Sidgwick & Jacks
Ltd., 1972); and John Hickey's *Urban Catholics* (London: Geoffr
Chapman Ltd., 1967). L.P. Curtis Jr. examines the development a
intellectualization of Anglo-Saxon racism in Britain and its Americ
implications in *Anglo-Saxons and Celts: A Study in Anti-Catho*
*Prejudice in Victorian England* (Bridgeport, Conn.: Conference
British Studies, 1968). The two most important volumes on an
Catholic American nativism are Ray Allen Billington's *The Protest*
*Crusade, 1800–1860,* paperback ed. (Chicago: Quadrangle Boo
Inc., 1964) and John Higham's *Strangers in the Land: Patterns*
*American Nativism, 1860–1925,* paperback ed. (New York: Athene
Publishers, 1965).

David W. Miller has published a number of interesting and inf
mative articles on Catholic religious practices and values in ni
teenth-century Ireland. His book, *Church, State, and Nation in ]*
*land, 1898–1921* (Pittsburgh: University of Pittsburgh Press, 197
discusses the complex relationships between the Catholic church
Ireland, the British government, and the Irish nation from the cl
of the nineteenth century to the signing of the treaty establishing
Free State. Desmond Fennell, editor of *The Changing Face of Cath*

*Private Faces, Public Places,* paperback ed. (New York: Curtis Books, 1973) reveals the life and political styles of the Irish in the northern Midwest, indicating that they were more liberal and intellectual than their eastern cousins. Alfred Connable's and Edward Silberfarb's *Tigers of Tammany* (New York: Holt, Rinehart & Winston, 1967); Mike Royko's *Boss,* paperback ed. (New York: New American Library, a Signet book, 1971); and Len O'Connor's *Clout* (Chicago: Henry Regnery Company, 1975) are studies of machine politics, the last two dealing with Mayor Richard J. Daley's Chicago. In my comments on John F. Kennedy I relied on Arthur M. Schlesinger Jr.'s *A Thousand Days: John F. Kennedy in the White House,* paperback ed. (New York: Fawcett World Library, Premier Books, 1971); Theodore H. White's *The Making of the President, 1960,* paperback ed. (New York: Atheneum Publishers, 1961); and Benjamin C. Bradlee's *Conversations with Kennedy* (New York: W.W. Norton & Company, Inc., 1975).

Thomas N. Brown's *Irish-American Nationalism,* paperback ed. (Philadelphia: J.B. Lippincott Company, 1966) is the best study of its subject in print. *America and the Fight for Irish Freedom, 1886–1922* by C.C. Tansill (New York: The Devin-Adair Company, 1957) provides information on Irish-American financial contributions to freedom movements in Ireland. Leon Ó Broin's *Fenian Fever* (New York: New York University Press, 1971) uses British government documents from Dublin Castle to present a history of the IRB. *Fenians and Fenianism,* edited by Maurice Harmon (Seattle: University of Washington Press, 1970), is a multiauthored volume of essays, and William D'Arcy's *The Fenian Movement in the United States, 1858–1886* (New York: Russell & Russell Publishers, 1971) offers a detailed discussion of the American wing of the republican movement. Brian Jenkin's *Fenians and Anglo-American Relations during Reconstruction* (Ithaca, N.Y.: Cornell University Press, 1969) and Alan J. Ward's *Ireland and Anglo-American Relations, 1899–1921* (London: George Weidenfeld & Nicolson Ltd., 1969) are both excellent studies of the impact of Irish-American nationalism on diplomatic relations between the United States and the United Kingdom.

Andrew M. Greeley writes most frequently about the contemporary Irish-American community. His optimistic views about the future of Irish identity in the United States have been published in *That*

*Most Distressful Nation* (1973); *Why Can't They Be Like Us* (New York: E.P. Dutton & Co., Inc., 1971); and *Ethnicity in the United States* (New York: John Wiley & Sons, Inc., 1974). Although it is mainly concerned with Slavs and Italians and is suspicious of the Irish as half-WASPs, Michael Novak's *The Rise of the Unmeltable Ethnics,* paperback ed. (New York: The Macmillan Company, 1973) contains intelligent distinctions between the Catholic ethnic and Anglo-American Protestant views of the world.

Creative literature is rich in insights into Irish ethnicity, and not all good Irish-American writers have soured on their own community. Edward McSorley's *Our Own Kind* (New York: Harper & Row, Publishers, 1946) is a sympathetic portrait of Irish-American, working-class family life in Providence, R.I. Many of the volumes in James T. Farrell's Danny O'Neill series present accurate studies of Irish-American family life. His *Father and Son* (New York: Vanguard Press, Inc., 1940) must be included with Pete Hamill's *The Gift,* paperback ed. (New York: Ballantine Books, Inc., 1974) and William Gibson's *A Mass for the Dead* (New York: Atheneum Publishers, 1968) as excellent studies of the relationships between Irish-American fathers and their sons. Joseph F. Dinneen's *Ward Eight* (New York: Harper & Row, Publishers, 1936); Thomas J. Fleming's *All Good Men* (Garden City, N.Y.: Doubleday & Company, Inc., 1961); and Wilfrid Sheed's *People Will Always Be Kind,* paperback ed. (New York: Dell Publishing Co., Inc., 1973) are political novels as good as Edwin O'Connor's *The Last Hurrah,* paperback ed. (New York: Bantam Books, Inc., 1969). Actually, O'Connor's best Irish-American novel is probably *The Edge of Sadness,* paperback ed. (New York: Bantam Books, Inc., 1970), a study of a priest. J.F. Powers's volume of short stories *The Prince of Darkness* (Garden City, N.Y.: Doubleday & Company, Inc., 1947) and his prize-winning novel *Morte D'Urban,* paperback ed. (New York: Popular Library, 1963) are also examinations of clerical life. Thomas J. Fleming's last novel about the New Jersey Irish, *The Good Shepherd* (Garden City, N.Y.: Doubleday & Company, Inc., 1974) discusses a bishop trapped by the need to serve many constituencies in an evolving Irish-American Catholicism. Elizabeth Cullinan's *House of Gold* (Boston: Houghton Mifflin Company, 1970) is a portrait of a destructive Irish matriarch. Mary

McCarthy's *Memories of a Catholic Girlhood,* paperback ed. (New York: Berkley Publishing Corporation, 1957) describes an Irish-Catholic childhood in St. Paul and Seattle. She gives credit to Catholic education for stimulating her creative imagination by emphasizing history and mystery. Finley Peter Dunne's portraits of the Chicago Irish are as much social history as literature. His *Mr. Dooley at His Best,* edited by Elmer Ellis (New York: Charles Scribner's Sons, 1938), contains some of Dunne's best essays.

As far as the theater is concerned, all of Eugene O'Neill's works reflect an Irish-American consciousness, particularly *Long Day's Journey into Night,* paperback ed. (New Haven: Yale University Press, 1969) and *A Moon for the Misbegotten* (New York: Random House Inc., 1952). During the 1920s and 1930s, Philip Barry presented a number of plays with Irish themes and characters to American audiences. More recently, Frank D. Gilroy's prize-winning *The Subject Was Roses,* which appeared on Broadway in 1965, and William Alfred's 1966 play *Hogan's Goat* successfully utilized Irish-American themes.

In addition to the authors and novels recommended above, readers will appreciate the works of Jimmy Breslin, Robert Byrne, Mary Deasy, Edward Hannibal, Tom McHale, Ralph McInerny, and John R. Powers.

# Notes

## 1. Introduction: Irish Pioneers of the American Urban Ghetto

1. The Irish of South Boston are one obvious exception to the successful assimilation of Irish-Americans. Their protests against busing blacks into their schools exhibits intense ghetto identity and paranoia. In the course of this book, I will discuss why the New England Irish have not experienced the same kind of upward mobility as Irish-Americans in other parts of the United States and why the Irish in Boston are the Irish-American exception rather than the rule.

2. This is a frequently expressed observation. In *The Rise of the Unmeltable Ethnics* (New York: Macmillan Publishing Company, Inc., 1973), p. 163, Michael Novak states: "More than one person has noted that anti-Catholicism is—or perhaps was—the anti-Semitism of the intellectuals." In his *American Catholics and the Intellectual Life* (Chicago: The Heritage Foundation, Inc., 1956,) pp. 16–18, John Tracy Ellis discusses the anti-Catholic prejudices of American intellectuals. He quotes a statement made by Arthur M. Schlesinger, Sr. to him: "I regard the bias against your Church as the most persistent prejudice in the history of the American people."

3. Other Catholic ethnics, resentful of the long Irish domination over the church and urban politics, share the anti-Irish sentiments of academic and intellectual liberals. Arguing that the Irish are half WASP and not true ethnics, they also exclude them from minority-group culture programs and seminars. Anti-Irish attitudes among some Catholic ethnics are expressed in Michael Novak's *The Rise of the Unmeltable Ethnics* (New York: Macmillan Publishing Co., Inc., 1973). In pursuing his case against the Irish as contaminated Catholic ethnics, Novak often goes to ridiculous lengths. For example, he argues that Slavic ethnicity resembles Italian more than Irish culture.

In fact, the Polish historical experience and the Polish link between Catholicism and national culture are much more like the Irish than the Italian experience.

4. American Jews represent one exception to this statement. Although the Jews and the Irish share many experiences and grievances —their literary expressions, for example, are often similar—Jews arrived in the United States already equipped with much experience in urban situations and with a rich, cultural sophistication. The Irish, on the other hand, were more typical of European immigrants; they were unsophisticated, culturally and technologically impoverished peasants.

## 2. Ireland: English Conquest and Protestant Ascendancy, 1169–1801

1. Irish poets and playwrights like to trace the source of Ireland's woes—the coming of the English—to the fruits of adultery, jealousy, and vengeance. In William Butler Yeats's "Dreaming of the Bones" in *Four Plays for Dancers* (London: Macmillan & Co., 1921), the poet-dramatist relates how MacMurrough seduced Dervorguilla, wife of O'Rourke, king of Brefni, and how the husband gained his revenge by aiding Rory O'Connor, high king of Ireland, to crush the king of Leinster in an Irish civil war. Although MacMurrough did seduce O'Rouke's wife and the king of Brefni was a decisive factor in the defeat of MacMurrough in 1166, O'Rourke's reasons for opposing the king of Leinster were probably more associated with the politics of Irish clan society than responses of a jealous cuckold.

2. Gaelic or Celtic Ireland as used in this book refers to a culture, not to a race. The Irish like other Europeans are a mixed breed. Celtic invaders in the Bronze Age determined the popular language and institutions but pre-Celts remained to influence the cultural trappings of the Irish heritage.

3. Not all Protestants in Ireland, however, were equal. Those who were not members of the Church of Ireland could own property but were still less than first-class citizens in the community. The Church of Ireland Ascendancy and power monopoly promoted significant Presbyterian emigration to North America in the eighteenth century. But nonconformists were reluctant to combine with Catholics in a

common front against the Church of Ireland establishment. Anti-Catholicism forged a kind of Protestant unity more powerful than disputes between the established church and its Protestant dissenters.

4. Although Irish peasants were loyal to the Catholic church, they were not as diligent at participating in religious observations as were their late nineteenth- and twentieth-century descendents. According to data gathered by Prof. David Miller of Carnegie Mellon University, in the early nineteenth century only a minority of people in remote parts of Ireland attended Sunday mass regularly. In fact, had every Catholic attended mass, there would not have been enough chapel space.

5. In the border counties of Ulster, where both Catholic and Protestant peasant populations were of almost similar sizes and competed for land, economic grievances were often mixed with sectarian hatred. This resulted in frequent party fights between Catholics and Protestants, leading to the formation of secret societies primarily devoted to religious interests. In 1795, a clash between the Catholic Defenders and the Protestant Peep O' Day Boys in County Armagh, dubbed the Battle of the Diamond, resulted in a Protestant victory followed by the formation of the Orange Order. The group began as a Protestant peasant movement designed to force Catholics to abandon Ulster for Connacht, but it was quickly taken over by the Protestant aristocracy and used as a terrorist tool to intimidate Catholics and to preserve Protestant Ascendancy. The order spread into England as an expression of Anglo-Saxon Protestant nativism, and a member of the royal family even became the grand master of the order.

6. According to Poynings' Law, originally passed in 1494 but later modified, an Irish parliament could not pass legislation without the approval of the English government. The Declaratory Act passed by the British Parliament in 1720 also asserted the right of British M.P.s to legislate for Ireland. In the eighteenth century, the British Parliament used the Declaratory Act to force the Irish economy to fit the patterns of British mercantilism.

7. Although Catholics lacked direct political power, Cornwallis and Castlereagh talked with leaders of the Catholic hierarchy, because a favorable Catholic response to the Union with Britain would certainly facilitate its achievement. Bishops and influential Catholic laymen did

lean toward the Union as a step toward emancipation, believing that a United Kingdom would give their grievances a more objective hearing than would an Irish Protestant legislature committed to anti-Catholicism and Protestant Ascendancy. Daniel O'Connell, a young Catholic barrister, objected to this point of view. In 1800, against the wishes of his Uncle Maurice, head of the Kerry O'Connell clan, he argued that the maintenance of the Irish nation was more important than Catholic Emancipation. As a Whig patriot, O'Connell was optimistic about the long-range tolerance of the Irish Parliament and eventual friendship between Catholics and Protestants.

### 3. Ireland: The Rise of Irish Nationalism, 1801–1850

1. O'Connell's reputation extended far beyond the shores of Ireland. As tribune of the Irish-Catholic masses, he was the only successful radical, democratic politician in the era of Metternich. European liberals and radicals of the time respected his achievements and took inspiration from them.

2. Many anti-O'Connell nationalists have used the disfranchisement of the "40s freeholders" as an issue to attack his reputation. They claim that by not resisting the government's attack on peasant democracy, he betrayed both Irish nationalism and liberal principles. But O'Connell never had been enthusiastic about the 40s franchise, because he believed that without a secret ballot it was too open to intimidation. Of course, in 1826 and again in 1828 the Irish masses had resisted landlord pressures at the polls, but there was no guarantee that they would have continued to do so. And another factor must have influenced O'Connell's decision not to resist the disfranchisement of the 40s freeholders: many upper and middle-class Catholics active in the emancipation effort were not friends of political democracy. If O'Connell had fought to retain the tenant-farmer franchise, he might have antagonized this faction and split the association on the brink of victory.

3. Daniel O'Connell to Archbishop John MacHale, 25 July 1840, in W.J. Fitzpatrick, ed., *The Correspondence of Daniel O'Connell,* 2 vol. (London: John Murray, 1888), p. 246.

4. In addition to his respect for British political and economic thought, O'Connell recommended that the Irish people abandon their

native language for the exclusive use of English. Although he was fluent in Irish—Young Irelanders were not—O'Connell decided that English was a more utilitarian form of expression and communication and would further the progress of the Irish people.

5. This thesis proposing Young Ireland ecumenism has recently been challenged by Ailfrid MacLochlainn, deputy director of the National Library of Ireland. In a paper, "Thomas Davis and Irish Racialism," delivered before the Annual Conference of the American Committee for Irish Studies held at Stonehill College, Easton, Massachusetts, on 25 April 1975, MacLochlainn convincingly argues that despite the tolerant front projected by Young Ireland, Davis's interpretation of Irish history in his poems and essays encouraged racial distinctions and animosity between native Gaelic Catholics and Anglo-Irish Protestants. In another revisionist paper, "The Catholic Nationalism of Thomas Davis," Maurice O'Connell told a meeting of the American Catholic Historical Association at Boston College on 5 April 1975 that Davis had encouraged religious and class divisions between Irish Catholics and Protestants. O'Connell also pointed out that although Young Irelanders pretended to be more culturally Irish and anti-British than O'Connell, they used British upper-class versions of their names—Charles Gavan Duffy, Thomas D'Arcy McGee, William Smith O'Brien.

6. The Queen's Colleges plan also included a Belfast campus for Ulster Presbyterians.

7. Young Irelanders may have been the most talented group of nationalists ever to serve Ireland, often proving their abilities in exile. Duffy remained in Ireland until the mid-1850s, editing the *Nation* and helping to create an independent Irish parliamentary party devoted to the tenants' rights issue. Frustrated by Catholic clerical influences in Irish nationalist politics, he finally left for Australia, where he became prime minister of Victoria. John Blake Dillon returned from exile in America and was a prominent parliamentary nationalist in the 1860s. His son John Dillon was chairman of the Irish Parliamentary Party on two occasions. Thomas D'Arcy McGee became a prominent journalist in the United States and then migrated to Canada, where he became a founding father of and a cabinet minister in the Dominion of Canada. He was assassinated in April 1868 by a Fenian sympa-

thizer who resented McGee's hostility to revolutionary Irish republicanism. Thomas Francis Meagher served as a Union army general during the American Civil War and was drowned in the Missouri while on his way to assume his duties as territorial governor of Montana. John Mitchel escaped from Australia and came to the United States, where he became a strong journalistic defender of the Confederacy. In the 1870s, voters in Tipperary twice voted him their M.P. (his first election victory occurring even before he returned to Ireland from the United States), but the government denied him his seat as a convicted felon. Mitchel's brother-in-law John Martin was an early leader of the Home Rule movement and a member of the Irish Parliamentary Party in the 1870s. Thomas O'Hagan became lord chancellor of Ireland. Although most Young Ireland leaders rejected revolution after 1848, some of them were the founders of the Irish Republican or Fenian Brotherhood.

8. Quakers were particularly generous in their famine relief efforts, but not all Protestant groups were as charitable. Before distributing bowls of soup, some of them demanded that Catholics renounce their faith in favor of Protestantism. The Irish still use the term "souper" to describe a man who sells his convictions or renounces his Irish identity for personal advancement. "Souper," "informer," and "land grabber" are the worst forms of insult in Ireland.

9. British government famine policy in Ireland would fit the concept of ideological terror and murder as defined by Albert Camus in *The Rebel* (New York: Knopf, 1957).

## 4. Refugees from Disaster: The Irish Immigrants, 1822–1870

1. E. Estyn Evans, *The Personality of Ireland* (Cambridge: Cambridge University Press, 1973), p. 82.

2. Compared to other European immigrants in the 1840s, 1850s, and 1860s, the Irish were a wretched lot. But according to Philip Taylor, *The Distant Magnet* (New York: Harper, 1971), pp. 35–36, they were on a higher economic level than those peasants who remained in Ireland. Emigration still involved some expense, enough to prevent many Irishmen from finding refuge in America. In "Inland Urban Immigrants: the Detroit Irish, 1850," *Michigan History,* 57: 121–139, 1974, Jo Ellen Vinyard explains that the prefamine Irish in Detroit,

"the largest national group in the city," experienced significant social mobility: "Among the pre-famine immigrants, forty percent worked as laborers, whereas seventy-nine percent of those who had come after 1846 were in that category" (p. 125). In *To The Golden Door* (Westport, Conn.: Greenwood, 1974), George W. Potter also emphasized the business and professional success of the prefamine Irish.

3. The role of the Irish in the 1863 and 1871 New York riots is discussed in Chapters 10 through 21 of Joel Tyler Headley's, *The Great Riots of New York: 1712–1873,* introduced by Thomas Rose and James Rodgers (Indianapolis: Bobbs-Merrill, 1970).

## 5. *The New Immigrants, 1870–1922*

1. Traditional ballad, source unknown.

2. "Lament for the Molly Maguires." Words and music by Will Millar and George Millar, 1971, Antrim Music Ltd., Calgary, Alberta, Canada.

3. In "The Devotional Revolution in Ireland, 1850–1875," *The American Historical Review,* 72:625–652, June 1972, Emmet Larkin presents evidence to show that pietism and authoritarianism in Irish Catholicism are Roman features which Cardinal Cullen brought with him to Ireland. Desmond Fennell, ed., *The Changing Face of Catholic Ireland* (London: Geoffrey Chapman, 1968), argues that certain things frequently designated as Irish Catholic—authoritarianism, clericalism, puritanism, anti-intellectualism—are not uniquely Irish but post-Council of Trent Romanism mixed with British Protestant Evangelicalism.

4. Since the 1950s, American-Catholic, liberal intellectuals, demanding reform and relevance in their church, have attacked Irish domination of American Catholicism as the cause of most of its troubles. They insist that the Irish have inflicted authoritarianism, puritanism, conservatism, and anti-intellectualism on Catholicism in the United States. In a number of articles and in *The Rise of the Unmeltable Ethnics* (New York: Macmillan Publishing Co., Inc., 1973), Michael Novak, a leading Catholic intellectual and ethnic-studies scholar, describes "chill and bleak and death-centered" Irish Catholicism as a "Celtic heresy," an aberration of true Catholicism. He claims that while the Irish were originally "pagans like the Slavs,

the Italians, the Greeks," they have "allowed their church to make Christianity an agent of order and cleanliness, rather than an agent of mystery, ghostliness, fear, terror, and passion, which at best it was."

5. In attempting to discover the source of the Irish obsession with sex as something evil and filthy, Sean O'Faolain in "The Priest," a chapter of *The Irish: A Character Study* (Harmondsworth, Middlesex, England: Penguin Books Ltd., 1969), blamed Jansenism, a seventeenth-century, neo-Calvinist heresy originating within Dutch Catholicism, which promoted a puritanical attitude toward sex. He argued that when the penal laws were in force, Irish candidates for the priesthood had studied in Continental seminaries permeated with Jansenist theology. Later, when the Irish Parliament established a Catholic seminary at Maynooth and the Irish bishops selected a faculty, they appointed a number of Continental clerical refugees from France, many of whom were advocates of Jansenism. O'Faolain's thesis has been very popular with both Irish and Irish-American intellectuals, although the excessive asceticism of medieval Celtic Christianity has also been offered as an explanation of the Irish rejection of the flesh.

6. Although Irish social conduct improved in the course of the nineteenth century, alcoholism remained a serious problem. No doubt the Catholic church's emphasis on sexual puritanism and its tolerance of drinking encouraged the Irish to seek joy and solace in the bottle. Drinking in Irish pubs and American saloons and the male companionship offered there served as partial substitutes for social and sexual relationships with women.

7. Stephan Thernstrom, *Poverty and Progress* (Cambridge, Mass.: Harvard University Press, 1964), pp. 184–185.

8. Throughout this book there is an emphasis on the relationship between Irish-American success and failure and American regionalism. When I was a graduate student at the University of Iowa, Prof. James E. Roohan first suggested to me the importance of diversity among the American Irish and the effect of westward movement on that diversity.

9. In "American Catholics, Native Rights, and National Empires: Irish-American Reactions to Expansion, 1890–1905," a history Ph.D.

dissertation submitted to the University of Iowa in 1975, David Doyle offers the following class breakdowns: Upper middle class: native white, 7.4%; German-American, 5.8%; Irish-American, 5.7%. Lower middle class: native white, 10.5%; German-American, 14.2%; Irish-American, 14.4%. Doyle's class categories are not traditional. He classifies people more by income than by vocation, placing skilled laborers in the ranks of the lower middle class, but his definition of middle class fits the ordinary American citizen's view of class as an economic rather than an occupational definition.

10. Since Sir Robert Peel as chief secretary for Ireland from 1812 to 1818 established the Peace Preservation Force that evolved into the Royal Irish Constabulary, the paramilitary guardians of British law and order in Ireland, the Irish referred to policemen as "Peelers." When Peel was home secretary in the 1820s, he took steps to establish a professional police force in Britain. That is why the English today call a policeman a "bobby."

11. Although they came from Irish backgrounds, I have excluded F. Scott Fitzgerald and John O'Hara from my list of important Irish-American writers. While they both reflected Irish ethnic origins in the contents of their literary work—especially O'Hara—both men had values and aspirations that were more upper-class, Anglo-American Protestant than Irish Catholic.

## 6. Communities in Conflict: American Nativists and Irish Catholics

1. Guy Fawkes, leader of a Catholic conspiracy in England, on 5 November 1605 attempted to annihilate the British Parliament and kill James I with a gunpowder explosion. Authorities foiled the plot, arrested, and executed Fawkes. Since that time, the British have celebrated 5 November as Guy Fawkes Day, burning him and sometimes the pope in effigy. Now the occasion is more one of fun than of malice.

2. Of course the conflicts between individual consciences, religious and secular, and the pragmatism of the state is not unique to Catholics. Such conflicts have provided themes for great literature since the times of Plato and Sophocles.

3. There were Catholic nativists. Eastern and Kentucky Anglo-American Catholics and French Catholics in Louisiana despised their Irish coreligionists as barbarians who by their presence lowered the quality of American Catholicism. Many members of these Catholic groups expressed their animosity toward the Irish by joining the American Party. Although Know-Nothings were antiforeign as well as anti-Catholic, a number of European immigrants became nativists because they disliked Catholics, particularly the Irish variety.

4. The most bitter part of the quarrel over Americanization in European Catholicism came after the publication of a French translation of Walter Elliott's biography of Isaac Hecker. Abbé Felix Klein, a French, liberal, Catholic cleric, wrote the introduction and in it distorted the views of Hecker and American, progressive Catholics to score debating points against conservatives in his own country. In condemning the "American heresy," Leo XIII cited the French translation of Hecker's life as evidence for his decision.

5. Stories and songs about the Mollys contain more legend than fact. During the 1870s, Irish coal miners did react to brutal working conditions in the Pennsylvania coal fields by organizing a secret society modeled, even in name, on agrarian terrorist movements in the old country. But Molly Maguire violence was as much motivated by ethnic rivalries—Irish against Welsh and English—and Irish factionalism as by a search for social justice or the desire for revenge against the coal companies and their rapacious agents.

6. The existence of the Papal States independently of Italy with the pope as temporal monarch gave some credence to the charge that Catholics were loyal to a foreign ruler. As a result, in 1870 many American Catholics were happy to see the Papal States incorporated into a united Italy. But the pope continued to claim sovereignty over the lost territories and to live as an exile in the Vatican.

7. Some Irish-Americans like Ignatius Donnelly of Minnesota, Patrick Ford of New York, and Denis Kearney of California were associated with populism, and the latter two freely expressed prejudices. Ford's attacks on capitalism frequently took on anti-Semitic tones, and Kearney led the fight to exclude Chinese labor from California. But on the whole, Irish politicians and labor union leaders were in the

vanguard of those opposing restrictions on immigration. Along with many Americans, however, they feared cheap Chinese labor competition.

8. Both of these quotes are taken from L. P. Curtis, Jr., *Anglo-Saxons and Celts* (Bridgeport, Conn: the Conference on British Studies, 1968). Freeman is quoted on page 81, the Webbs on page 63.

## 7. Irish-America and the Course of Irish Nationalism

1. Thomas Flanagan, "Rebellion and Style: John Mitchel and the *Jail Journal,*" *Irish University Review,* Vol. I, Autumn 1970, pp. 4–5. Flanagan took this quote from William Dillon's two-volume *Life of John Mitchel* published in London in 1888.

2. O'Connell was an accurate prophet. He understood that while emigration was an Irish disaster, it would also haunt the British. In *States of Ireland* (New York: Random House, Vintage Books, 1973), Conor Cruise O'Brien remarks that "The beginnings of the Irish revolution—that is the revolution of the Catholic Irish—are as much in America as in Ireland." (pg. 45) O'Brien argues that most of the postfamine emigration came from the least-Anglicized regions of Ireland. He claims that "the original Gaelic stock of Ireland split into two branches, one of which learned English and the other American." They did communicate with each other and "those who stayed at home were encouraged to rebel by those who left." (pg. 44) O'Brien quotes Sir William Harcourt, the British home secretary in the 1880s, on the connection between emigration and Irish nationalism: "In former Irish rebellions the Irish were in Ireland . . . We could reach their forces, cut off their reserves in men and money and then to subjugate them was comparatively easy. Now there is an Irish nation in the United States, equally hostile, with plenty of money, absolutely beyond our reach and yet within ten days sail of our shores." (pg. 45)

3. The Ecclesiastical Titles Bill, which threatened to prosecute Catholic clergymen who accepted territorial diocesan titles derived from the United Kingdom, was a cheap and flashy effort by Whig Prime Minister John Russell to exploit the anti-Catholic hysteria that engulfed Britain after Pope Pius IX decided to create a diocesan structure for the Catholic church in Britain. The pope's decision was

determined by the increasing number of Catholics in Britain, largely the product of Irish immigration.

4. In their newspaper *The Irish People,* Fenian journalists like Charles Kickham, John O'Leary, and Thomas Clark Luby attacked clericalism. They did not reject the spiritual authority of bishops and priests but insisted that the church must remain outside politics. Fenianism made a substantial contribution to Irish nationalist anticlericalism which started in the conflict between O'Connell and Young Ireland and reached a high point in the 1890s when Irish Catholic bishops and priests joined British Protestants and the Liberal Party in demanding that Charles Stewart Parnell leave his post as leader of Irish nationalism because he was named correspondent in a divorce case involving his mistress, Katharine O'Shea.

Despite the commands of their bishops, many priests sympathized with the Fenians and gave them the sacraments. Like most American Irish bishops, John MacHale, archbishop of Tuam and an old enemy of Cullen in the Irish hierarchy, refused to take a hard line against the republicans. In addition to many churchmen, however, a number of respected lay nationalists like William Smith O'Brien, Thomas D'Arcy McGee, Thomas Meagher, John Blake Dillon, and A. M. Sullivan, proprietor of the *Nation,* condemned Fenianism.

5. Patrick Ford and Michael Davitt, both disciples of nineteenth-century American economist Henry George, wanted land nationalization rather than peasant proprietorship. But Irish Catholicism and the land hunger of the peasant masses negated a socialist solution to the Irish land question.

6. Alan J. Ward, *Ireland and Anglo-American Relations, 1899–1921* (London: Weidenfeld and Nicolson, 1969). In a recent paper, "Ireland and America," delivered to the thirteenth annual meeting of the American Committee for Irish Studies at Stonehill College, Easton, Massachusetts, on 26 April 1975, Ward discussed how Irish-Americans pioneered in the use of ethnic power to manipulate congressional attitudes toward American foreign policy.

7. On Easter Monday, 24 April 1916, a small number of men and a few women representing the IRB-dominated, anti-Redmond wing of the Irish Volunteers and James Connolly's socialist Citizen Army

started a revolution in Dublin and proclaimed the Irish Republic. After six days of fighting, the Republicans led by Padraic Pearse and the socialists by Connolly surrendered. At first Irish public opinion opposed the revolution as a stab in the back of the British who were fighting the Germans, but after the British authorities brutally executed the leaders of the Easter Week rebellion and imprisoned many other Republicans, Irish people began to glorify the dead and imprisoned men as heroes and martyrs. Pearse, a poet, had preached that a successful revolution was not necessary; he wanted a blood sacrifice to wash away the taint and corruption of parliamentary nationalism and to inspire the youth of the country to throw off British tyranny. Pearse proved a prophet. The execution of republican idealists did nurture the spirit of Irish nationalism. British responses to the Home Rule crisis in 1912–1914 and to Easter Week destroyed constitutional nationalism in Ireland and made revolution almost inevitable.

8. Sinn Fein officially came into existence in 1908. Its founder, Arthur Griffith, a Dublin journalist, preached a dual-monarchy approach based on the Austro-Hungarian model as the solution to the tensions between Ireland and Britain. Sinn Fein means "we ourselves," emphasizing the economic nationalism preached by Griffith. Shortly after Sinn Fein's beginnings, members of the Irish Republican Brotherhood infiltrated the new group, changing its goals from dual monarchy to complete separation from Britain. After Easter Week, republicans opposing the Irish Party campaigned as Sinn Feiners, and Griffith, although remaining a member, surrendered the leadership of the party to Eamon de Valera, the only surviving commandant of the 1916 uprising.

9. In the midst of the Anglo-Irish War, the British government tried to compromise the Irish Question with a Government of Ireland Bill which partitioned Ireland into twenty-six and six-county Home Rule territories. This partition was a consequence of the 1912–1914 Home Rule crisis and debates. It was an act of hypocrisy for British politicians to accept the argument that a United Ireland would be unfair to a 25 percent Protestant minority and then proceed to create a Northern Ireland with a 33 percent Catholic minority. During the treaty negotiations with Sinn Fein, Lloyd George promised a Boundary Commission and strongly suggested that such a group would

return Catholic majority areas to the Irish Free State (including Fermanagh, Tyrone, South Down, South Armagh, and West Derry). In the early 1920s a Boundary Commission did meet but refused to honor the verbal promises of Lloyd George, who was no longer prime minister. Right from its beginning, the Protestant leaders of Northern Ireland began to discriminate against Catholics in economic and political areas, creating "a Protestant nation for a Protestant people." Although Northern Ireland was part of and responsible to the United Kingdom, British politicians refused to protect the civil rights of the Catholic minority in that area. The result is the current crisis in Northern Ireland.

10. Cohalan's statement is quoted in Alan J. Ward, *Ireland and Anglo-American Relations, 1899–1921* (London: Weidenfeld and Nicolson, 1969), p. 219.

## 8. Irish-American Politics

1. To the Irish, "honest graft" refers to taking a little off the top in exchange for services rendered, a kind of fee. It assumes a just compensation for useful and constructive efforts. "Dishonest graft," on the other hand, means appropriating large sums of public money without compensating the taxpayer. The distinctions between honest and dishonest graft often become so subjective that they are really matters of private conscience.

2. Spring-Rice's comments on Irish-American political power and Anglo-American relations are presented and discussed in Alan J. Ward, *Ireland and Anglo-American Relations, 1899–1921* (London: Weidenfeld and Nicolson, 1969), pp. 93–96.

3. In "Urban Liberalism and the Age of Reform," *The Mississippi Valley Historical Review,* 49: 231–241, September 1962, J. Joseph Huthmacher argues that the poverty experience of Catholic ethnics, their religious values, and their welfare-oriented political machines made them the main force challenging *laissez faire* liberalism. Huthmacher suggests that Protestant progressivism was much more concerned with conformity, making ethnics one-hundred percent American, than with social improvement. He pointed out that progressive nativism attacked parochial schools as divisive, imposed prohibition and other puritan panaceas as remedies for social disorders, and

placed Anglo-Saxons above lesser "breeds." Naturally Catholic ethnics responded negatively to such nativist, puritan reform rhetoric.
Huthmacher shows how Catholic ethnic politicians in state legislatures sponsored and supported bills to improve the working conditions and social security of the proletariat. During the administration
of Gov. Alfred E. Smith in the 1920s, New York previewed the New
Deal. And during the 1930s, Franklin Delano Roosevelt, who was
tutored by Smith, was able to change the direction of American social
policy from self-help individualism to semi-collectivism because he
had the loyalty, encouragement, and votes of Irish-dominated urban
political machines. In *Urban Liberalism and Progressive Reform*
(New York: Charles Scribner's Sons, 1973), John B. Buenker applies
Huthmacher's thesis to urban machine politics in cities like Providence, Cleveland, Chicago, New York, and Pittsburgh. Ethnic Catholic communalism in contrast with Anglo-American Protestant individualism and the political, social, economic, and cultural
implications of these two conflicting value systems is the main theme
of Michael Novak's *The Rise of the Unmeltable Ethnics* (New York:
Macmillan Publishing Company, 1973) which concentrates on analysis of Italian and Slav attitudes. Although many Catholic bishops,
priests, and journalists have advocated extremely conservative positions regarding private property and social change, such conservatism
seems to be more eastern than nation-wide. In general, Catholic laymen in the United States, like those in Ireland, do not follow the
dictates of bishops and priests on political, economic, or social questions unless the opinions of priests and prelates conform to the interests of the total Catholic community. Irish-American workingmen
took their social gospel from labor unionism, not from papal encycli-
cals.

    4. In an article, "Thanks to the Irish," in *America,* 14 May 1966,
Philip Gleason, professor of history at the University of Notre Dame,
refutes Catholic intellectuals and literati who argue that Irish control
over American Catholicism has made it authoritarian and conservative. He insists that it was fortunate that the Irish were the first
Catholic ethnics to arrive in the United States because "they were the
best equipped among all the immigrating Catholic groups to assist the
church in effecting a positive adjustment to American life." Continen-

tal Catholics came from ultraconservative political environments where church and state were united, serving as twin agencies of upper-class government control. In America, they found the separation of church and state to be strange and hostile. As reluctant citizens of the United Kingdom, the Irish on the other hand had successfully learned to organize and operate within the Anglo-Saxon Protestant political system and to sustain a church dependent on private financial support, free of state money and control. Because of their experience in Ireland, their familiarity with the Anglo-Saxon mind and political system, and their command of English, the Irish could communicate and compete with Anglo-Americans. Irish political expertise protected Catholic interests in the United States and in the process "Americanized" Catholic ethnics. Gleason reflected on the alternatives to Irish power in the American Catholic community:

> In this connection, it might be salutary to reflect for a moment on how much more radically the Catholic Church would have been cut off from American society—how much higher the ghetto walls would have been—if the Germans or French or Poles had occupied the overwhelmingly dominant position the Irish have historically enjoyed. And this not simply because of the difficulties of linguistic communication, but even more fundamentally because of the psychic identification of Catholicism with a language and culture that seemed so deeply opposed to that of the larger American society.

## 9. *From Ghetto to Suburbs: From Someplace to No Place?*

1. In the early 1960s, after the failure of a bombing campaign in the North, which had very little support from the Catholic community, the IRA, adopted the party designation "Sinn Fein" and abandoned terrorism for socialist politics in the South. During the civil rights phase of the Catholic protest in the six counties, the IRA kept a low profile, promoting the cause of civil liberties as a tactic for mobilizing the ghettos. In 1969, after the IRA resumed its role as a nationalist guerrilla army, it split into Official and Provisional wings. Officials apply a Marxist interpretation to the Northern Ireland situation, arguing that sectarian conflict is the product of capitalist divisive

tactics and projecting an All-Ireland socialist republic as a solution. They directed their violence against symbols and agents of British authority, carefully avoiding attacks on Irish Protestant civilians. Provisionals also claim to be socialists but not of the Marxist school. Despite their workers'-republic rhetoric, they seem to advocate a traditional nationalism which views the British as Ireland's main problem, one that can best be eliminated through bombs and bullets. While Provisionals denounce sectarianism and suggest a nine-county Ulster regional assembly as part of a federated Irish republic, they do not discriminate in their violence, killing Protestant civilians as well as British soldiers. Officials claim that Provisionals originally received funds from some members of the Fianna Fail government in the South as a way of directing IRA activities away from Socialist politics in the North. Fianna Fail, a political party which de Valera founded to combat the treaty, has dominated Irish politics since 1932. At present Ireland is ruled by a Fine Gael (descended from pro-treaty Sinn Fein) and Labour coalition.

2. British and American newspapers have not always been fair in covering the violence in Northern Ireland. Primarily, by concentrating on IRA terrorism they neglect Protestant atrocities. In all parts of the six counties, Protestant gangs have been and still are killing Catholics. As of May 1975, more than four Catholics were being killed for every Protestant. The British government has not been as concerned with curbing Protestant unionist violence as it has been Catholic republican terrorism.

3. "Four Green Field" refers to a song of the same name written by Tommy Makem in which Makem refers to Ireland as an old woman (the Cathleen ni Houlihan tradition) asking her sons to recover the fourth green field (Ulster) stolen by an alien invader (the British). This song is now among the most popular of nationalist songs sung in Irish pubs in Ireland, Britain, and America.

4. Most contemporary IRA support in the United States seems to come from Irish people who really do not understand the complexities of the situation in Northern Ireland or its connection with problems in other parts of the globe, including the United States. Their nationalism is very provincial without much humanitarian idealism. Many of them are conservatives, even reactionaries in terms of the American

political spectrum. This type of IRA apologist ignores the socialist goals of the IRA and the fact that the terrorist group has much in common with other violent groups like the Viet Cong. He or she also avoids the obvious comparisons between Northern Ireland Catholics and American blacks as well as the influence of the American civil rights movement on Catholic protest tactics.

5. Other Catholic ethnic groups followed the Irish from urban to suburban America, transforming parochial schools from ethnic centers into white enclaves and finally into black institutions. Such rapid racial changes prompted criticism of Catholic education from liberals both inside and outside the church. Some argued that Catholic schools encouraged segregation; others claimed that the existence of Catholic schools in the inner-city hurt the quality of public education by siphoning off the talents of the best students and most concerned parents. These criticisms reflect more emotion than reason and certainly ignore the real contributions of Catholic education to the difficult task of preserving the American city. For a long time Catholic schools helped maintain ethnic neighborhoods, placing a brake on exodus, retaining urban pluralism. Now they present black parents with an alternative to often-miserable public school systems. The closing of Catholic schools would depress rather than lift the quality of culture and hope for the future in black ghettos.

6. The FBI and CIA offered educated Catholics the opportunity to demonstrate their patriotism in good civil service positions. For years a popular joke has said that Irishmen from Catholic colleges and universities join government security agencies to spy on WASPS (White Anglo-Saxon Protestants) from Harvard. Conservative journalist Garry Wills has claimed that the late J. Edgar Hoover, former head of the FBI, and Pres. Richard M. Nixon liked to employ Catholics because of their intensive, almost neurotic loyalty to the United States. (Garry Wills, "Rose Mary's Creed: Serving the 'Boss'," Chicago *Sun Times,* December 6, 1973.)

7. Theodore H. White, *The Making of the President, 1960* (New York: Pocket Books, Inc., 1961), pp. 312–313.

8. Kennedy lost California—Nixon's home state—Wisconsin and Ohio. Some Catholics who voted against Kennedy feared that if he were an unsuccessful president, the entire Catholic community would

suffer the blame. Others, many of them clerics, believed that Nixon as president might try to court Catholics with aid to parochial schools while Kennedy would refuse money to Catholic education to prove that he was committed to separation of church and state.

9. Many Anglo-Americans and even some Irish-Americans refused to accept Kennedy as Irish. They believed that his wealth and ivy league education had for all practical purposes converted him into an Anglo-American. However, journalist Benjamin C. Bradlee's *Conversations With Kennedy* (New York: Norton, 1975) makes it clear that JFK emotionally and culturally identified himself as Irish and had a real distrust of Anglo-America.

10. Msgr. Ellis received strong support in the debate over the quality of Catholic education from Thomas F. O'Dea, *The American Catholic Dilemma* (New York: Sheed & Ward, 1958). A sociologist, O'Dea like Ellis emphasized the immigrant, peasant character of American Catholics. He agreed with Ellis that the Catholic hierarchy possessed the anti-intellectual biases of the working class from which it came. O'Dea also argued that the authoritarianism, clericalism, moralism, and defensiveness that pervaded the church as a teaching institution frustrated intellectual freedom and the formation of creative, imaginative minds, both so essential for first-rate art and scholarship.

11. Distinctions should be made between the Coughlin and McCarthy movements. To a certain extent, the same kind of insecure people were attracted to both Catholic demagogues, but unlike Coughlin, McCarthy was not an anti-Semite—Roy Cohen and David Shine were his chief lieutenants—and he appealed to anticommunist, cold-war anxieties that pervaded both the liberal and conservative camps.

12. In "Catholics, Neutrality, and the Spanish Embargo, 1937–1939," *The Journal of American History,* 54: 73–85, June 1967, J. David Valaik presents evidence to show that a majority of American Catholics rejected the counsel of the pulpit and Catholic press by not favoring Franco's attack on the Spanish Republic.

13. Greeley's analyses of Irish-American opinion and attitudes are discussed in a number of his publications, including *That Most Distressful Nation* (Chicago: Quadrangle Books, 1973); *Why Can't They*

*Be Like Us* (New York: Dutton, 1971); *Ethnicity in the United States: A Preliminary Reconnaissance* (New York: Wiley, 1974); "Portrait of the Neighborhood, Changing," *The Critic,* 30: 14–23, September/October 1971; "The American Irish Since the Death of Studs Lonigan," *The Critic,* 29: 27–33, May/June 1971; and "Making it in America: Ethnic Groups and Social Status," *Social Policy,* 4: 21–29, September/October 1973.

14. In February, 1972, I gave an Irish culture test to about 100 students in a large ethnic history course at Loyola University of Chicago. All of those who took the test identified themselves as Irish and had attended Catholic secondary schools. Less than three percent could identify important Irish political figures such as O'Connell, Parnell, Pearse, or de Valera, and only about fifteen percent had some knowledge of literary personalities such as Joyce, Yeats, or O'Neill.

15. The American Polish community shares with its Irish counterpart many of the Old and New-World relationships between ethnic and religious identities. Both countries were conquered by foreign, non-Catholic enemies, resulting in tighter bonds between sectarianism and patriotism. Polish-Americans, however, still remain in urban ghettos to a greater degree than the Irish. Since contemporary Poles are less assimilated into the American mainstream than the Irish, their commitment to Catholic dogma and their resistance to clerical activism in leftist social and political causes is more intense. Today young, Polish-American men and women are more likely to enter seminaries and convents than the Irish, who tend to seek opportunities in professional and graduate schools. More than half of the American Catholic hierarchy today is still Irish, but the future leadership of the church belongs to the Poles.

16. In Thomas Fleming's novel, *Romans, Countrymen, Lovers* (New York: William Morrow & Co., 1969), Jim Kilpatrick described his humanities education in an urban, Jesuit university:

Ah, literature, he imbibed great quantities of it, mostly Catholic. *The Hound of Heaven* was dissected and examined as if it were another *Iliad.* Belloc, Chesterton and Newman were our intellectual triumvirate, men who had weighed the modern world and found it wanting. The answers they failed to supply were infallibly guaranteed by that other modern thinker, Thomas Aquinas (1225–1274).

Although there are a number of first-rate Irish writers, many Catholic colleges and universities still do not offer courses in Irish literature.

17. Many Irish and other ethnic Catholics who support parochial schools do so not because they represent a unique and valuable cultural contribution to a pluralistic America but because they are an escape from the conflicts and tensions of the contemporary metropolitan environment.

18. In the January 1975 issue of *The Critic,* Andrew M. Greeley reports that a National Opinion Research Center survey of American Catholic opinion has revealed that in the last ten years Sunday mass attendance has dropped from 71 to 50 percent and monthly confessions from 31 to 17 percent. Only 32 percent of American Catholics believe that the pope is infallible on questions of faith and morals. Eighty-three percent of them approve of artificial contraception, an increase of 38 percent since 1963. Ten years ago, 56 percent of the American Catholic population considered religiously mixed marriages to be unwise; today that number has been reduced to 27 percent.

# Index

Abbey Theatre, 83, 120
Abortion, 88
Act of Union, 30–31, 42–43, 46
Acts of Supremacy, 17
Adams, Henry, 104
Adrian II, 12
Agrarian secret societies, 24, 53
Aisling poems, 53
Alcohol addiction, 80
Alfred, William, 84
Alien and Sedition Acts, 89, 139
Allen, W. P., 124
*All Good Men*, 147
American Catholicism: Irish influence in, 5, 9, 75, 76, 88–91; and intellectualism, 81, 166–68; accommodation to American culture, 97–100; and ethnicity, 176–78
American Civil War, 64, 68, 95–96, 120–21
American Minute Men, 106
American nativism: 6, 85–106 *passim*, 159–60, 163
American Protective Association, 105–6
American Revolution, 86
Amnesty Association, 124
Anglo-American patriotism, 25
Anglo-Irish, 14–18, 24–26, 29, 45, 58
Anglo-Irish War, 136–37, 152
"Anglo-Saxon and Celt," 44
Anti-Catholicism, 85–95; among scholars and intellectuals, 5; motivation for union with England, 29; as obstacle to reform, 31–32; strengthened by Catholic Emancipation, 40; Peel and, 47; and populism, 102; propaganda, 159
Anti-slavery movement, 69
Asquith, Herbert, 134
Athletics, 81

Ballads, 70–71
Beecher, Lyman, 92
Berlin, Isaiah, 153
*Beyond the Melting Pot*, 146, 147, 165
Biggar, Joseph, 127, 129
Blacks, 68, 81, 159
Blaine, James G., 144
Bocock, John Paul, 145
Boston, 63, 68, 140, 147
Boston House of Correction, 68
Boycott, Charles Cunningham, 129
Breslin, Jimmy, 84, 169
Britain, 60, 153
British government, 31, 70, 112, 116, 123, 125, 126, 136, 155
British Parliament, 29, 30–31
Brogan, Denis W., 166–67
*Brooklyn Tablet*, 170
Brown, Edmund G., Jr., 166
Brown, Thomas N., 147
Bruce, Edward, 13
Butt, Isaac, 125, 127

Canada, 122–23
Captain Moonlight, the, 24
Carson, Edward, 135
Carey, Hugh L., 166
Carroll, Charles, 87, 89
Carroll, John, 87, 89–90
Castlereagh, Robert Stewart, 29
Catholic Association, 37–40
Catholic churches, 77–78, 94
Catholic Committee, 35, 36, 37
Catholic education, 173–76
Catholic Emancipation, 27–40 *passim*, 111–12
Catholic ethnics, 151, 158–60, 171
Catholicism: and Irish identity, 8, 138–39, 172–73; in Gaelic Ireland, 12, 15; as 1960

election issue, 161–63. *See also* American Catholicism; Irish Catholicism
Catholic Relief Bill, 39
Catholic University, 97, 98, 99
*Catholic World, The,* 99
Celtic Christianity, 12, 13
Central Intelligence Agency, 160
Charitable Bequests Act, 47
Charles I, 20
Charles II, 20
Chicago, 140, 143, 144, 147
Civil rights, 3, 154, 155
Clan na Gael, 126, 129, 130, 137, 144
Cleveland, Grover, 101, 144
Cohalan, Daniel F., 137
Cohan, George M., 81–82, 136
Collins, Jerome J., 136
Collins, Michael, 152
*Commonweal,* 170
Condon, Edward, 124
Confederation of Kilkenny, 20
Connell, Kenneth H., 54
Conover, S. B., 126
Cornwallis, Charles, 28
Corrigan, Michael, 98, 99, 100
Coughlin, Father, 88, 170
Covenanters, the, 106
Crawford, William Sharman, 113
Crime, 68, 76
Crimean War, 117
Cromwell, Thomas, 16, 20
Cullen, Paul, 75, 115, 116, 119, 120
Cullinan, Elizabeth, 84
Curran, Sarah, 33

Dail, the, 136
Daley, Richard J., 140, 161
*Davenport Messenger,* 170
Davis, Thomas, 43, 44, 49, 83, 109
Davitt, Michael, 129, 130
Deasy, Timothy, 124
Debs, Eugene V., 101
De Clare, Richard fitz Gilbert, 11
Defenders, the, 24, 53
Democratic Party: intellectuals vs. Irish in, 5; Irish loyalty to, 108, 136, 144; bosses, 139; machines, 139, 161; Irish leadership of, 140; Irish contribution to, rewarded by FDR, 160; minority coalitions in, 163
De Valera, Eamon, 137

Devon Commission, 47, 48
Devoy, John, 119, 126, 127, 128, 144
Dillon, John Blake, 43, 44, 49, 115, 134
Disestablishment Act, 116
Doheny, Michael, 117, 118
Draft law of 1863, 68, 69
Drummond, Thomas, 42
Duffy, Charles Gavan, 43–50 *passim,* 109, 113, 114
Dunne, Finley Peter, 84

Easter Week "blood sacrifice," 136
Ecclesiastical Titles Bill, 114
Economic depression of 1880s, 100–1
*Edinburgh Review,* 103
Edward VI, 17
Elizabeth I, 17, 19
Ellis, John Tracy, 166–68, 174
Emigrants, Irish, 40, 58, 62, 64
"Emigrant's Letter," 71
Emigration, Irish, 55–56, 59–62, 71–72
Emmet, Robert, 32–34, 109, 117
Emmet, Thomas Addis, 32
Entertainment business, 81
Evans, E. Estyn, 63

Fabian Society, 104
Famine, 55–58, 61, 67, 73, 112
Farley, James J., 160
*Farragan's Retreat,* 169
Farrell, James T., 84, 168
Federal Bureau of Investigation, 160
Federalist Party, 89, 94, 139
*Felon's Track, The,* 117
Fenian Brotherhood, 117–24, 126
Fillmore, Millard, 95
Fitzgerald, C. E. Vesy, 38
Fitzgerald, Earl of Kildare, 16
Flaherty, Joe, 84
Fleming, Thomas J., 84, 147
Ford, Patrick, 128
40s franchise, 26, 27, 39
*Forum, The,* 145
France, 27, 28, 99
Franciscans, 18
Freeman, Edward A., 102, 103
*Freeman's Journal,* 113
French Catholic clergy, 90
French, Percy, 71
Froude, James A., 102

*Gaelic American,* 144
Gaelic Christianity, 17
Gaelic culture, 53
George III, 31
George IV, 31, 39
Ghettos, American urban, 6, 10, 62, 65–68, 107, 140, 159, 175
Gibbons, James Cardinal 97, 98, 100
G. I. Bill of Rights, 158
Gibson, William, 84
Gilroy, Frank D., 84
Gladstone, W. E., 116, 131, 133
"God Save Ireland," 124–25
Goff, John W., 126
Government of Ireland Bill, 154
*Governor, The,* 141
Grant, Ulysses S., 126
Grattan, Henry, 26, 29, 35, 36
Gray, John, 113
Great Depression, the, 152, 159
Great Famine, the, 55–58, 61, 73
Greeley, Andrew M., 168, 171
Green, John R., 102
Grey, Edward, 145
Guardians of Liberty, 106

Hamill, Pete, 84
Handlin, Oscar, 63, 68
Harrison, Benjamin, 144
Hartford Convention, 89
Haymarket Square riot, 101
Hecker, Isaac, 99
Henry II, 11
Henry VIII, 14, 16–17
Holland, John, 126
Holmes, Oliver Wendell, 96
Home Rule movement, 125–35 *passim*
Hughes, Charles Evans, 145
Hughes, John, 94, 120
Humbert, General, 28
Humphrey, Hubert, 162

Immigrant Restriction League, 104
Immigrants, Irish: reflect Irish history and culture, 7–10; numbers of, 59, 62, 70; stimulate further emigration, 61–62; as urban dwellers, 63–66, 87; vocational opportunities, 64, 65, 79–82; poverty of, 68; educational level, 72; improved quality of, 73, 77, 111, 140; property ownership,

77; political experience, 138, 147–48
Immigration, Irish: pre-1815, 59; post-1815 increase, 60; 1870–1901 rate of, 70; restrictions on, demanded, 101; decrease of, 152–53
Immigration legislation, 94, 104, 152
Independent Irish Party, 113–14
Industrial Revolution, 54, 64, 96, 102
Infant mortality, 54
Ireland, 11–29; rural poverty, 52, 73–74, 127–28; marriage age and rate, 54, 61; population, 54, 61, 73; education, 72–73; literary revival in, 83; geography, 108; parliamentary candidates in, 114–15; combat-trained Irish-Americans in, 121; suffrage, 132; die-hard Republicans in, 152; place in Western civilization, 174, 175
Ireland, John, 65–66, 97, 98, 99
Irish-American nationalism: as identity search, 105, 137, 138; and hatred for England, 110; history of, 111–12; and American foreign policy, 117; revived nativism sustains, 126; no longer vital force, 156
Irish-Americans: ethnic studies and, 3–7; and Irish nationalism, 8–9, 111, 130, 132, 134, 136, 152; social mobility, 76, 77, 79, 151, 157–59, 161, 171–72; vocational opportunities, 79–80; military service, 135–36, 158, 159; disassociation from Irish affairs, 152, 153; and present crisis in Northern Ireland, 154, 156–57; in literature, 168–69; politics of, 170, 171
Irish Brigade (U.S. army), 95–96
Irish Brigade, 113–14
Irish Catholic clergy: Peel's concessions to, 47; encourage rural life in U.S., 65, 90, 91; loose discipline of, 74; opposition to Fenianism, 119–20; justify empathy for republicans, 125; opposition to Parnell, 133
Irish Catholicism: Romanization of, 17–18, 148, 149, 173, 174; revitalization, 23; essential to Irish life-style, 53–54; changes in, 72–76; vs. European Catholicism, 87; and British nonconformism, 115–16; foe of Fenianism, 119; sense of community, 149–50
Irish Catholics, 20–23, 35, 47, 51–52, 60, 154, 156

Irish Confederation, 48–51
Irish ethnic identity, 107–9, 172–78
Irish Free State, 154
Irish government, 153
Irish history, study of, 8, 174–76
*Irish Melodies,* 109
Irish Municipal Reform Bill, 42
Irish National and Industrial League of the United States, 130
Irish nationalism: Irish-American commitment to, 8–9, 111, 152; early leaders, 32; principles of liberal democracy in, 40, 148; and Catholic Emancipation, 46–48; response to famine disaster, 56, 57; cultural, development of, 107–9; returns to constitutional channels, 113, 125; clerical politics in, 114; agrarian strategy, 128–29; hostile to politics, 144; posttreaty brand, 153
Irish Parliament, 24, 26–27, 29
Irish Parliamentary Party, 125, 132, 133–34, 136
*Irish People, The,* 122
Irish personality and character, 52–54, 63, 72–74, 76, 102–3, 139, 150
Irish Poor Law, 42, 43
Irish-Protestant nation, 27–28
Irish Republican Army (IRA), 136, 154–57
Irish Republican Brotherhood (IRB), 118, 122–26 *passim*
Irish Volunteers, the, 136
*Irish World,* 128
Italians, American, 4

Jackson, Andrew, 139
James I, 19
James II, 20–21
Jesuits, 18, 99
Jews, American, 81, 102, 171, 172
John XXIII, 164
John Birch Society, 170
Joyce, James, 83, 84

Keane, John, 97, 98
Kelly, "Honest" John, 140
Kelly, Thomas J., 124
Kendrick, Francis, 94
Kennedy, John Fitzgerald, 93, 161–65
Kennedy, Robert, 166
Kennedy, Teddy, 166

Kickham, Charles, 83, 109
Kilmainham Treaty, 131
Knights of Labor, 98
Knights of Luther, 106
*Knocknagow,* 109
Know-Nothing Party, 94–95
Ku Klux Klan, 106, 159

Labor movement, 79, 98, 101
Labour Party, 104
*Laissez faire* capitalism, 98, 99
Lalor, James Fintan, 49, 129
Land acts, 116; 131
Land system of Ireland, 47–54 *passim,* 65–66, 70, 73, 108, 115, 116, 128, 129, 131
Land war, 130–31
Larkin, Michael, 124
*Last Hurrah, The,* 141
Lavelle, Patrick, 120
Lazarus, Emma, 96, 97
Leo XIII, 100
Liberation Society, 115
Lichfield House Compact, 41
Literature, Irish-American, 83–84, 109
Lodge, Cabot, 104
Loyal National Repeal Association, 43, 46
Lucas, Frederick, 113

Macaulay, Thomas, 102
McCarthy, Eugene, 100, 166, 170
McCarthy, Joseph, 170
McCarthy, Justin, 133, 134
McCarthyism, 88
McCready, William, 171
McHale, Tom, 84, 169
McManus, Terence Belew, 120
MacMurrough, Dermot
McQuaid, Bernard, 98, 99, 100
Maguire, John Francis, 115
Manchester Martyrs, 124
Mangan, James Clarence, 109
Mansfield, Mike, 166
Marechal, Ambrose, 90
Mathew, Theobold, 43
Meagher, Thomas Francis, 50, 95
Melbourne, Lord, 42
Melting pot thesis, 96–97, 100
Messmer, Sebastian, 99
Military service, Irish in, 64, 160
Mitchel, John, 49, 50, 109, 110

Molly Maguires, the, 24, 101
Monk, Maria, 93, 105
*Moon Gaffney*, 168, 169
Moore, George Henry, 113, 115
Moore, Thomas, 33, 83, 109
Moriarty, David, 119
Morse, Samuel F. B., 92
"Mountains of Mourne, The," 71
Moynihan, Daniel Patrick, 146, 147, 165–66
Murphy, Frank, 160
Murray, John Courtney, 100

*Nation*, 43–45, 51
National Association, 115, 119
Nationalism. *See* Irish-American nationalism; Irish nationalism
National Land League, 129–32
Naturalization, 89, 95, 104–5, 126
New Departure, the, 128–29
New England, 77–79
New York City, 69, 91, 140, 143, 147
Northern Ireland, 30, 154–57
Notre Dame (University of), 99

O'Brien, Michael, 124
O'Brien, William Smith, 49, 50, 51
O'Casey, Sean, 84
O'Connell, Daniel, 34–46, 48, 98, 107, 112, 138, 148–49
O'Connell, Denis, 97, 98
O'Connor, Edwin, 84, 141, 160, 161
O'Connor, Frank, 84
O'Connor, Rory, 12
O'Faolain, Sean 84
"Oh, Breathe Not His Name," 33
O'Mahony, John, 117–19
O'Neill, Eugene, 84
O'Neill, Thomas P. (Tip), 166
Order of the Star Spangled Banner, 94
Oregon boundary dispute, 117
O'Shea, William, 133
*Our Sunday Visitor*, 170

Packenham, General, 28
Pale, the, 14, 16
Papacy, the, 170
Parliamentary elections, 114
Parliamentary nationalism, 127, 132, 133
Parnell, Charles Stewart, 114, 127–33, 149
*Passing of a Great Race, The*, 105

Paul VI, 164, 177
Paulists, 99
Peel, Robert, 38, 39, 42, 45, 46–47
Penal Laws, 8, 22–24, 26, 28, 31, 35
Penal laws (U.S.), 88
Phoenix Society, 188
*Pilot, The*, 95
Pitt, William, 28–29, 31
Pius IX, 75, 116
Pius X, 100
*Playboy of the Western World*, 83
Plunkett, George Washington, 143–44
Poles, American, 4
Policemen, Irish-American, 80
Political machines, 143, 160, 161
Political reformism, 142–43
Politicians, Irish-American, 140, 142, 145–48
Politics: Irish-American, 8, 9, 138–51, 160; Irish, 148
*Population of Ireland, The*, 54
Populism, 102
*Poverty and Progress*, 76–77
Powderly, Terence, V., 126
Power, O'Connor, 129
Powers, J. F., 84
*Principatio*, 169
Protestant Ascendancy, 22, 23, 24, 38, 42
Protestant church of Ireland, 116
Protestant radicalism, 27, 28
Protestants: Anglo-American, 3, 58, 105, 149–50, 151, 163; Anglo-Saxon, 8, 18, 19, 31, 58, 66; Irish, 21–23, 29, 40, 57, 59–60, 69; Ulster, 135
Protestant Unionist government, 155
Provisional IRA, 156

*Quarterly Review*, 58
Quebec Act, 86
Queen's Colleges, 47
Queen's University, 154

*Races of Europe, The*, 105
Racism, 102–6
Rebellions, 20, 27–28, 58, 113, 119
Reconstruction, 106
Redmond, John, 134
Reform bills, 30, 132
Reformation, the, 17
"Remorse for Intemperate Speech," 110
Religious orders, 99

Repeal movement, 111–12. *See also* Penal Laws
Republicanism. *See* Fenian Brotherhood
Republican Party, 139
Restoration, the, 20
Revolutionary Directory, 126
Revolutionary nationalism. *See* Fenian Brotherhood
Ribbonmen, the, 24, 53
Riots, 69, 101
Ripley, William Z., 105
Roberts, William R., 122
Roosevelt, Franklin D., 160
Rossa, Jeremiah O'Donovan, 118
Royal Irish Constabulary, 136
Ryan, John, 100

Salisbury, Lord, 104
*Sally Cavanagh,* 109
Sarsfield, Patrick, 21
Schools: Irish national, 41–42, 72, 82; parochial, in U.S., 82, 92, 158, 167; Catholic clergy support public, 98
Scots, 13
Senior, Nassau, 57–58
Seward, William, 91
Sheehan, Edward R. F., 141
Sheil, Bernard, 100, 170
Sheil, Richard Lalor, 37
"She Is Far From the Land Where Her Young Hero Sleeps," 33–34
"Shores of Americay, The," 71
Simmons, William J., 106
Sinn Fein Party, 136
Six Counties, the, 19, 155, 156
Smith, Al, 106, 159, 165
Society of Priests of St. Sulpice, 90
Society of United Irishmen, 27, 32, 35, 89
"Soldier's Song, The," 125
Spalding, John Lancaster, 97, 98
Special Powers Act, 154–55
*Speeches from the Dock,* 109
Spellman, Francis Cardinal, 170
Spring-Rice, Cecil, 145
Statutes of Kilkenny, 14
Stephens, James, 117–19, 122, 123
Stevenson, Adlai E., II, 161
Stubbs, William, 102

Sullivan, A. M., 144
Sullivan, T. D., 109, 124
Sylvester, Harry, 168
Synge, John Millington, 83, 84

*Tablet,* 113
Tammany Hall, 140
Thernstrom, Stephan, 77–79
Tone, Theobold Wolfe, 27, 32, 33
Tories: Irish, 28, 31; British, 32
Treaty of Limerick, 21
Trevelyan, George, 57
Tweed Ring scandals, 140

Ulster, 14, 16, 19, 27, 53, 59–60, 135, 155–56
Ulster Orangemen, 156
Unionist Party, 104
Union with Ireland, 28–29. *See also* Act of Union
United Irish League, 134
*United Irishman, The,* 50
Urban problems, 145–48
U.S. Government, 123
U.S. Supreme Court, 106, 160

Vatican II, 100, 177
Volunteers, the, 26

Walker, Franklin, 104
Walsh, Frank, 160
Washington, George, 86
Webb, Beatrice and Sidney, 104
Wellington, Duke of, 38, 39
Whig Party (U.S.), 86, 94, 139
Whigs, 42, 57
Whiteboys, the, 24, 53
William III, 20, 21
Wilson, Woodrow, 136, 144–45
Wolsey, Thomas Cardinal, 16
World War I, 135
World War II, 159, 160
*World Without End Amen,* 169
Wyse, Thomas, 37

Yeats, William Butler, 83, 84, 110
Young Ireland, 43–45, 48, 50–51, 83, 107, 109, 119